Philosophy: Key Themes

Philosophy: Key Themes

Second edition

Julian Baggini and Gareth Southwell

palgrave
macmillan

First edition published 2002
Second revised edition published 2012 by
PALGRAVE MACMILLAN

Palgrave Macmillan in the UK is an imprint of Macmillan Publishers Limited,
registered in England, company number 785998, of Houndmills, Basingstoke,
Hampshire RG21 6XS.

Palgrave Macmillan in the US is a division of St Martin's Press LLC,
175 Fifth Avenue, New York, NY 10010.

Palgrave Macmillan is the global academic imprint of the above companies
and has companies and representatives throughout the world.

Palgrave® and Macmillan® are registered trademarks in the United States,
the United Kingdom, Europe and other countries.

ISBN 978–0–230–29663–3 hardback
ISBN 978–0–230–29664–0 paperback

This book is printed on paper suitable for recycling and made from fully
managed and sustained forest sources. Logging, pulping and manufacturing
processes are expected to conform to the environmental regulations of the
country of origin.

A catalogue record for this book is available from the British Library.

A catalog record for this book is available from the Library of Congress.

10   9   8   7   6   5   4   3   2   1
21   20   19   18   17   16   15   14   13   12

Printed and bound in Great Britain by
CPI Antony Rowe, Chippenham and Eastbourne

Contents

Contents

Preface to the Second Edition

This book is designed to help the reader approach key themes in Western philosophy. Its aim is to give brief, accurate and informative overviews of the major arguments given and positions held in each area.

The introduction contains some advice on how to read and make sense of philosophical arguments. Philosophy is not a museum of ideas or an intellectual pick and mix. Arguments need to be carefully examined and assessed and this section helps provide some of the tools to do this.

Each chapter comprises a discussion of the main areas in each theme, a summary, a glossary of key terms and suggestions for further reading.

The discussions combine two main features. First, they summarise and explain the main arguments of each theme, clarifying and distilling their core. Second, the discussions also contain critical points, questioning the validity or soundness of arguments, and highlighting potential weaknesses and problems in the positions examined. The main purpose of this is not to provide an exhaustive catalogue of criticisms, but to highlight potential weaknesses and to encourage the reader to question the claims being made for themselves.

There is also a glossary of key philosophical words at the end of the book, along with suggestions for further reading in philosophy.

This second edition adds a sixth theme (Aesthetics) and includes revisions and additions to the chapters on the original five.

Acknowledgements

Terka Acton, Priyanka Gibbons, Penny Simmons and the anonymous readers at the publishers who helped make this book possible and then better than it otherwise would have been.

Julian also thanks his former students whose feedback on the teaching materials that formed the bases of the first edition of this book encouraged him to develop them further.

Gareth thanks Julian, for his generosity and support; Mam and Mike, for their frequent and timely help; Dad and Dor, for the sumptuous shed, wherein most of this was written; Phill and Carol, for the kind loan of their laptop, on which most of this was written; the Royal Literary Fund and the Society of Authors, for their literary alms; and Jo, for her only very occasionally daunted optimism (I loves you, babes).

Introduction

If you went to a driving school, you might well expect to be taught about the highway code and some basics about car maintenance, but what you'd expect to spend most of your time doing would be actually learning to drive. If you pick up an introduction to philosophy or enrol on a philosophy course, however, you'll find that you spend a lot of time being presented with philosophical arguments but very little time, if any at all, learning how to actually philosophise. The presumption seems to be that to do philosophy, you just have to dive into some of it and find your way around yourself.

Being thrown in at the deep end is not always the best way to learn and even being thrown in at the shallow end, which is what happens to most readers of introductions, is not much better. So before going on to discuss the six themes covered in this book, this introduction will give you a crash course in the basic skills of philosophising. Of course, these skills will be best developed when applied to the arguments presented in the rest of the book. But at the very least, they should give you a head start in being able to make the most of them.

Where do we start?

One of philosophy's distinguishing features is that it questions everything and assumes nothing. Philosophy exposes and questions the assumptions which underlie our everyday thinking about the world, ourselves, our values and our beliefs.

But at the same time, one cannot always be questioning everything or else we would only ever be able to consider the most fundamental questions in philosophy. These questions include many of those discussed in the chapter on theory of knowledge, such as how we can

1

have knowledge and whether the external world exists or not. These are vital questions in philosophy. But if we are considering, for example, the question of the mind's relation to the body, we will get nowhere fast if we insist we first have to justify our belief in the existence of an external reality.

So although it is true that philosophy questions everything and assumes nothing, this questioning has to be kept in its place. The time to question the existence of the external world is when we are doing epistemology (theory of knowledge) or metaphysics, not usually when we are doing the philosophy of mind.

The problem is that there is no formula for determining which questions should be put to one side and which are central to the issue being discussed. Here, as with so much in philosophy, good judgement is required. Unfortunately, good judgement is more like a knack one needs to develop than a technique that can be directly taught.

Nevertheless, merely being aware of the problem is a good start. Too often people start doing philosophy and come to think that a few easy points can be scored by simply questioning any assumption an argument rests upon. But except when we are considering the most basic questions of philosophy (and perhaps even then too), we always need to make some assumptions to even get started. The question is whether these are appropriate or inappropriate assumptions to make.

Premises

Some people say that philosophy is about ideas. In fact, it's more accurate to say that philosophy is about arguments. It's no good having what sounds like a great philosophical idea – for example, that we have no free will, or that everything in the universe is composed of one single substance – unless you can provide arguments to support it. Arguments are basically rational justifications for conclusions. There are many ways in which this process of rational justification can proceed. But before we even get to that stage, we have to start with what the argument is arguing from – premises.

The premises of an argument are those fundamentals which have to be accepted as true in order for the justification to get started. For example, consider the argument that God cannot exist because there is evil in the world and a good, all-powerful God would not let this happen (see Chapter 4). There are at least three premises required for this argument: that if God exists, God is all-powerful; that if God exists, God is Good and loving; and that there is evil in the world. From these three premises, the argument tries to demonstrate that God cannot exist.

In other words, the premises are used to provide a rational justification for the conclusion that God doesn't exist. But if one rejects any of these premises, the argument cannot work. If you think there is no evil in the world, for example, the argument fails to get off the ground.

How does one decide whether to accept the premises of an argument? There is no simple answer to this. Sometimes, we are asked to accept a premise on the basis of evidence. In this example, it just does seem to be true that there is evil – in some sense of the word – in the world. To say that there isn't flies in the face of the evidence of the holocaust, genocides and other terrible acts recorded in history. On other occasions, we are asked to accept premises on conceptual grounds. In the example above, it just does seem to be an essential part of the concept of God that God is all-powerful and all-loving. Some premises are justified on the grounds of basic logic. The fact that something cannot both be and not be at the same time, for example, is an elementary logical truth. And sometimes we are asked to accept a premise because it is itself the conclusion of another argument.

Sometimes premises are stated clearly, on other occasions they are tacitly assumed. In either case, when assessing an argument one needs to be able to identify what its premises are and whether they should be accepted. Only then should you move on to consider whether the rational justification is sufficient for the conclusion.

Forms of rational justification

All arguments move from premises to conclusions, but there are different ways of making this movement. The three most important forms are deduction, induction and abduction.

Deduction is the most rigorous of the three. In a deductive argument, the movement from premises to conclusion should be as precise and as rigorous as in a mathematical sum. Just as $1 + 1 = 2$, no dispute, so in a deductive argument, premise + premise = conclusion, no dispute. Consider as an example:

Brechin City is the greatest football team in Britain.
Roddy Grant plays for Brechin City.
Therefore, Roddy Grant plays for the greatest football team in Britain.

Note that in an argument such as this, 'therefore' stands in the same relation to the premises and conclusion that '=' does to the sum and its product.

In this example, it should be clear that the conclusion follows from the premises as surely as 2 is the sum of 1 + 1. This means that if the premises are true, the conclusion must also be true. Such an argument is said to be valid. That does not mean, however, that the conclusion has been shown to be true. Its truth is only demonstrated if the premises are true. (In this example, it seems sadly to be the case that at least one of the premises is not true.) If the premises are true and the argument is valid, then the argument is sound. A sound argument is a philosophical bull's-eye.

Because deductive arguments are the most rigorous of all arguments, it is ideal if one can justify one's conclusions by using them. However, it is not always possible to employ a deductive argument, for reasons that will become clear when we look at the second form of argument: induction.

Inductive arguments do not have the same necessary link between the truths of the premises and the conclusions. In an inductive argument, the premises are considered to be good evidence for the truth of the conclusion but not a guarantee of its truth. Take the following as an example:

No-one has ever run 100 metres in less than 9.5 seconds.

Jenny Jones is running 100 metres tomorrow.

Therefore, Jenny Jones will not run 100 metres in less than 9.5 seconds tomorrow.

The conclusion of this argument may seem so secure that you'd bet your last dollar on it. But the conclusion does not follow with any necessity from the premises. It is possible that both the premises are true and yet the conclusion is false – Jenny Jones could confound us all and run an amazing 100 metres. (Indeed, seven years after the first edition of this book set the time in the premise at 9.7 seconds, Tyson Gay ran 100 metres in 9.69.) The argument is thus deductively invalid.

However, on this occasion, the fact that the argument is invalid probably doesn't bother us. We don't require the conclusion to follow as a matter of necessity from the premises. It is enough that the premises give us overwhelmingly good reasons to accept the conclusion. Inductive arguments, therefore, do not require the same rigorous standard of proof as deductive ones.

Why should we ever accept one of these inductive arguments if they are less rigorous than deductive ones? The answer is that we often have no choice. When we reason about matters of fact, we have to base our arguments on experience of the past. This experience is always limited, in that we cannot know everything that has happened in the past and we do not have experience of what will happen in the future. Nonetheless, we assume that the unobserved past, present and future will resemble the observed past and present in certain vital respects. Unless we did this, we would be unable to make any generalisations about the world about us. But any generalisation about the world based on our limited experience has to fail the test of deductive validity. That is because all such arguments are basically of the form:

Every time we have observed X in the past, Y has been true of X.
Therefore, Y is true of X in the future and the unobserved past.

Clearly, this is an invalid argument. But if we didn't reason in this way, we would not be able to conclude that, for instance, all water freezes at zero degrees centigrade, or all people are mortal. In both these cases, as in all other generalisations about matters of fact, we are making a generalisation about all cases on the basis of a limited, though often large, number of other cases.

There are many interesting and important philosophical disputes about the status and justification of inductive arguments. All we need to be clear about here is that inductive arguments do have their place and that they differ in their justification from deductive ones. They are not valid, but we still have to judge whether the premises provide sufficient evidence to justify the conclusions.

A third form of argument is known as abduction. This is often known by its more descriptive name 'argument to the best explanation'. For example, several years back people discovered strange markings in fields. These so-called 'crop circles' seemed to appear overnight, from nowhere. Where did they come from?

No deductive argument could help here. From the fact that these circles existed and no-one knew where they came from, no facts about their origins could be deduced by means of a valid argument. Standard inductive arguments were also inadequate, since no past experiences directly corresponded to these new phenomena. The only alternative way to reason was by abduction, where we look for the best explanation of the phenomenon.

In this case, the main candidates were alien visitations, human pranksters, or natural forces such as wind vortexes. The evidence would later show which of these explanations fitted the facts, so eventually induction provided the solution. But before this evidence settled the matter, we could only ask which hypothesis best explained their appearance.

Here, abduction provided a temporary, provisional solution until enough evidence could be gathered for an inductive explanation. But when it comes to issues such as whether God exists, or whether other people have minds, we may have to rely permanently on arguments to the best explanation. This form of argument is the best kind of rational account we can give for a conclusion if it cannot be demonstrated by a deductive argument or if there is insufficient evidence to construct an inductive one.

Deduction, induction and abduction thus provide three models for arguments. Each provides a different way of producing a rational account which justifies the drawing of a conclusion from premises. One needs to be able to recognise when each type of argument is being used, whether it is appropriate that it is being used in the context, and whether it is satisfactorily executed.

Critiquing arguments

What has been sketched out so far provides only a brief account of the basics of philosophical argumentation. However, if one takes on board all the lessons from it, one is provided with a wide range of tools for the critique of arguments.

First, one can show that the argument depends upon a false premise. This attacks the argument at its root and prevents it from getting off the ground. Sometimes, it is necessary to show that a premise is actually false. On other occasions, it can be enough to show that the premise has not been established. For instance, if one wants to argue that baboons should be granted full human rights because they demonstrate the capacity for abstract thought, the argument fails if the truth of the premise has not been established. One doesn't need to show that baboons don't have the capacity for abstract thought, it is enough to show that it has not been established that they do. (The argument that we should grant baboons full human rights because they *might* have the capacity for abstract thought is importantly different.)

Second, one can show that the argument depends upon a premise which has not been recognised and is either false or not established as true. For example, in the baboon argument, it may simply have been assumed by the person putting forward the argument that full human rights should be granted to creatures that can demonstrate the capacity for abstract thought. If this is so, then the argument rests on an unstated and unrecognised premise. The critic can then show that this premise is in fact necessary for the argument to work and then show that it is either false or has not been shown to be true.

Third, if the argument is deductive in structure, one can show that the argument is invalid. One does this by showing that the premises do not guarantee the truth of the conclusion. For example, someone might argue:

> If John got drunk last night, he'll look a wreck this morning.
> John looks a wreck this morning.
> Therefore, John got drunk last night.

This can be shown to be invalid because it is possible that both premises are true yet the conclusion is false. For instance, it may be true that John always looks a wreck in the morning if he gets drunk the night before and that John looks a wreck this morning, but in this instance he looks terrible because his neighbours kept him awake all night playing Johnny Mathis albums at full volume, not because he got drunk. Therefore the argument is invalid. (Note that the argument is invalid even if, as a matter of fact, Johnny did get drunk last night. The point is the conclusion doesn't follow from the premises and so is not necessarily true, not that it is necessarily false.)

Fourth, in an inductive argument one can show that the premises do not provide sufficient evidence for the conclusion. If I reason that everyone who has ever lived has died and therefore I too will die, this is a justifiable inference. But if I reason that everyone I've ever met called Simon has been an arrogant fool and that therefore everyone called Simon is an arrogant fool, this is clearly not a justifiable inference. What makes an inductive inference justifiable is a matter of debate, but it essentially hinges upon the argument being based on the kind of evidence from which we can reliably generalise from. A limited acquaintance with a few people with the same name is not the kind of evidence from which one can generalise to all people with the same name.

Fifth, in an abductive argument one can argue that there is a better explanation than the one offered. One can do this by showing that the alternative explains more, relies on fewer coincidences or makes fewer assumptions, for example. In the crop circles example, the explanation that winds caused the circles requires one to suppose that freak weather caused some remarkably intricate patterns to be created. That seems as likely as imagining that a great abstract painting was caused by the chance spillages of some paint buckets. The explanation that hoaxers did it explains more because it explains not only the appearance of the circles, but also their intricate design.

Sixth, one can argue that an inappropriate or inadequate form of justification has been used. Different issues call for different types of argument. In some cases the firm proof of a deductive argument may be needed, but only an inductive argument is offered. This is most evident when someone is offering an argument as a firm proof but the argument fails to be deductively valid. One might also criticise someone for trying to provide a deductive argument when the subject matter demands an inductive one. Matching the right form of argument to the right issue is a skill as important as constructing one's arguments well.

Beyond demolition

From what has been said so far, it may seem that examining philosophical arguments is a rather negative enterprise. The focus has been on critique and finding mistakes. But surely the aim is to hit upon the truth, not simply to pull apart arguments?

It is certainly true that philosophy is not just a negative enterprise. But it is wrong to see its critical aspects as being wholly negative. When we examine arguments from all sides and attempt to find faults in them, we do not (or at least should not) do so for the mere pleasure of finding fault. The function of such critical examination is more like the function of a quality control department in a factory. A company which spends a lot of its resources rigorously testing its own products to ensure they stand up to hard use is a company which is likely to produce superior goods. Philosophy Inc. hopefully follows this model. We examine arguments as rigorously as possible because we want the ones that do get out and enjoy an intellectual life to be as durable and effective as possible.

Nevertheless, more often than not it is decided that an argument doesn't quite make the grade. Does that mean it should simply be thrown out? Not at all. We can almost always learn from a close examination of an argument, even if we end up rejecting it. There are at least three ways of doing this.

First, the major arguments in philosophy have all, for some time at least, been put forward and believed by some of the smartest people in society. It is extremely unlikely that these people were wholly wrong. Even when an argument fails, there is usually at least a part of it which hits upon a truth. So it is always worth looking for the truth or insight which lies behind the flawed argument. For example, the behaviourist thesis that all mental concepts refer to behaviours rather than inner mental events does not have many supporters today. But a sympathetic reader will see that what motivated this view was the realisation that we need something public to fix the meaning of mental concepts for them to have any shared meaning at all (see Chapter 3). Seeing what is true in behaviourism is therefore essential if we are to learn anything from it.

Second, if an argument is flawed, it may just be that it needs a little improving. For example, if one is arguing in applied ethics and one uses the premise 'It is always wrong to kill a human being' in an argument about euthanasia, most people would reject the argument, since very few people think it is always wrong to kill a human being. Self-defence, for example, may be an instance where killing is permitted. But instead of simply rejecting the argument, it can be much more fruitful to revise it. In this case, the premise could perhaps be changed to, 'It is always wrong to kill an innocent human being'. This process of revision and strengthening of the argument could go on for a long time. But unless one at least tries to construct the strongest possible argument for a position before rejecting it, one hasn't given that position a fair chance.

This point is particularly important in the context of a book like this, where each theme is only introduced. You will not read here the most sophisticated and elaborate arguments for the positions discussed simply because to have presented these would have changed the book from a brief introduction to a detailed, advanced text. Therefore, if one finds some of the arguments too simplistic and obviously wrong, that may well be as much a product of the relatively unsophisticated nature of the text as a lack of better arguments for the positions themselves.

A third reason to look beyond the failures of an argument is that, even if the argument is indeed irredeemable, we can often learn from its mistakes. The argument from design, for example, which attempts to show that God must exist because the universe is so orderly, is, most would agree, a poor argument (see Chapter 4). But understanding why it is poor increases one's understanding of how inductive arguments work and of the limits on arguments from analogy. We can learn from its inadequacies and should take the opportunity to do so.

Becoming a philosopher

From what has been said so far, it should be clear that there is no difference between reading philosophy properly and doing philosophy. Hence, the skills a reader needs to develop are the skills of philosophising. To conclude, I will sum up what some of those skills are.

To be a philosopher one needs to treat the philosophy one reads, not as authoritative texts to be ingested and learned, but as one side of a conversation to be participated in. One needs to approach the text critically but constructively. A balance needs to be struck between looking for what might be wrong in the argument and looking for any truths or insights it may nonetheless contain.

It is important to go beyond exactly what is written on the page before you. One should try and see what is motivating the arguments, what unstated premises, if any, lie behind them, and how one might take the argument forward. What one reads is almost always a start for an enquiry and not the end.

If all this makes reading philosophy sound quite demanding, then that is only because, done properly, reading philosophy *is* demanding. Philosophy requires you to draw on all your intellectual resources, for the intellect is the only resource we have to do philosophy with. However, though demanding, many find it rewarding, sometimes exhilarating even.

This book should provide a set of keys to unlock the door to some of philosophy's riches. As such it is an entrance only, but one that we hope you find yourself glad to have gone through.

1
Theory of Knowledge

What is the theory of knowledge?

If I were to ask you whether you know anything, you might understandably find my question odd. Of course we know things. We know where we live and what our names are. We know that $2 + 2 = 4$ and that the square root of 9 is 3. We know Rome is the capital of Italy, that there is a blackcurrant bush in the garden and that we had a cup of coffee for breakfast this morning. It's one of the basic facts about humans that they know things.

Philosophers have always found this common-sense idea rather problematic. Socrates is reputed to have gone so far as to say that the only thing he knew was that he knew nothing. How can we explain this stark contrast between common sense and the doubts of philosophers?

The root of the problem is that knowledge seems to require a special kind of certainty which ordinary belief doesn't have. But once you ask what could justify this certainty, you begin to find that it's very difficult, if not impossible, to find an answer.

It's easy to see why so many thinkers have argued that knowledge requires certainty. 'Know' is what we could call a success verb. 'Learn' is such a verb. To say someone has learned something is to say that they have studied it successfully and have now taken on board whatever it is they were learning. (To say someone *is learning* obviously doesn't imply this mastery has been attained, only that it is being worked towards.) Another example of a success verb is 'remember'. To say someone has remembered something is to say that they have successfully recalled information about it acquired in the past.

Because such verbs imply success, it doesn't make sense to use them if success has not been achieved. To say someone has learned to speak

Italian implies they can speak Italian, or at least could speak it before they got out of practice. If we 'remember' drinking coffee but in fact drank tea, then strictly speaking we didn't remember at all, but just *seemed to remember*. You can only genuinely remember what actually happened.

The success required to genuinely 'know' is disputed, but at minimum it implies that what we know is in fact true. I can't know that Auckland is the capital of New Zealand if the capital is in fact Wellington. I can only know that there is a blackcurrant bush in my garden if there is actually such a bush there.

When we are wrong about what we claim to know, we say that we merely believe, incorrectly. Beliefs can be true or false. But I can only *know* what is true.

This is where the problem comes in. If I am to claim to know anything, I should really only make such a claim when what I know is definitely true. If I can't be sure it is true, I should really say I believe it, not that I know it. This means that knowledge seems to require a certainty that what is known is actually true.

The problem, as we shall see throughout this chapter, is that such certainty is hard to come by. But if we can't find it, surely we can't claim to have knowledge?

The relationship between knowledge and belief will also be considered in more detail. We have seen that knowledge is not the same thing as belief, but there does seem to be a strong connection between the two. Knowledge seems to be a special kind of belief, belief which carries a seal of certainty.

The theory of knowledge (epistemology) is a central theme in philosophy. In some senses, all philosophy leads back to the question, what can we know? Hence, the considerations of this chapter are of interest to all themes in philosophy, not just epistemology.

To begin, we will consider a fundamental question in epistemology: where does our knowledge come from?

Rationalism

A recurring theme in philosophy is the relationship between our minds and the world. Philosophers as different in their outlook as Descartes and Locke have agreed that it is our nature as thinking beings which distinguishes persons from animals and that philosophy is largely about the questions that arise in the minds of such beings when they consider how the faculty of thought works.

In epistemology, two different accounts of this faculty are offered by two traditions: rationalism and empiricism.

Rationalism is most closely associated with seventeenth- and eighteenth-century philosophers such as Descartes, Leibniz and Spinoza. However, the defining characteristics of rationalism can be detected in many thinkers before and after.

Rationalists believe that the way to attain knowledge is to rely on the resources of logic and the intellect. Such reasoning proceeds from basic truths which are not grounded in experience, and don't need to be. This form of reasoning and the principles it starts with are therefore described as *a priori*, since the reasoning occurs 'prior to' experience. One example of an *a priori* proposition is that $1 + 1 = 2$. We can know this to be true just by thinking about what the sum means. We do not need to look and see if the real world provides evidence for or justifies the sum. Similarly, basic principles of logic such as 'nothing can both be and not be at the same time' are *a priori*, since they are not justified by, or grounded in, facts about the world.

The caricature of the rationalist as an 'armchair philosopher' is not wholly unjustified, since their approach to philosophy does suggest that all the important truths about reality can be discovered by thought alone, without any need to go off and examine the world.

Rationalism can appear a bit dotty to the modern mind, which is used to the idea that science, with its emphasis on experimentation and observation, is vital to the advance of knowledge. However, it can appear a little less cranky if one disabuses oneself of some common misconceptions about rationalism.

First, the rationalist does not say that one could reason without having had any experience whatsoever. We need to be taught language and educated properly if we are to have any chance of success in philosophy. The point is not that philosophers need have no experience at all of the outside world. It is rather that, once they have been equipped with good reasoning skills, language and a basic understanding of things like maths and geometry, they can go on to reason without any further reference to experience. Such *a priori* reasoning starts from first principles rather than from the evidence of experience.

Second, the rationalist does not say that one can discover particular facts about the world without going out into it. No-one could know how far London is from Paris, for example, without referring to the evidence of experience. But when it comes to knowledge about the most basic features of reality, such appeals to experience are not required. To know what the time is now, for example, I need a clock. But to understand the nature of time itself, I need only think carefully about the concept of time. To know what substance my kettle is made of, I need to test the metal it is made of. But to understand what the general nature of substance is, and whether mind and matter are different substances, I need only think carefully about what substances mind and matter are.

To see how rationalism can be intuitively appealing, consider an example of a rationalist argument derived from an Ancient Greek philosopher, Zeno (*c.*470 BCE). There is a race between Achilles and a tortoise. Achilles runs quickly, the tortoise slowly, but constantly – he is never at rest. The tortoise has a head start. In order for Achilles to overtake the tortoise, he must first get to where the tortoise started from. This will take him a certain amount of time, during which the tortoise will have moved on, however slowly. At this point in time, then, the tortoise is still ahead of Achilles. For Achilles now to overtake the tortoise, he must once again first get to where the tortoise has moved on to. This takes him a period of time, however short, during which the tortoise will have moved on a little more. Having got to where the tortoise was, to overtake, Achilles must once again first get to where the tortoise has moved on to, and so on. The point of the argument is to show that, according to what seems to be impeccable logic, Achilles can never overtake the tortoise.

At this point you might think that this is a terrible advertisement for armchair-style rationalism because we all know from experience that Achilles would have overtaken the tortoise. But the argument is not completed. It is true that Achilles would win the race. So what is wrong with the argument? One suggestion is that the argument depends on the assumption that you can divide up time and space into infinitely small parts. No matter how short a space of time you have or how short a distance, you can always talk about Achilles needing to travel that distance in a certain time. The argument thus depends upon the idea that space and time can be divided up into ever smaller parts.

So, in fact, the conclusion of the argument is not the absurdity that Achilles cannot overtake the tortoise, but the startling revelation that time and space cannot be infinitely divisible. So, it seems we have learned something about the fundamental nature of reality just by thinking in our armchairs.

This example is intended to show how rationalism may not seem quite so daft after all. However, it should be pointed out that the argument does require a small appeal to experience (the knowledge that people can overtake in races). Curiously, Zeno also put forward arguments that showed time and space cannot consist of indivisible parts, directly contradicting the conclusion of this argument! However, he believed he could resolve this by claiming that time and space are themselves indivisible, capable neither of being infinitely divided, or made up of a number of indivisible things. (In this, he was supporting the monism of his teacher Parmenides, who taught that what appear to be separate things are in fact merely aspects of a single underlying reality.)

There are some other key features of rationalism which need to be highlighted. The first is that it takes as its model of rationality deductive reasoning (see Introduction). That is to say, one advances arguments by very precise steps, only accepting conclusions which strictly follow from the premises. The model here is mathematics, whereby every stage of the calculation has to be proved and where there is no room for guesswork or 'more or less' answers.

The second is that rationalism rests on the assumption that only one conception of reality will be consistent with the findings of reason. Just as only one answer is correct to any given sum in arithmetic, so the rationalist believes, if you reason properly, only one account of reality will fit the deductions of reason. If this weren't the case, then you could never be sure that you had arrived at a proper understanding of reality, since it would be possible that equally sound reasoning could have led you to a different conclusion.

This last assumption of rationalism has come under considerable attack. Most philosophers now believe that there are many accounts of ultimate reality which are all logically consistent. To decide which one is true, therefore, we need to appeal to more than reason. We also need to appeal to the evidence of experience. This conclusion fits in with the main rival tradition to rationalism – empiricism.

Empiricism

It sounds like a poor joke, but the adversaries of Descartes, Leibniz and Spinoza were an Englishman, an Irishman and a Scotsman: Locke, Berkeley and Hume. The empiricists rejected the idea that reason alone had the power to understand reality. Instead, they gave the main role in knowledge to experience.

Locke started his great empiricist work, *An Essay Concerning Human Understanding* (1690), by rejecting the then popular theory that the mind contained certain ideas and concepts from birth. We are obviously not aware of these so-called 'innate ideas' from birth, but it was thought we needed them in order to be able to reason.

Locke's critique of innate ideas attempted to show that the mind is a 'clean slate' (or *tabula rasa*) and is furnished by experience, through our five senses. There is no need to postulate the existence of innate ideas since every idea we have can be explained in terms of experience. Locke's argument appeals to a principle known as Ockham's Razor, which states that if there are two competing explanations, then, all other things being equal, one should prefer the one which is simpler. (In Ockham's original version, the principle is strictly that one should prefer the principle which postulates fewer entities.) In Locke's view, it is just a far simpler explanation to suppose we get all our ideas from experience, by mechanisms we can understand and explain, rather than that we get some innately, through mechanisms we can neither know nor explain.

Locke's essay was the first salvo in the empiricist attack on rationalism. By showing how much we depend on experience for our knowledge, it challenged the rationalist view that experience could be set aside when reasoning philosophically. However, one should not think that Locke's idea of the *tabula rasa* is essential to empiricism. David Hume (1711–1776) believed that we were born not with ideas as such, but instincts which shape our knowledge. For Hume, the mind is not a *tabula rasa*, but is predisposed in certain ways to understand the world. He offered a different challenge to rationalism, one which again put experience over reason.

Hume's main argument was that deductive reason, which the rationalists thought was the route to all knowledge, was actually a very limited instrument. Mathematics, logic and geometry all depended on deductive argument. But knowledge of the world required a different form of reasoning, what we now call induction.

To see the difference, consider first this deductive argument:

All professional athletes are fit.
Angela is a professional athlete.
Therefore, Angela is fit.

In this deductive argument, the conclusion must follow from the premises. If all professional athletes are fit and Angela is a professional athlete, then Angela must be fit.

Now consider this inductive argument:

There has never been a year without rain in England.
Therefore, it will rain next year in England.

This argument is different. We may think that the premise provides a good reason to accept the conclusion, but it doesn't necessarily follow from the fact that it has rained every year in England that it will rain next year in England. The possibility, however slight, remains open that next year it won't.

As we saw in the introduction, in such an inductive argument we are relying on something other than pure deductive reason to reach our conclusions. These things Hume calls variously custom, habit and experience. What is perhaps surprising is that Hume thought all knowledge of the world was based on this kind of reasoning. We can never prove by deductive reasoning that every event must have a cause, that fire burns or that water quenches thirst. Rather, we learn these things through experience. Further, this learning from experience does not usually take the form of using the evidence of our senses to provide premises for deductive arguments. Reasoning about experience is wholly distinct from deductive reasoning and is therefore not 'rational' in the traditional sense at all.

Empiricism is a pretty radical hypothesis. If true, it shatters the rationalist dream that by reason alone we can discover the ultimate nature of reality and that only one such account of the world will be compatible with reason. If experience is our main guide and experience is not about forming deductive arguments on the basis of the evidence of our senses, then humans are much less rational creatures than the rationalists could ever have imagined.

The main weakness of empiricism is that there do seem to be many truths and principles of thought absolutely essential to good reasoning which are not justified or grounded in experience. The basic rules of logic, for example, are not judged to be true or false on the evidence of the real world. The empiricist needs to explain why they are permitted to help themselves to these intellectual tools while at the same time maintaining that experience provides the grounds for all knowledge.

Foundationalism

Although the rationalists and empiricists were directly opposed to each other in key respects, many of them had in common a commitment to what is sometimes called foundationalism.

The basic idea behind foundationalism is simple. Epistemology is about answering the questions of what we can know and how we can know it. It is natural to try and answer this by identifying what the basis of our knowledge is. If we can do this and demonstrate that these foundations are secure, then we can build up our knowledge confidently.

The rationalists believed that reason provided the foundations for our knowledge. All that we know is built on the rock of rationality. This rock is secure because, in its essence, reason is ultimately based on nothing more than self-evident truths. The basic principles of good reason are obvious propositions, such as 'nothing can both be and not be at the same time', and simple rules of deduction, such as 'if A and B are true, then B is true'.

The empiricists, on the other hand, believed that the foundations of our knowledge are set in experience. This may not be as immediately reassuring as rationalism, since experience can lead us astray. But by accepting that we have to base our knowledge on the fallible lessons of experience and that reason cannot do all the work, we arguably have a more realistic, attainable foundation for our knowledge.

However, we might question whether the whole foundationalist assumption is a mistake. Building from the bottom up is only one way to construct. Consider an analogy with a wall. One way to build a wall is to build it up, brick by brick, laying the foundations first. This is how foundationalists see knowledge – an intellectual edifice built up from a secure base. However, another way to build a wall is to use four boards to create a mould, fill it with concrete and then remove the boards once the concrete is set. In this way, the wall is created all at once, not from the bottom up. Could this provide a different model for understanding how knowledge is possible?

Over the last two centuries, many philosophers have rejected the foundationalist assumption and have tried to understand knowledge in a different way. They have sought to find pragmatic alternatives to foundationalism.

Pragmatism with a capital P is most closely associated with the American philosophers of the late nineteenth and early twentieth centuries, C. S. Peirce, William James and John Dewey. Pragmatism is rooted in a reaction against the correspondence theory of truth, which is an important part of the philosophy of language as well as epistemology.

The correspondence theory understands words (and by extension sentences and the beliefs we have) as standing in a relation to the real world. When our thoughts correspond correctly to the real world, they are true. So, if I have a thought, 'the bug is on the rug', and the bug is indeed on the rug, my thought is true. However, if I have the thought which doesn't correspond to the way the world is, such as 'Britain is bigger than America', my thought is false.

The theory sounds like common sense, but it is actually very difficult to give a satisfactory account of what correspondence comprises. One problem is that it seems hard to see what exactly the theory is explaining. What it says is something like this:

'The bug is on the rug' is true if the bug is on the rug.

What is not explained here is how the sentence in inverted commas – 'the bug is on the rug' – actually corresponds to the fact of the bug being on the rug. Nor is there any indication here of what the fact corresponding to the sentence is, since the fact is simply the sentence repeated.

For our purposes, we need not dwell on the problems of the correspondence theory. What we need to do is consider the pragmatist alternative. Pragmatism rejected the idea that it is correspondence which makes sentences true. Rather, the truth is what works.

For instance, what makes it true that water freezes at zero degrees centigrade? Rather than say it is because the sentence 'water freezes at zero degrees centigrade' somehow corresponds to a fact or the truth, the pragmatists answer is to say that it is true because taking it to be true allows us to successfully do certain things, such as make ice-cubes or predict on the basis of a thermometer reading whether a water sample will be liquid or solid.

Likewise, 'Britain is bigger than America' is false, not because it fails to correspond, but because one will fail to do anything like plan a journey or make a decent map if one takes it to be true.

Apart from Pragmatism with a capital P, there are many other lower-case pragmatisms. The coherence theory, for instance, says that beliefs are true if they cohere together into a whole system of beliefs which are compatible with experience. Instrumentalism says that beliefs are true if they allow us to do things in the world which we couldn't do unless we took them to be true. All can be called pragmatic theories because they define truth in terms of what works, not in terms of any determinate connection they have with objective facts.

To make the connection between pragmatism and knowledge, one needs to consider the role of truth in knowledge. Remember that at the start of this chapter we said that to know implies that what one knows is true. Foundationalism provides a way to show why what we think we know is true – it is built on solid foundations of experience, rationality or both. On pragmatic conceptions of truth, knowledge does not rest on such foundations. Put crudely, truth is what works, and what works is determined by trial and error, not by building up from secure foundations. Knowledge, which is of what is true, is therefore similarly not foundationalist in nature.

The tripartite account of knowledge

One can see another way in which conceptions of truth plug into conceptions of knowledge by considering one of the most enduring conceptions of what knowledge is – the so-called 'tripartite account of knowledge'. The tripartite account of knowledge has a very noble pedigree. A version of it appears in Plato's dialogue, *Theaetetus*. In it, Socrates and the eponymous interlocutor test out the theory that knowledge is true belief plus a rational account. On this view, knowledge has three parts: a belief, the fact that the belief is true and the fact that one can provide a rational account to show the belief is true.

The modern counterpart of this theory dresses it up in a little jargon. The tripartite account aims to provide the necessary and sufficient conditions for propositional knowledge. By necessary and sufficient conditions, we mean what is required to be the case for something to count as knowledge. By propositional knowledge, we mean something that can be expressed in the form, 'X knows that P', where P is a proposition or sentence. This contrasts with knowledge by acquaintance, which is where I say 'I know X' because I am familiar with it through direct experience. So, 'I know London' is an example of knowledge by acquaintance whereas, 'I know that London is the capital of Britain' is an example of propositional knowledge.

The tripartite account claims that propositional knowledge has three necessary conditions: Justification, truth and belief. Expressed formulaically, this means:

S knows that P if and only if:

1.   S believes that P.
2.   P is true.
3.   S is justified in believing that P.

As we have seen, because 'know' is a success verb, condition (2) must hold. At this point, one may be tempted to ask, 'but how do we know something is true?' This is a legitimate question, but not relevant to the project of providing necessary and sufficient conditions for knowledge. What we are looking for here is not a way of *verifying* whether we do actually know anything or not, but rather what conditions would have to be fulfilled *if* one were to know something. The question is thus 'what is it to know?', not 'how do we know that we know?'

Condition (1) also appears to be necessary. After all, many things are true and justifiable, but if I have no beliefs about them, I cannot know that they are true. This is the *entailment* thesis, that knowledge entails belief or something similar, such as certainty, conviction or acceptance.

However, some hold that there is an *incompatibility* between knowledge and belief, so belief can have no part in knowledge. There are at least three arguments for this.

First, it is claimed that knowledge is by definition infallible. If one knows, one cannot be wrong, as that would simply mean one never knew in the first place. However, belief implies fallibility. Therefore, belief and knowledge are incompatible.

This does not seem to be very persuasive. As belief is only one part of knowledge, there seems no problem in holding that fallible belief plus the other conditions of knowledge add up to infallible knowledge. It's like saying that a bolt can't be part of a mansion, because bolts are cheap and mansions are expensive!

The second argument is that the words have incompatible meanings, illustrated by the familiar protest, 'I don't believe it, I *know* it!' But again, this has an alternative explanation. In such utterances, we are simply pointing out that what we have is not *just* belief, but something more. It doesn't mean belief is not involved. Compare, 'we didn't beat them, we destroyed them!' This means we didn't *just* beat them, we did something more, but still, beating was involved.

The third argument is that since belief entails uncertainty and knowledge entails certainty, knowledge cannot involve belief, as we cannot be both certain and uncertain of the same thing at the same time. However, the premises of this argument are dubious. Some people are certain of their beliefs, even though they cannot be said to know that they are true. Conversely, it doesn't seem impossible for someone to know and yet be uncertain. It is surely possible for there to be two people who believe the same thing to be true with the same justifications. If one just happens to be more confident than the other, it would surely be odd to say that person knows and the other one doesn't. It is unclear that the certainty a person feels has any relevance to whether they know something or not.

This is an interesting point, because there is a tradition in philosophy, found in Plato, for example, of characterising knowledge as if it were a certain special state of mind, of which certainty is one characteristic. On this view, if we could see into people's minds, we would find that knowing is a different mental state to believing, for example. This seems improbable, because whether one knows must surely depend at least partly on what is true of the world. That means that knowing requires something to be true outside of your head as well as in it. So just looking at your state of mind will never be enough to tell us if you know or not – we also need to know what is true of the world.

In addition to the entailment and incompatibility theses, there is the separability thesis. This doesn't go so far as to say that knowledge and belief are incompatible, but it does claim that they can be separated. This would mean that belief cannot be an essential part of knowledge. The idea here is that the test of whether someone knows something is whether they can answer questions correctly about it, whether they can use that knowledge and so on. Now, someone may be able to do these things and yet lack the belief that they know the facts in question. As an example, consider the student who insists they don't know, and the teacher says, 'Yes you do, have a go.' The student then offers what they feel is a guess, and the teacher replies, 'Correct. You see, you did know all along.' This account sounds odd, because one wouldn't normally claim to know something if one didn't believe it and was pretty sure of it. But perhaps there is no contradiction in claiming that one may not be justified in claiming one knows something, even though one does in fact know it. In order for Jack to *say* 'I know', he has to believe and have certainty, but for it to *be true* that 'Jack knows' these conditions may not apply.

The third component of the tripartite account, that the true belief be justified, is probably the most problematic. The main question here is what constitutes justification. People justify their claims to knowledge in all sorts of ways, some good and some bad. However, although this clearly is a thorny issue, it could be said to be irrelevant to the present purposes. We would need to know whether our justification was a good one or not if we are to decide whether we know that P in any particular cases. So, to know that we know we would need to be sure our justification was sound. But we are only concerned here with what is required for knowledge in general. Hence, all we need to consider is whether justification is required, not what *sort* of justification is required. That question can come later.

Against the tripartite account

Many have criticised the tripartite account by showing there are counter-examples where knowledge does not fit the mould of justified true belief. For instance, in D. H. Lawrence's short story, 'The Rocking Horse Winner', a child correctly predicts the winners of horse races time after time. Although there is nothing to justify his beliefs, he is nevertheless right. Hence, we seem to have knowledge without justification. (I owe this example to Michael Proudfoot.)

One reply to this is that this knowledge is justified. It is simply the case that the justification – repeated success – is not available on the earlier occasions. The fact that the justification is temporally after the time of the knowing doesn't mean there is no justification. We cannot *say* that the boy knows until the justification arises, but there is still a justification. The problem with this reply is that had the boy chosen to make just one prediction, then the justification would never have arisen and without the justification the boy could not be said to have known at all. But if the boy knew when he made one prediction which happened to be followed by others, then surely he would have known if he had made the identical prediction but not gone on to make any more. Whether he knows or not surely cannot be determined by what happens after he makes his prediction and the prediction comes true. Whether one knows cannot depend upon facts other than those pertaining to the relationship between fact and knower.

This example presents the possibility of knowledge without one of the three conditions in the tripartite account. Edmund Gettier, however, came up with some counter-examples to show how even if all three conditions are fulfilled, there can still be a lack of knowledge.

In one example, two people – call them Blib and Blob – apply for the same job. Blib justifiably believes that Blob has ten coins in his pocket and that he will get the job. Therefore, by simple logic, he is justified in believing that the person who gets the job has ten coins in his pocket. As it turns out, Blib also has ten coins in his pocket and gets the job. Given that Blib wrongly thought Blob would get the job and didn't know he himself had ten coins in his pocket, it would seem absurd to say he knew that the person who got the job had ten coins in his pocket. Yet he did believe this, his belief was justified and his belief was true. So it seems we have justified true belief without knowledge.

One obvious reply to Gettier is that his examples feature inadequate justifications. The problem here, though, is that if we are to reply to Gettier by specifying what constitutes an adequate justification, we risk either making our requirements so strict that we could never have knowledge, or that further counter-examples will be produced until we do reach these over-strict requirements. For example, if we claim that knowledge requires justification which *guarantees* the truth of the proposition, then at best we would only be able to know necessary truths of logic, definition and mathematics, as no empirical knowledge of the world is justified in such a way as to guarantee it to be true.

Solving Gettier's problems is frustratingly difficult. For instance, one attempt is to add a fourth condition to the three of the tripartite account which specifies the importance of causation, such as:

4.   P is the cause of S's belief that P is true.

In the Blib and Blob example above, Blib would not have knowledge because what caused him to have his true justified belief was not the fact that it was true. One objection to this is that it is unclear whether a proposition or fact is the right kind of thing to be a cause of a belief. Facts and propositions do not really cause anything. Another objection comes in the form of a counter-example devised by Alvin Goldman:

> Suppose Sam spots Judy across the street and correctly believes that it is Judy. If it were Judy's twin sister, Trudy, he would mistake her for Judy. Does Sam know that it is Judy? As long as there is serious possibility that the person across the street might have been Trudy rather than Judy . . . , we would deny that Sam knows.
>
> (*Epistemology and Cognition*, 1986)

Here, Sam is justified in his true belief that it is Judy, and Judy is the cause of this belief. But he doesn't know it is Judy because there was a large element of luck involved. He would have been just as inclined to say that it was Judy if it had been Trudy, which shows that he doesn't really know who it was – he was just lucky. All three conditions of the tripartite account plus the causal condition are all in play, yet we don't have knowledge.

One odd feature of an enquiry such as this is that when we decide whether or not a set of criteria for knowledge is a good one or not, we seem to already know what counts as knowledge! We confidently assert that Sam doesn't know it is Judy, for example. But how do we know he doesn't know? Because we know what knowledge is and it isn't *that*!

We are able to use the concept of knowledge and know when it is applied correctly, and yet every attempt to define it seems to end in failure.

Maybe this is because knowledge is indefinable, or at the very least there are no precise conditions which specify its correct application. It could be a primitive concept; that is to say, a concept so basic that it cannot be defined in even simpler terms.

Wittgenstein (1889–1951) would claim that to know what a word means is simply to be able to use it properly, even if we can't precisely define it. Consider the noun 'game'. Games have many different features. Not all involve winning, teams, competition or entertainment, for example. Hence, defining 'game' is very difficult. But someone unable to define what a game is (which is almost all of us) still knows what 'game' means. What ultimately enables us to use 'game' (or 'know') correctly is our familiarity with a word's various uses in everyday contexts and the fact that humans share common activities and interests, and that there is a 'family resemblance', as Wittgenstein later called it, between the various correct usages of 'game' which we come to recognise and this enables us to use the word correctly. If Wittgenstein is right, then we are wrong to think that we need to specify precisely what knowledge is. We know how to use the word 'know' and so already know what knowledge means. It is a kind of philosophical sickness that makes us believe we don't.

The nature of belief

Whether or not some clear definition of knowledge is possible, and whether or not knowledge necessarily entails belief, knowing generally seems to involve holding an opinion, having a certain attitude toward something, or adopting certain ways of behaving. If I know that it is going to rain, then I may feel depressed or frustrated, I may bring in the washing or cancel my trip to the beach, and so on. Knowing can therefore arguably be cashed out in terms of what I believe. But understanding belief is not itself so very simple.

There are two main philosophical approaches here. The first defends what we might think of as the common-sense picture, where belief consists in a mental state; the second, on the other hand, thinks of belief in terms of behaviour or physical dispositions to behave one way or another.

Firstly, the mental state view sees belief as consisting of two aspects, and is therefore sometimes called the *dual-component* view. For instance, my belief in Santa Claus consists in a certain proposition ('There is a man named Santa'), and a particular attitude to it (I think that it is true – he exists). Therefore, belief is what is called a *propositional attitude*, similar to hope, disapproval, doubt or envy. The only difference between these is the attitude that I adopt to the proposition in question. This account seems plausible. Simply having a thought is not enough to make it a belief – a mental image of Santa does not actually say anything at all (whether he exists, whether he thinks you've been naughty or nice). Belief therefore involves thinking or feeling something *about* a certain possible state of affairs.

However, we might argue that not all beliefs are propositional. As well as *believing that* something is the case, I may also *believe in* something. An example here might be religious faith: belief in God does not necessarily mean 'I believe that there is a supernatural force that is omniscient, omnipresent...', but can also imply a sense of trust or emotional investment. But this is not a fatal point to thinking of belief as a propositional attitude. I might simply accept that there are different forms of belief, but that the one that is relevant for an understanding of knowledge is *belief that*, or *propositional* belief.

But there are still problems here. First, talking of belief as a sort of mental state seems to treat beliefs as 'things' or real objects. Later on, in the chapter on philosophy of mind, we'll see that this idea of the mind as a mental space where ideas 'live' – which owes much to Descartes – is a problematic one. I can talk of something being 'in' my mind, but that's just a metaphor, isn't it? Science suggests that whatever beliefs and other forms of mental content really are, they certainly aren't immaterial entities floating around my mind. If the mental state approach implies thinking of thoughts as some sort of special mental 'stuff', then most philosophers would reject it. However, the view need not imply this, and beliefs may still be 'real' things in another sense. The mental state that my belief consists of may be reflected in the structure of the brain, in the arrangement of neurons. 'I believe in Santa' is therefore perhaps some identifiable neurological pattern, and someone might scan my brain and find the area of electrical activity that corresponds to my belief. On this view, the mental state is therefore simply the conscious experience of the belief that is 'encoded' in my physical brain.

However, whether brain states or ghostly thought forms, the idea is that beliefs have a specific definable content. What defines a belief is the fact that it is about *this* not *that*, about Santa not Satan. But beliefs do not always seem to be crisply defined. For instance, say that I hold the belief 'It is going to rain'. Now, when it rains, I fetch the washing in. To make sense of this, must I also consciously hold the belief that 'Rain will make the laundry wet', or 'Wet laundry will mean that I'll have no clean clothes to wear'? And so on. Any single belief can be seen to be connected to all sorts of related beliefs which are required to give it its fullest sense. In other words, to make sense of one belief, we must make sense of a wide range of others – in fact, arguably, our whole set of beliefs. But these cannot all form a part of my conscious mental state – I don't hold all the various implications of 'it's raining' each time I have that belief. We might respond here that just because a belief is vague or open-ended does not mean that it is not a real, defined thing. A crowd may be an amorphous loosely connected thing, but it still makes sense to talk of 'it'. However, if we cannot isolate a belief from other beliefs, or give it a specific character, then the idea that it is a definite, individual 'thing' seems to be undermined. Therefore, given these and other difficulties, some philosophers have preferred to think of beliefs in a different way.

The second main approach views beliefs in terms of dispositions to behave in certain ways. This does away with the idea that a belief is a 'thing' or consciously held attitude of mind. Faced with finding out what someone believes, instead of getting them to communicate their mental state, we may observe their behaviour under certain conditions. Do I think violence is occasionally necessary? Let's find out! Whether I respond to your sudden and unprovoked attack by breaking your nose or blithely turning the other cheek, my response will tell you what I believe. We may also find out about my opinions on certain matters by asking me or raising the subject in my presence. Such an approach aims to do away with what is mysterious about belief and the mind in general. Beliefs are not 'in here', but reveal themselves 'out there'. All belief is therefore reducible to how I might or actually do behave. This *dispositional* approach (a form of *behaviourism* – see Chapter 4) therefore marks a general move away from the internal and private, and toward the external and observable; from the subjective toward the (supposedly) objective. A good thing, surely? The problem with this view is that simply because external evidence is more readily available does not mean that this is all there is to belief. The fact that the private, subjective side of belief is slippery and difficult to pin down should not rule it out of our analysis. To focus solely on what is objectively observable, and to assume that this is all that matters, is like looking for my car keys where there is more light, not where I may have lost them. But external behaviour doesn't always give us the full picture. For instance, my external actions may mask a very subtle and hidden motive, or my actions might have some personal significance that remains hidden. Now, the behaviourist will argue that such differences must come out under relevant circumstances – they will eventually reveal themselves through behaviour and communication. But this assumes what it wants to prove: that all mental experience can be cashed out in terms of dispositions. But can it? We'll consider this question again later in the book, but many philosophers now find this approach generally unsatisfactory.

Other accounts of belief have built upon the dispositional approach. *Instrumentalism*, for instance, argues that speaking about the mind in terms of intentions, desires and beliefs is simply a useful 'stance' to adopt (this view is held by Daniel Dennett). So, such things as beliefs do not *really* exist, but such a way of talking provides a useful model of explanation: Tim's biological urge to procreate is usefully couched in terms of his belief that Jenny is attractive.

Another more radical approach, *eliminativism*, agrees that beliefs aren't real, but claims that by rejecting these false notions, and adopting the language of neuroscience, we can arrive at a more objective view of the world. So, just as cosmologists abandoned the idea that the Sun goes round the Earth, or children eventually realise that storks don't deliver babies, philosophical and scientific progress will one day relegate the range of terms we currently use to describe mind and human behaviour to the scrap heap. Belief in 'belief' will die out. Again, we'll look at these issues later, but you can see that how we account for belief is central to the philosophy of mind and the metaphysical question of *what* we are.

A more epistemological question – concerning the nature of knowledge – is whether belief is voluntary. David Hume argued that it is not. I may hold almost any idea in my mind, but it is not really up to me as to whether I believe in it. Does this mean that we have no choice in what we believe? Well, I can withhold belief in something, even something I am strongly inclined to believe. This was in fact Descartes's project in his *Meditations*: to avoid error, we must assent only to those things which appear to be completely certain. But intellectually keeping an open mind is different from actively *disbelieving*. I may consider the idea that the world is a dream a possible one, and thus at an intellectual level *withhold my assent* from my belief that the chair I am sitting on is real, but I cannot actively *disbelieve* its reality.

But perhaps there are in fact ways in which I can seek to change my beliefs. The fact that something is automatic doesn't mean that it is unalterable. I do not consciously make my heart beat, but I can speed it up or slow it down by vigorous exercise or relaxation. Similarly then, could I therefore choose to take action that will at some point cause me to believe differently? We may think here of evangelical conversion, or aggressive sales techniques. It's not that you have rationally come to accept that you need double glazing or the need to be born again in Jesus Christ, but the pressure brought to bear through appeal to emotion and other irrational elements may bypass your rationality. And who is to say that reason has the biggest say in these matters? The American pragmatist philosopher William James argued that the precise amount of evidence for this or that belief is ultimately immaterial. A single criticism may be enough to undermine a belief that is weakly held, but sure faith may survive a tide of contradiction. The grounds for belief may therefore be subjective. James is not rejecting the possibility of truth here, but merely pointing out that not all things are rationally decided matters of fact. Belief in God, appreciation of literature and art, the plausibility of various proposals in politics and business – often, in such cases, the facts do not fully decide matters for us, and the rest is up to us.

This leads us nicely on to the question of the possible extent of knowledge. As the above examples suggest, we are all limited in various ways when it comes to what we can know with any real certainty. However, whilst most of us will accept this in relation to certain questions, there is a certain brand of philosopher who wants to go further. So, rather than merely accepting that knowledge can have its limits, this view argues that – for various reasons – it is impossible to have knowledge at all. This is called *scepticism*.

Scepticism concerning knowledge

There is an important difference between ordinary scepticism and philosophical scepticism. Ordinary scepticism distinguishes between sources of knowledge which are reliable (such as good science) and unreliable (such as newspaper astrologers). Philosophical scepticism, on the other hand, calls into question the reliability of our system of knowledge in general. In this way, philosophical scepticism is quite indiscriminating. What reasons could we possibly have for accepting such a pessimistic and undermining position?

Many arguments have been advanced for scepticism but as A. J. Ayer (1910–1989) repeatedly pointed out, the basic form of most sceptical arguments is the same. They start by asking what would justify us being certain that any particular belief or proposition was true. They then show that no such justification is possible.

For instance, we might think we would be justified in being certain of statements which are self-evident. Self-evident propositions are those which stand in need of no further justification – they justify themselves. Examples include '2 + 2 = 4', or 'All bachelors are unmarried'.

However, the sceptic can argue that we cannot even be certain of the truth of these statements. In each case, all we are relying on is an intuitive sense that they must be true. But can we trust these intuitions? When we dream, aren't we just as certain about things which we later discover to be manifestly false? Couldn't we be mad people, who are both convinced of the self-evident truth of certain absurdities and totally unaware of their own madness? Could we not have been brain-washed or hypnotised to believe things to be self-evidently true which we would otherwise not accept as such?

The pattern of the sceptic's argument is the same when she turns her attention to the basis of our beliefs in sense experience, as we shall see soon. By showing that there are no certain foundations to our knowledge, the sceptic makes the whole possibility of knowledge problematic, if not impossible.

The sceptic follows the same line when considering how we use reason to give us knowledge of the world. The sceptic, following Hume, starts by observing that all reasoning about the world is inductive in form (see the section on empiricism above). But inductive reasoning, as we have seen, does not guarantee the truth of its conclusions. That means we can never be certain that what we have concluded from a piece of inductive reasoning is true, so again we have cast doubt on the possibility of our having knowledge.

Put these three strands of scepticism together and it seems we have no knowledge at all. We cannot be certain that self-evident statements are true. We cannot be certain that what we perceive exists. We cannot be certain that the conclusions of our reasoning about the world are true. In short, we cannot be certain of anything.

Scepticism is not short of critics. Gilbert Ryle (1900–1976), for example, argues that the sceptic robs the idea of 'certain knowledge' of any meaning by insisting that it doesn't exist. He uses the analogy that the concept of false coins only makes sense if there are genuine ones. The philosophical sceptic, however, labels all our supposed knowledge as 'false coins', which would seem to make no sense if there is no true knowledge for it to contrast with. Ignorance implies knowledge, so by denying we have any knowledge the sceptic robs the idea of ignorance of any content.

In reply to this, it could be argued that scepticism is not the claim that nothing is true, it is rather the claim that we cannot distinguish truth and falsehood. This means that, as far as we are concerned, we

can never be sure that we have knowledge. But the objection could still hold. Returning to the coins analogy, if there is no possible means of distinguishing between false and true coins, isn't the distinction meaningless?

This discussion reinforces the point made earlier about the difference between ordinary and philosophical scepticism. The philosophical scepticism I have outlined is not justified by experience. A scientist may cast doubt on a theory by citing other empirical evidence, but the sceptic cannot cast doubt on the existence of the world itself by citing empirical evidence. The sceptic considers what empirical evidence can and can't do, not whether any particular piece of empirical evidence casts doubt on our knowledge. The sceptic's general doubt makes all evidence suspect, not only in cases where we appear to be deluded. In essence, then, the sceptic does not base her argument on experience, but bases it on the hypothesis that our standards of proof are logically defective.

At the root of the sceptic's doubts lies the quest for certainty and the conviction that such certainty cannot be attained. The quest for certainty has been seen as a fundamental part of the theory of knowledge, the idea being that without certainty, we cannot have knowledge. Thus, it appears the sceptic only needs to remove certainty to remove our claim to knowledge. It is this which seems to make scepticism inevitable. As Ayer says: 'There can be doubt so long as there is the possibility of error.'

Perhaps this is the problem. There are many different concepts all getting tangled up in the sceptic's web. First, there is knowledge, which is about a relation the knower has to information or facts. Then there is certainty, which in its primary usage is about a state of mind. (We can say 'it is certain' rather than 'I am certain' and thus not refer to a state of mind, but this is another usage of certain.) Next there is doubt, which is also a psychological state.

The point is that certainty, knowledge and doubt are all distinct. It does not seem to be self-contradictory, for example, to say that I know something, even though I'm not certain of it. Similarly, I can be certain of something and yet not know it, since I am in fact wrong. Could it, then, be that in tying the idea of certainty and immunity from doubt so closely to the idea of knowledge, the sceptic – and those she attacks – have made a fundamental mistake?

It is also possible to rebuke the sceptic by rejecting the foundationalist approach to knowledge (see the section on foundationalism above). Scepticism works by undermining the foundations of our knowledge. But if we accept a pragmatic, coherence or instrumentalist conception of knowledge, then perhaps we can sidestep the sceptic's challenge. If our knowledge has no foundations to undermine, then the sceptic's attack leaves no sting.

Scepticism concerning perception

Scepticism has perhaps been most influential in arguments concerning perception. The sceptic's prime target here is naïve realism. Naïve realism is the view that the world is more or less as we perceive it to be. This view is threatened by the widely held idea that we do not perceive the world directly. If this is true, then there may be sceptical repercussions. It may be that we don't perceive the external world at all, or it could even be true that there is no external world.

Many philosophers have, in fact, concluded that we do not perceive the world directly. It is rather that we have perceptions, and from these perceptions we infer the existence of the external world. Those things which we perceive have variously been called ideas (Locke, Berkeley), impressions (Hume) or sense data (Russell, Moore).

Sense data are not things in the mind which have been discovered by science. There is no experimental way of distinguishing between seeing an object and seeing a sense datum. So why then introduce sense data? The most popular argument for sense data is the argument from illusion, one primitive version of which is:

> When I look at a distant house, what I see is small.
> The house is not small.
> Therefore, what I see is not a house.

This is clearly unsound, as it begs the question to say that what I see *is* small. Surely, all I can say is that it *appears* small. If the first premise is thus amended, the argument then becomes invalid, unless we add a third premise which states: 'If a house is large, and what I see does not appear to be large, then what I see cannot be a house.' However, it is far from clear why we should accept this as a premise.

Similar objections can be raised against this subtler version of the argument:

> We often perceive something not as it really is.
> In such cases, we are perceiving something.
> Therefore, it cannot be the object itself we are perceiving.
> Therefore, we must be perceiving something else, that is, sense data.

We can take this one stage further and argue that we always see sense data. If it is true that in such cases when we perceive something not as it really is that we perceive sense data, and there is nothing to distinguish such perceptual experiences from veridical perceptions, then it would seem that we always perceive sense data. It would be very odd if perception sometimes were of sense data and sometimes of the object itself, even though the experience was identical in both cases.

Unfortunately, this argument is also flawed. The argument is only valid if we accept the rulings, 'in every case where an object seems to be perceived there is something directly perceived,' (which is required for the second premise to be true) and 'that which is directly perceived cannot appear otherwise than as it is' (which is required for the first conclusion to follow).

In the first case, it is not clear that we can give any sense to the idea of direct perception unless we can contrast it with indirect perception. If it is true that ordinary perception of objects is indirect, then what would it mean to perceive them directly? The problem is that perception is always, in some sense, indirect. The whole point about perception is that it is awareness of an object through the medium of one or more senses. This is as direct as perception can ever get. It may make sense to talk about perception via a reflection or television, for example, as being indirect. But to talk about ordinary perception as being indirect as opposed to direct seems to be making a contrast with something that doesn't exist.

As for the second ruling – 'that which is directly perceived cannot appear otherwise than as it is' – there just seems to be no good reason to accept it. Extraordinary though it may seem, many philosophers seem to have assumed that something like this must be true. If I see a castle through a heat haze, for instance, it seems perfectly acceptable to say I am directly perceiving the castle, yet it is not appearing as it really is, since it isn't actually shimmering. There just seems no good reason to deny this possibility.

A further version of the argument for sense data is:

Every time I see an X, it is possible that X may not be there.
So I should say, 'I seem to see an X'.
This can also be phrased as 'I see a seeming X'.
This seeming X is a sense datum.

For example, did Macbeth see a dagger? Well, he seemed to see a dagger, so we could say he saw a seeming dagger, that is a sense datum of a dagger. But this could be dismissed as unnecessary 'reification'. Reification is the process of taking a phenomenon to be a certain kind of object. In this case, we are taking the phenomenon of 'seeming to see a dagger' and creating an object 'a seeming dagger'. But to seem to see an X is not the same as to see a seeming X, as the latter supposes that there is something there to be seen, whereas the former does not. We could equally say of Macbeth that he saw nothing, or thought he saw a dagger. The point is that to have a visual experience does not entail that there is something which one is seeing.

Ryle makes this objection even more convincing when he talks of the sense data theorist making a 'logical howler'; namely, 'assimilating the concept of sensation to the concept of observation'. With observation, the thing observed is not immediate to the observer. For example, one can have a good or bad view of what one is observing, one's observation can be more or less clear or striking. These things are not true of sensations. Sensations are immediate to the person having the sensation. One does not introspect to *observe* one's pain, one simply *has* the pain.

Ryle argues that the having of a perception is more like a sensation than an observation. It cannot be a form of observation for the following reason: perception requires the object perceived and the perception of that object. If having a perception is like an observation, then the perception itself must be observed or perceived. We would then have the perception and the perception of the perception. But then the perception of the perception would also have to be observed, so we would need a perception of the perception of the perception, and so on. To prevent this infinite regress (a never-ending requirement for the perception to be perceived), we have to conclude that a perception cannot itself be perceived or observed.

The upshot is that we should think of a perception as more like a sensation which is simply 'had' than an observation of sense data. This removes the regress. But then the sense data model would have to be rejected, as this model assumes that in perception, it is sense data that are directly perceived, which follows the observation model.

A. J. Ayer has a good reply to this objection. He claims that there is no general principle that the having of a perception itself entails a further perception. It is simply that in the particular case of perceiving physical objects, we have grounds for believing it is not the objects themselves which are perceived.

Who is right? There is no consensus on this debate. If Ayer is right, then we do not perceive the world directly, and the world may well be different to the way it appears. Hence, naïve realism would be defeated. But if Ryle is correct, that wouldn't necessarily mean naïve realism triumphed. There are other competing models for perception.

Ryle's view is compatible with the causal theory of perception, which states that:

1. Objects have those properties which science indicates that they have.
2. Perceived qualities are caused by these actual properties interacting with the environment and the observer.

This seems compatible with a weak form of naïve realism, which simply claims that objects are directly perceived. Although the physical properties causing perception are not themselves perceived, nevertheless, the object itself is the direct cause of our perceptions, and so in a sense objects are directly perceived. There is nothing between the perceiver and object as there is in the sense data theory.

Although the scientific view which informs the causal theory is arguably itself based on observations of sense data, the fact that science explains and predicts so well gives us good reasons to believe our scientific view is correct.

One potentially serious difficulty for this view is that it still creates a huge chasm between the world as it is and the world as it is actually perceived. The world appears as a collection of solid, coloured, textured objects, not a seething mass of colourless particles in motion. It appears then, that no strong form of naïve realism can really be compatible with this view. Yet part of the appeal of the causal theory is that it seems to be based on a scientific realism which is the natural successor to naïve realism. But if scientific realism is true, surely naïve realism is false. The world just isn't as it appears.

On the other hand, it could be said that scientific realism is compatible with naïve realism. Just because science says a table is a collection of molecules, does that mean that the table isn't 'really' hard, brown, square and so on? Possibly not. Science is concerned with micro-properties, whereas hardness, shape and so on are macro-properties, not there on the molecular level but certainly real on the macro level. After all, what does it mean to say the table is not 'really' brown? This makes sense if we mean that it is in odd light, for example, or that it has been painted over. To say it is not really brown is to suggest it has a real colour or no colour at all. The scientific view does not suggest either. As colour is something only evident to those who perceive an object, what science says about an object's deep structure cannot have any bearing on whether it really has colour or not.

We are beginning to move away from the centre of epistemology and into metaphysics, which considers questions surrounding the fundamental nature of reality. Epistemology and metaphysics are very closely related and many universities offer classes in both, nicknamed 'ep and met'. Continuing this chapter, we will look at three major metaphysical positions – realism, idealism and phenomenalism – and see how they tie in with epistemological arguments.

Realism

Realism is simply the view that objects exist independently of our perceptions of them. An optimistic realist would say that we also are able to know about the nature of this real world. The basic assumption of realism is actually shared by moderate sceptics, whose doubt that we can have knowledge of the real world rests on the belief that it nonetheless exists.

Realism is a common-sense view and one tends not to see many positive arguments for it. Rather, people defend realism by arguing against rival positions, such as idealism and phenomenalism. So, much of what can be said about realism will be covered in what is said against idealism and phenomenalism.

One example of a positive argument for realism comes from John Searle (see his *Mind, Language and Society*). He offers a kind of transcendental argument. A transcendental argument starts from what we know to be true in experience and then goes on to show what must be the case in order for this to be true.

In Searle's argument, the starting point is that ordinary discourse is meaningful and allows us to do certain things. For instance, if we arrange to meet up at a certain time and place, then assuming we have accurate watches, maps and so on, we will do so. None of this makes sense, argues Searle, unless we make the assumption that 'there is a place, in space in time, that is independent of us and we can meet at that particular place', as he put it in an interview (collected in *What Philosophers Think* by Baggini and Stangroom). That assumption is precisely what realism is.

Realism is obviously very attractive, even though it creates space for the sceptic. However, it faces many challenges, the most illustrious of which is idealism.

Idealism

The empiricist philosopher John Locke (1632–1704) distinguished between the primary and secondary qualities of objects. Primary qualities are those of size, shape, solidity, number and motion. These were thought to be properties objects had regardless of whether anyone was observing them or not. Secondary qualities, however, depend upon the perceiver. Colour, texture and temperature, for instance, all vary according to the nature of the perceiver. The colour of what we call a red ball, for instance, looks very different to a normally sighted person, to someone who is colour-blind or to a dog. The same water feels tepid if your hand is cold, yet cold if your hand is hot. A surface smooth for a human can be a rough, rugged landscape for an ant.

Locke's view was essentially a realist one. He thought that primary qualities were the real properties of objects and that these existed independently of any minds. Secondary qualities accounted for the fact that objects may appear differently to us but they do not cast doubt on the basic independent reality of things.

However, Bishop George Berkeley (1685–1753) disagreed, and turned Locke's arguments against him to support a decidedly non-realist alternative. Berkeley contended that, to be consistent, Locke should have acknowledged that what he called primary qualities were really secondary qualities. Consider shape. In what way can we talk about shape independently from sense experience? If a box is square, that is because it looks and feels square. Take away the idea of look and feel from the idea of square and what are you left with? Nothing, contends Berkeley. That means you need sense perception to have the idea of an object's shape, so the idea that shape is a primary quality which exists independently of sense perception doesn't make sense. Shape, therefore, has to be a secondary quality, like colour and taste.

Berkeley said similar things about the other so-called 'primary qualities'. The root of his argument is that all properties of an object are only known to us through sense perception. They are all thus sense dependent, not sense independent.

This view has a remarkable upshot. If all the properties of an object are sense dependent, and an object is after all no more than the sum of all its properties, then that must mean that all objects are sense dependent. Realism is thus false. Objects do not exist whether they are perceived or not. Objects only exist because they are perceived. As Berkeley put it, *esse est percipi* – to be is to be perceived.

This thesis is known as idealism, so called because things which are perceived are ideas in some mind, rather than material objects in a mind-independent world. If true, it raises some odd questions. For instance, if objects only exist as ideas in minds, what happens if I leave an empty, windowless room and shut the door? With no-one there to perceive the objects in it, do they no longer exist? Berkeley thought that would indeed be true, but mindful of its absurdity, perhaps, he concluded that because the mind of God is all-perceiving, objects continue to exist at all times because God perceives them all.

The main weakness of Berkeley's view, as Bertrand Russell pointed out, is that it seems to misunderstand what it means for something to be in a mind. If I think about someone, there is a sense in which I have that person 'in mind'. Indeed, they have to be in my mind in some sense for me to think about them. But, obviously, that doesn't mean the actual person is walking around in my head.

In a similar way, when I perceive an object, I need certain ideas to be in my head. I need to have an idea of its shape, texture, colour and so on. But that doesn't necessarily mean that the shape, texture and colour themselves are actually in my head. It is a simple truism to say that to know an object I need to have mental ideas of that object. But it doesn't follow from this that the object is nothing more than these ideas.

Despite its intuitive implausibility, idealism has continued to be a theory with many supporters. It also has a distinguished cousin, which it is sometimes confused with: phenomenalism.

Phenomenalism

Phenomenalism has a different starting point to idealism; namely, the acceptance that there are sense data. However, it tries to avoid the scepticism that sense data can introduce when it seems that sense data stand between us and a direct perception of the real world. It does this by claiming that sense data do not stand between us and objects because talk of objects is no more than talk of sense data. The phenomenalist thesis is that physical objects are logical constructs out of sense data. Mill expressed it by saying that objects were 'permanent possibilities of sensation'. All talk of objects, according to the phenomenalist, is reducible to talk about sense data. So, for example, everything I say about my house can be reduced to statements about sense data. There is no further reference to an object beyond those sense data.

Consider, for example, 'ice-cream'. Once you add up all the sense data associated with ice-cream – its texture, consistency, flavour, smell, colour, temperature and so on – you have actually said all there is to say about it. You don't need to add 'and all these sense-data correspond to an object which we call ice-cream'. The object just is all those sense data.

An obvious objection to this theory is that it is in the very idea of an object that it can exist unperceived. Therefore, it cannot be true that all talk about sense-independent objects can be reduced to talk of sense-dependent experience. The phenomenalist would reply that, on their view, objects can exist unperceived. All they insist on is a hypothetical clause, so that to say X exists is to say that, under the right circumstances, the appropriate sense data would occur. The idea of an object that would never produce any sense data is, on their view, meaningless.

Note that phenomenalism is thus a logical thesis about what it means for something to exist. Idealism, though closely related, is an ontological thesis, as it is about the nature of things which exist. Phenomenalism merely claims talk of objects is a logical construct of sense data – it doesn't deny that objects exist. This is a simple, fundamental and important difference and one worth getting clear about to avoid confusing idealism and phenomenalism.

The introduction of the hypothetical clause doesn't seem convincing. As Isaiah Berlin said, the existence of objects is not hypothetical but categorical. To say something exists is to say it exists, full stop, not that it would exist if perceived. The implausibility of phenomenalism is that it claims categorical talk of public objects is a construct of hypothetical talk about private experience.

There are two other swift and incisive objections against phenomenalism. First, as the having of a sense datum does not logically entail that the object exists (think of hallucinations, etc.), it is clear that statements about objects cannot be just logical constructs of sense data. Second, the existence of an object does not logically entail that a sense datum must occur. Thus, there is a clear logical independence of sense data and objects.

Kant and the Synthetic *A Priori*

Given the problems with each of the above accounts of reality, and how we perceive it, we may consider an alternative approach. The *transcendental idealism* of Immanuel Kant sits somewhere in between realism and idealism, in a sense, in that it agrees that there is a mind-independent reality (as realism does), but argues that we cannot experience this reality as it is in itself. We can only experience reality as it is filtered through our perceptions. This is different to representative realism, for our perceptions do not indirectly 'represent' reality at all. 'Things in themselves' exist in the *noumenal* world, which is inaccessible to us. We live entirely in the *phenomenal* world, of things as they appear.

This approach also seems to take the best from both rationalism and empiricism; we may acknowledge our indebtedness to sense experience for most of our knowledge, whilst at the same time conceding the rationalist point that there must be substantial knowledge which cannot be derived from experience. The way Kant sought to achieve this was by reversing the relationship between the world and the observer. We usually think that our experience corresponds to objects in the world. Kant's radical suggestion was that, in fact, objects in the (phenomenal) world are made to fit the way in which the mind itself shapes and make sense of experience. So, for example, we experience the world in terms of three dimensions, but three-dimensionality is not a property we should ascribe to the world based on experience, but rather a *precondition* of experiencing the world in the only way possible to us. The phenomenal world appears to us as shaped by the innate tendencies of the mind to structure experience in certain ways: in space and time, related by cause and effect, and so on. As Kant put it in the *Critique of Pure Reason*, 'Thoughts without content are empty, intuitions without concepts are blind', where by 'intuitions' he meant all our experiences of the world. In other words, we must have sense experiences to think and reflect, but without the mind's built-in ability to frame and shape experience, perception would be a complete mess.

Building on this, Kant attempts to introduce a distinct category of knowledge: the *synthetic a priori*. A priori knowledge, which does not stem from experience, is usually thought of as being 'analytic', meaning that it doesn't really tell us anything more than can be found out from *analysing* the terms. So, for example, knowledge that 'brown is a colour' is analytic, because it is part of what 'brown' means that it is a colour, and so you don't gain any genuine new knowledge from saying that it is a colour. In contrast, 'that coat is brown' is synthetic, not analytic, because it tells us something new by producing a *synthesis* of two concepts that might otherwise be unrelated. Such knowledge is not *a priori*, because it is only through experience that you could learn that a particular coat was brown.

However, Kant thought there could be knowledge that was both *a priori*, in the sense that it does not stem from experience, and also *synthetic*, and so provides us with additional knowledge. The synthetic *a priori* therefore describes knowledge which, whilst it cannot be doubted, comes through experience. Mathematics is an example. That $79 \times 23 = 1817$ is an analytic truth: given the meaning of all the terms, it must be true. But the knowledge that these two numbers multiplied have this sum creates genuine new knowledge. It is not the case that we already implicitly knew the answer, just because it was in some sense already contained in the sum.

Kant's solution is ingenious, and is more sophisticated than we have had room to suggest here. There is also some evidence to back it up. Take the famous optical illusion of an image that can look like a vase or two faces looking at each other, but not both at the same time. Even if you see neither, you will see some collection of forms and lines – your mind will struggle to impose some sort of pattern on it. The point is that, just as Kant suggested; we are pre-programmed to try to make sense of experience. However, there are possible problems with Kant's view. It is one thing to identify that such mental predispositions play a role, and quite another to suggest that those dispositions have a fixed and definite form. Perhaps, for instance, it is possible for different people (from different cultures, perhaps) to see the world differently. If so, the way we see the world may not in fact relate to innate tendencies, but rather develop *through* experience.

The Sapir-Whorf Hypothesis

A related but alternative view to Kant's was proposed by linguist Benjamin Whorf (1897–1941), building upon the theories of his mentor Edward Sapir (1884–1939). The Sapir-Whorf Hypothesis, as it has become known, suggests that different cultures evolve different fundamental concepts as to the nature of the world, which entails that they structure their experience differently. As with Kant, there is therefore some factor which structures experience and determines what is thinkable and communicable; but unlike Kant, these sets of concepts or *conceptual schemes* do not spring from innate capacities of the mind but are formed through the development of language. One quite radical consequence of this view is therefore that a person's language and culture will determine how and what it is possible for them to think. Thus, for instance, we might argue that a culture that has no word for future time would also lack that concept. So, rather than inheriting a fixed set of conceptual possibilities, as Kant thought, the Sapir-Whorf Hypothesis proposes that concepts are culturally inherited, and relative to that culture's language, and for this reason it is sometimes described as *linguistic relativism*. Since (it is argued) language is acquired through experience, then this approach may also be thought of as a form of empiricism.

Whorf's own examples were drawn from his study of the Native American Hopi language and culture (among others). He argued, for instance, that the Hopi had a different concept of time, which did not break it down into distinct units (hours, minutes, days) as European cultures do. In his study of the Inuit language, he also famously argued that they have numerous names for 'snow'. This, he claimed, showed that reality might be broken up in different ways according to the different practices and traditions of the culture in question.

Whorf's claims have been controversial, with some researchers arguing that (for instance) he misinterpreted linguistic practices, and that the Inuit in fact have a similar number of names for snow as Western societies do. But a more telling criticism springs from the philosophical difficulty involved in accounting for exactly how we can actually know about the existence of these different conceptual schemes. If, as according to Whorf, we are each bound to the conceptual scheme we have acquired, then we cannot get outside of it. But, as Donald Davidson has argued, if we can realise that others possess what seems to be a different conceptual scheme, then perhaps the ideas concerned cannot be as fundamentally different as thinkers such as Whorf suppose. If an Inuit were to teach me the different words for snow (if they in fact exist), or a Hopi their different concept of time, then where is the problem? The differences would obviously not be fundamental. And yet, if they were, then I would arguably be unaware of their existence, and fail to understand the language of the other culture. If I notice such differences, I can try to understand them; if I don't, I cannot. Linguistic relativism therefore seems flawed, but Kant's basic insight that the mind shapes experience in order to understand it seems to contain a great deal of truth – even if that shaping is not fixed or representative of how it is possible for us to experience or conceive of the world.

The linguist Noam Chomsky has argued that the mind shapes experience in another, more limited way. It is not that we are born with a fixed set of concepts, or that languages narrowly limit what we can think. But it is true that the brain is 'hard wired' for language – that, in order to learn language in the first place, we must possess its basic structures (verb, noun, tense and so on). No matter what language we speak, we are all born with an in-built 'universal grammar', and this is what enables children to learn languages so easily and quickly. This would explain why a child learning language makes mistakes such as saying 'runned' instead of 'ran'. This suggests that it understands grammatical rules to do with the formation of tense in regular verbs, of roots words and suffixes, and so on. No one needs to teach the child the rules; what the child needs to learn are the exceptions.

Some philosophers and linguists reject this approach. For instance, we may account for a child's linguistic behaviour by simply assuming that humans are good at spotting patterns. This is still perhaps an innate tendency, but does not imply a 'universal grammar'. Other research suggests that there exist languages which do not possess certain key features common to others. If so, then this would seem to argue against any genetic or inbuilt tendency common to all humans. However, the controversy in this area is ongoing, and there is still no definite consensus as to the role played by any inbuilt tendencies which humans may possess.

Objectivity and relativism

No survey of the theory of knowledge can avoid looking at the question of whether objective knowledge is possible, or whether we must accept some form of *relativism*. Here, for the purposes of discussion, we may consider objective knowledge to be that which is the same to any rational observer, regardless of cultural background, personal opinions and so on. The fact that the Earth goes round the Sun, some philosophers argue, is not dependent on any value or viewpoint, but is an objectively verifiable fact. Similarly, the self-evident ideas beloved of the rationalists were self-evident to whomever was capable of clearly perceiving them – which all rational people should be. Relativism, on the other hand, argues that there is nothing that is absolutely true or false: everything depends on what perspective you adopt. Something may be true for you, true for human beings, true in the twenty-first century and so on, but nothing is just true, full stop.

Relativism is a sort of philosophical bogeyman. Like scepticism, the relativist position is generally seen as counterproductive: if everything is relative, then what is the point of doing philosophy in the first place? Most philosophical ink has therefore traditionally been spilt in *avoiding* relativism, or rebutting it.

However, relativism and scepticism, whilst they have points of overlap, are not necessarily related. In general terms, if something is relative, then it may be subjective, dependent on certain factors, or true only in relation to something else. Is it a warm day? Well, if you've just come from the Bahamas, perhaps not; if from Alaska, probably. The fact that some things are relative is not itself a sign that all things are. I like coffee, you like tea. The whole fabric of truth and reality does not fall apart simply because our tastes in common beverages differ. Philosophical relativism, however, is more fundamental. If, for instance, we argue that moral goodness is relative, we are saying that no moral action is *objectively* right or wrong, but rather that morality is always dependent on something else – a set of culturally defined values, an interpretative framework, a point of view. At its most extreme, then, relativism denies that objective knowledge is possible – and this is where it shares common ground with scepticism. But a relativist need not deny that we can have knowledge or meaning, but merely point out that it need not be the same to any independent observer (objective in the fullest sense). To do this, he might employ certain sceptical arguments – to show, for example, that self-evident truths are not in fact as self-evident or indubitable as we might think. But often undiluted scepticism is not the final goal of the relativist, but merely the means to undermine rigid objectivism.

The relativism/objectivism issue may apply to a number of different areas – to truth in general, to moral standards, to notions and concepts. As we saw above, the Sapir-Whorf Hypothesis was described as a form of 'linguistic relativism', in that the concepts available to a certain culture were seen as relative to its language, which in turn was seen to evolve differently according to historical accident, environment, tradition and so on. But other things might provide a basis for relativism. Friedrich Nietzsche (1844–1900) famously announced the death of God, and that we are therefore responsible for our own moral values. Existentialist Jean-Paul Sartre (1905–1980) termed this situation *abandonment*, and argued that we are therefore ultimately responsible for everything we do, every choice we make. Misquoting Dostoevsky, Sartre considered that 'If God does not exist, then everything is permitted' (*Existentialism is a Humanism*) – that is, there is no basis for objective truth or morality; everything is relative. Other forms of relativism may infect the search for knowledge itself. For instance, Thomas Kuhn (1922–1996) argued that science does not evolve by rational steps, but through what he termed *paradigm shifts*. At one moment in history, the Earth was the centre of the solar system; now, it is the Sun. But the transition from one view (paradigm) to another was one in which other, external factors played a part – social trends, developments in technology and commerce, and so on. If we interpret Kuhn radically, then our view of the world is not based upon sound rational principles, a picture edging ever nearer to 'truth', but more akin to a form of faith or communal belief, in which consensus and internal coherence are equally or more important than the concerns of pure science. Scientific truth is relative to its paradigm, which in turn may be driven by non-rational factors.

However, Nietzsche, Sartre and Kuhn were not relativist in the most extreme sense, in that they held that there were certain factors which made the search for truth far from arbitrary. Nietzsche advocated that our morality should express our 'will to power', our deepest sense of purpose and value, which in turn should reflect a joyous and positive conception of life; Sartre thought that we owed it to our consciousness of our own freedom not to choose attitudes or opinions which renounced it – by attributing our values to God or nature, we are guilty of 'bad faith'; and Kuhn denied the charge of relativism, and argued that he chiefly wished to point out that scientific advance was not a simple case of proposing and testing theories, proceeding calmly from superstition to enlightenment, but was a more complicated and less direct process than that. We would therefore say that such views have relativist elements, in that they reject certain notions of objectivity – of moral goodness, human nature, scientific truth – in favour of more complex accounts, but are not relativist in the strongest sense.

We may distinguish between two main forms of relativism: *descriptive* and *normative*. Descriptive relativism may describe certain features of a culture or belief system, and point out how different standards, concepts or values are at work. For instance, if Whorf was correct about the Hopi concept of time, then we could say that he was *describing* what 'time' meant *relative* to their language and culture. However, descriptive relativism need not imply that such concepts are in fact relative: we might look at the Hopi culture and say, 'well, they just don't really understand time'. To go the extra step, to adopt *normative relativism*, we need to say that the Hopi conception of time is as valid as any European conception, or that of any other culture. As for time, so for moral values, cosmologies, conceptions of truth, space, life and death, and so on. Merely to point out that people have different concepts need not therefore present a philosophical problem. It is normative relativism where the problems begin.

A typical relativist position might go like this: faced with the conclusions of descriptive relativism – that there are a wide variety of concepts and values – then we must conclude that there is no one objective truth, morality or set of concepts that is 'correct'. 'Truth', 'goodness', 'time' and so on have meaning and 'correct' application only in relation to the contexts within which they are applied. A 'good' man in ancient Greece might expose a sickly infant on a hillside to die; a 'good' man in modern Western cultures would do everything he could to care for and treat the infant. Each view is equally valid, because what is 'good' is relative to the standards of time and culture. This does not deny that 'goodness' or 'truth' exist, but merely points out that we must interpret them according to standards which are *internal* to the culture in which we find them. So, an anthropologist should not judge some remote cannibal tribe by modern standards, but by the standards which it has evolved in the struggle to survive within its environment.

We might, however, question whether it is in fact always possible to distinguish between what is 'internal' and what is 'external' to a framework. Once the anthropologist shows up on the doorstep of the cannibal tribe, he has 'contaminated' them. His very presence may influence their beliefs and question their loyalty to their 'internal' standards. In similar ways, today's modern multicultural societies show in fact how belief systems can intermix, change and influence one another. Once different cultures or viewpoints come into conflict or mutual influence, it is difficult to precisely distinguish what is intrinsic to this or that perspective, and the attempt to maintain various 'relativisms' breaks down. As with the Hopi Indians, if we can talk about their concept of time, then perhaps their worldview is not so alien after all. This does not necessarily lead us back to objectivism, but shows that it is not so easy to maintain the existence of completely separate 'paradigms' or belief systems. The fact that some remote tribe has evolved a distinct morality does not suggest that different cultures evolve completely distinct and *incommensurable* views of the world (which cannot interact or understand one another); rather, it simply suggests that different factors motivate cultures to evolve differently. However, the cannibal may give up his flesh-eating ways, or the anthropologist may come to understand the different conceptions of time held by the Native American. Things may still be relative *overall* – there is no 'right' morality or worldview – but the various relative perspectives are not completely distinct and alien to one another. This may still leave us with a broader view, where perhaps moral and metaphysical standards are relative to (for instance) human culture in general, but this is practically a consensus view among a large section of modern philosophers, and hardly merits the name 'relativism' at all.

But what, then, about full-blown relativism? Can *everything* be relative? If there are no objective standards, then perspectives may not only be relative to cultures, but to individuals, each of which may hold different moral or philosophical views, all of which are equally 'valid'. So, I could have my own moral code, my own standards of truth, or even my own meaning for terms and ideas – couldn't I? Perhaps not. Arguably, to hold different opinions about some things, I must hold similar ones about others. To have a different moral code, I must at least appreciate what a moral code is; to differ about 'right' and 'wrong', I must at least share the view that actions can be one or the other (even if I disagree as to which actions fall into which category). This is similar to a point made by Wittgenstein regarding the limits of scepticism. To doubt the existence of something, I must at least acknowledge its existence (in some form). Is this chair real? Well, 'this chair' must be real in the sense that it is a perception of a chair – that, at least, exists. Similarly, then, to differ in terms of morality or standards of truth or logic, I must at least share certain conceptions – as to what morality or logic are. I may reject the logical law of excluded middle, for example – that 'something must either be or not be the case' – as, in fact, do certain forms of ancient Indian philosophy. But these are points of difference. We can still talk about whether such a view is valid or not, and to do so we must share certain concepts of what logic is. It seems, then, that even individual relativism cannot be absolutely so – it must take some things as common (meaning of terms, concepts, shared values).

The main problem with this form of radical relativism, however, is that it is arguably self-defeating. To put the point in a simple, well-known way: 'everything is relative' is not itself a relative position, but an absolute one. In fact, it looks like an objective point of view, a fact that everyone must accept. This is paradoxical: in order to hold that position, I have to assume that there is at least one thing which is objectively true (relativism); to deny it (as relativism seems to entitle me to do), then I am also left with one objective view (relativism is false). As a result, we may argue, extreme relativism, like extreme scepticism, is simply incoherent, and both are positions for which the serious philosopher has little time.

Conclusion

Epistemology attempts to answer questions such as 'how can we have knowledge?' As we have seen, these are very tricky questions to answer. Much depends on how high a standard for knowledge we set. If knowledge requires certainty, perhaps it is unattainable. If knowledge must be of a reality independent of experience, maybe we can never have it, since all reality is mediated by experience. If knowledge requires a secure foundation, then maybe we can never have it, because no foundations are firm enough.

Whenever we are faced with a pessimistic option, however, there is usually a more optimistic, though perhaps less ambitious alternative. Maybe knowledge requires something less than certainty. Maybe we don't need to reach a world independent of sense experience to gain knowledge. Maybe knowledge doesn't build from the bottom up.

The choices we make when navigating through epistemology require us to strike a balance between setting the standard for knowledge so low that any old belief counts as knowledge, or setting the standard so high that we find it is unattainable. Getting the right attitude to knowledge therefore requires something more than just sound philosophical reasoning. It requires good judgement. Perhaps we might even call it wisdom.

Summary

The theory of knowledge is concerned with questions of the basis and justification of knowledge. Rationalists have argued that all knowledge is founded on reason, which does not need to appeal to the evidence of experience to demonstrate truths. Empiricists, in contrast, believe all knowledge derives from experience and that only truths of logic, geometry and mathematics can be known to be true without reference to experience. Both empiricism and rationalism can be seen as foundationalist, in that they attempt to discover what the foundation of knowledge is and build up from there.

An alternative to foundationalism is pragmatism, which defines knowledge and truth in terms of what works, without demanding a secure basis for this knowledge.

One of the most important definitions of knowledge is justified true belief – the so-called 'tripartite account of knowledge'. On this view, to know something is to believe something which is true and to be justified in this belief. There are several objections to this. Although some think that knowledge **entails** belief, others think that knowledge and belief are **incompatible**, since knowledge has features belief does not. There are also counter-examples where people seem to have knowledge without one of the components of the tripartite account, or where all three components are in place but we don't seem to have knowledge.

An alternative to the tripartite account is to take a Wittgensteinian approach, which claims that the meaning of 'know' is given by the way the word is used and just cannot be specified in a formulaic definition.

Linked to the question of how we know things is what knowing or believing involves. In the dual-component view, belief may be thought of as a **propositional attitude** or mental state. Problems with this view have led philosophers to deny the reality of such mental states, and to adopt a behaviourist or dispositional account according to which what we believe is constituted by what we do.

Sceptical arguments attempt to show that we do not have any knowledge at all. They work by claiming that certainty is required for knowledge and then showing that such certainty cannot be attained. Sceptics can claim we cannot be certain that **self-evident** statements are true, that what we perceive exists or that our reasoning is sound. Sceptical arguments concerning the existence of objects include the argument from illusion and more general arguments from **sense data**. Critics say that sceptics set an impossible standard for knowledge and that by making knowledge impossible they make meaningless the concept of ignorance.

Metaphysical views relate to the theory of knowledge. **Realism** is the view that objects exist independently of our experience. Optimistic realists believe we can know this reality; pessimistic realists are sceptics. **Idealism** is the view that everything which exists is mental in nature. **Phenomenalism** is the view that all talk of objects is really talk of sense data.

Kant's **transcendental idealism** attempted to synthesise elements of rationalism and empiricism by explaining how the mind has a pre-existing structure which shapes how we experience the world, but that nonetheless what we experience does furnish us with new knowledge.

The Sapir-Whorf Hypothesis of **'linguistic relativism'** presents an alternative account of how our language limits what we can think about the world by framing experience through certain fixed concepts, and which therefore may differ between cultures and linguistic groups. In contrast, Noam Chomsky's 'universal grammar' suggests it is the structure of language that is **innate**, not the concepts employed in it.

The idea that there can be objective knowledge, which is true for all people at all times, is opposed by **relativism**, which states that things are only true for certain people, at certain times. Full-blown relativism about everything is quite rare, but many are relativists about particular domains of belief, such as values or science. Relativism faces the charge of being self-defeating, since the claim that knowledge is relative is not itself a relative claim, but an absolute one.

Glossary

Causal/scientific realism   The idea that the perceived **qualities** of objects are caused by the actual properties possessed by objects (scientifically determined) interacting with the observer and the environment.

Coherence theory   The theory that a proposition is true if it coheres (or fits in with) other true beliefs.

Correspondence theory   The theory that propositions are true if they correspond to reality.

Entailment thesis   The idea that knowledge requires belief, in contrast to the views that knowledge can be separated from belief or that knowledge is incompatible with belief.

Epistemic   The adjective, meaning 'concerning knowledge'.

Epistemology   The technical name for the theory of knowledge.

First principles   Absolutely certain ideas which act as a basis for other forms of knowledge (playing a central role in rationalism).

Idealism   The view, associated with Berkeley, that all objects are perceptions in some mind, and that the only things that exist are minds and their perceptions.

Incompatibility thesis   The claim that knowledge and belief are incompatible, because (for example) belief is fallible and knowledge is not.

Innate ideas   Ideas we are born with rather than learn from experience.

Instrumentalism   The view that ideas should be judged in terms of their explanatory power and usefulness (a form of pragmatism). Also, the idea that ascriptions of intentions and beliefs to people should be viewed in this way (as not 'real', merely useful).

Linguistic relativism   The view, associated with the Sapir-Whorf hypothesis, that concepts are relative to separate cultures and their languages and customs.

Naïve realism   The belief that the world appears to us as it really is, and objects are directly perceived (often used disparagingly).

Phenomenalism   The idea that, whilst a mind-independent reality exists, it is inaccessible, and that all objects are merely constructions of sense data (or exist as the potential to be perceived).

Propositional knowledge   Knowledge of truths which can be expressed in statements or propositions; that is, to know that something is the case.

Propositional attitudes   Mental states which involve an attitude (belief, doubt, fear) toward a certain proposition.

Qualities   Primary qualities belong to the objects themselves. Secondary qualities only exist in our perceptions of objects.

Relativism   The view, in opposition to belief in objective knowledge, that concepts and values are relative to some framework, or even simply to each other.

Self-evident truths   Truths which do not require any further justification.

Sense data   Perceptions, which are arguably all we are directly aware of.

Separability thesis   The claim that knowledge and belief can be separated – that we can know things without believing them to be true, for instance.

Transcendental argument   An argument that starts from an experience we cannot deny we have and attempts to show what must be true for that experience to be possible.

Transcendental idealism   The view, springing from Kant, that reality in itself is unperceivable, and that we shape experience through inbuilt mental tendencies.

Further reading

In the companion volume to this book, *Philosophy: Key Texts*, we look at two books which focus on epistemology: Descartes's *Meditations* and Hume's *An Enquiry concerning Human Understanding*. Both can be read with care by a novice as well as by experts. Nietzsche's *Beyond Good and Evil* also contains important and relevant material to this debate, but is less accessible.

Other accessible twentieth-century texts include *The Problems of Philosophy* by Bertrand Russell (Opus), *The Problem of Knowledge* by A. J. Ayer (Penguin) and *The View from Nowhere* by Thomas Nagel (Oxford University Press), all three of which address the challenges of scepticism. Other classic texts worth reading include Berkeley's *The Principles of Human Knowledge*, which is the classic exposition of idealism, and Plato's *Theaetetus*, an instructive run through some early theories of knowledge.

A Companion to Epistemology, edited by Jonathan Dancy and Ernest Sosa (Blackwell) is an excellent reference book with entries long enough to be read as mini-essays. It is too detailed for the casual reader, but highly recommended for anyone seriously studying epistemology.

2
Moral Philosophy

What is moral philosophy?

Unlike many branches of philosophy, it is quite easy to express clearly the main question of ethics, or moral philosophy. It is found in the title of books on the subject, such as *How Should One Live?* by Roger Crisp and *How Are We to Live?* by Peter Singer. But, as ever, things are not quite as simple as they appear. This apparently simple question contains a concept which is highly problematic: 'should' or 'ought'.

As any parent knows, when you say someone *should* or *ought* to do something, that is often not the end of the matter but the beginning. The problem is that the status of this 'ought' is not clear. Is it an absolute command or is it in some way conditional?

Consider the first possibility. One might argue that when one says 'you ought to tell the truth', for example, the question 'why?' doesn't arise. You ought not to lie just because that is one of the things you ought not to do. Moral 'oughts' like this are simple, absolute commands. We follow them because morality demands that they be followed.

But this is an unsatisfactory response. When a parent tells their child they shouldn't hurt other children, for example, and the child asks why, it seems inadequate to reply by saying it is just wrong. It does not seem unreasonable to want to know why this moral rule should be followed. At the very least, we need to know why this is a moral rule at all, rather than just a piece of advice like, 'you ought to see the new George Clooney film'.

To offer an explanation of why we ought to do certain things is to make 'ought' somehow conditional. That would mean that every sentence of the form 'You ought to do X' is really a kind of shorthand for a sentence of the form, 'If you want Y, you ought to do X'. An example from moral philosophy should make this clear.

Consider the person who thinks morality is just what God commands. (This is known as the divine command theory.) On this view, to say, 'You ought to obey the Ten Commandments' is to say, 'If you want to obey God's will, you ought to obey the Ten Commandments'. You could, of course, ask why you ought to obey God's will, and the reason for this might be something like, 'You won't get to heaven if you don't' or 'God knows what's best for us'. This would mean an even more complete unpacking of the simple 'ought' sentence would be, 'If you want to get to heaven, you ought to obey the Ten Commandments' or 'If you want what's best for you, you ought to obey the Ten Commandments'.

Other moral theories will imply similar conditional statements. Utilitarianism, for instance, is the view that it is right to increase happiness and reduce suffering, and wrong to do the opposite. So if a utilitarian says, 'You ought not to hit people unprovoked,' what they really mean is 'If you want to increase happiness and reduce suffering, you ought not to hit people unprovoked'.

You may well have already noticed that this approach has its own problems. It is always possible to ask why one should want what follows the 'if' in such a sentence. Why should I want to get to heaven? Why should I want to reduce suffering and increase happiness? Why should I want what's best for me? When one asks a question like this, one is really looking at the basis for morality and asking why one should be moral at all. Here, it seems the 'ought' or 'should' cannot be justified any further. If we can't see why we ought to want to go to heaven, increase happiness or do what's best for ourselves, then we have some kind of moral blindness.

This touches on some fundamental issues of moral philosophy. First, there is the question of what the foundation of morality really is. Is it, for instance, just a way of getting to heaven, of increasing happiness on earth, or of serving our own self-interests? Second, there is the question of why we ought to be moral at all. At some stage it seems we have to confront the basic choice of whether to be moral or not. If someone rejects morality, have they done wrong? We may think someone is rash or foolish to reject their way into heaven or refuse to do what's best for them. We may despise the person who doesn't care for human happiness. But if we can't say why they ought to have chosen differently, can we condemn them?

As we can see, then, though it may be a simple matter to say moral philosophy is about how we ought to live, there is nothing at all simple about explaining what this 'ought' means.

The divisions of moral philosophy

Moral philosophy can be divided into three main levels of enquiry. At its most practical, it is about what we ought to do in any given situation. This we can call the level of applied ethics. Most ethical discussions in the media are conducted at this level and include questions such as: Is it ever right to clone a human being? Is euthanasia morally wrong? Can we justify our treatment of farmed animals?

To answer such questions, one often needs to go up a level and consider general theories about what the right or wrong thing to do is. This takes us to the level of normative ethics, where we find general theories about what kinds of things are right or wrong. So, for example, a normative ethical theory might say that it is always wrong to kill any creature that has the capacity to decide its own future and has not chosen to be killed. This is not a theory about which *particular* things are right or wrong, but what *kinds* of things are right or wrong. Someone working at the level of applied ethics who agreed with this normative ethic would then try and see what implications this rule has for specific issues, such as those of cloning, euthanasia and animal welfare.

However, the debate can go up another level again to what is called 'meta-ethics', which deals with the status of moral claims in general. For instance, when someone says it is wrong to kill any creature that has the capacity to decide its own future and has not chosen to be killed, what kind of claim are they making? Are they saying something that is true or false, or are they just expressing an opinion? Are they saying something which applies to everyone, or only to people from a particular culture or historical period? What is the basis of what they say? Is morality rooted in nature, human nature, God, or do we just create it ourselves? These are issues of meta-ethics. They are about the general nature and structure of ethics rather than what kinds of actions are right or wrong.

We could see meta-ethics, normative ethics and applied ethics as three levels of enquiry in moral philosophy. Alternatively, we could see them as describing three general areas on a continuum, running from the most specific questions of what we are to do, to the most general questions about the nature of ethics. The advantage of this way of looking at it is that it is almost always impossible to discuss ethics purely at one level. For example, when discussing the meta-ethical issue of whether moral principles are just opinions, examples from applied ethics – such as the fact that torture is wrong – are often invoked to criticise such a view. Like much in moral philosophy, the labels we apply here do not describe things which are entirely distinct but general areas which merge into each other.

Our approach here will be to start from the top down, first looking at issues in meta-ethics, then normative ethics and, finally, some issues in applied ethics.

Morality and realism

A fundamental question about the nature of ethics concerns whether or not moral values are real. In one sense, of course, they must be real since people hold them. The philosophical issue of moral realism, however, is the more specific one of whether or not moral values are independent from the people who hold them. Perhaps the easiest way to understand this is by an analogy with art.

When someone looks at, for example, Michelangelo's sculpture of David and says that it is beautiful, what do they mean? They could mean that there is some fact of the matter, that the sculpture is or is not beautiful and that they believe it is true to say that it is. On this view, beauty is a real quality of the sculpture and one can be right or wrong when one claims that the sculpture is or is not beautiful. On the other hand, they might think that they are merely expressing an opinion when they say it is beautiful. According to this attitude, beauty is in the eye of the beholder. If two people disagree about whether the sculpture is beautiful, it is not the case that one of them must be wrong. Rather, both have their opinions and that's all there is to say on the matter. From this perspective, beauty is not a real property of the sculpture, but a value judgement we each as individuals make.

The same kind of distinction can be made in ethics. if you say 'causing animals to suffer needlessly' is wrong, you could mean one of two things. You could mean that wrongness is a real quality of causing such suffering and one can be right or wrong when one claims that causing such suffering is wrong. On the other hand, you could mean that you are merely expressing an opinion when you say causing such suffering is wrong. On this view, morality is in the eye of the beholder. If your friend thinks causing such suffering is not wrong, it is not the case that one of you is making a mistake. Rather, you both have your opinions and that's all there is to say on the matter.

Those who think there are facts about right and wrong are known as moral realists. If, in addition, they believe that such facts can be known by us, they are known as cognitivists. Those who think there are no such facts about right and wrong are called non-realists, and since this means they do not think there is anything one can know about such facts (since they don't exist) they are also known as non-cognitivists. Non-cognitivism is perhaps best captured in the words of Shakespeare's Hamlet: 'There is nothing either good or bad, but thinking makes it so' (Act 2, Scene 2).

Historically, moral realism has been by far the more popular of the two theories. Indeed, it can appear to be quite shocking to deny that moral judgements are correct or incorrect. When we say that torture is wrong, for example, we do not generally think we are merely expressing an opinion. We think torture just is wrong, fact. So why have versions of non-cognitivism proved to be so popular in modern philosophy?

Non-cognitivism

One reason why non-cognitivism can be appealing is that, when we look at other cultures, we find that people hold very different moral views. For instance, while it is perfectly acceptable to charge interest on loans in Christian countries, such a practice is contrary to Islamic ethics. While polygamy is considered morally wrong in most Western countries, there are communities there and in other parts of the world where it is perfectly acceptable. If we hold the cognitivist view, it seems we are forced to say that some of these countries or communities are behaving immorally while some are behaving well. This smacks of Western imperialism. Who are we to say that people with different cultures than our own are wrong? Isn't that both arrogant and intolerant? Non-cognitivism provides a way out, since its implication seems to be that we should not judge other cultures by our own standards. Morality is in the eye (or the culture) of the beholder, it is not some independent thing which applies to everyone.

However, the view that non-cognitivism is the only route to tolerance is highly questionable. First, tolerance could well be a value in the one true ethical system. The mere possibility of that means there is no necessary link between tolerance and non-cognitivism.

Second, if morality is not universal, then that does not mean that the values we choose must include tolerance. We might think that there is no fact of the matter as to whether our ethics are right and someone else's are wrong, but that's not going to stop us fighting tooth and nail for our own values.

Valuing tolerance, then, is not a good enough reason to be a non-cognitivist. Better reasons are offered by thinking about what could make moral claims right or wrong. Compare ethical claims to ordinary, factual claims. If I say 'water freezes at zero degrees centigrade', there are ways of seeing if this is true, which involve going out and seeing if water does in fact freeze at this temperature. If I say 'the square root of 289 is 17', I can see if this is true by standard mathematical procedures. But how can I go about seeing if 'smacking children is wrong' is true? I cannot examine examples of such smacking to see if I can observe the wrongness. Nor can I prove it is wrong in the way in which I can prove a mathematical sum. It is no use conducting an opinion poll because that will only tell me what people *think* is wrong, not what *is* wrong. In short, it seems that whatever moral claims are, they are not the same kinds of things as facts. And if they are not facts, they cannot be true or false.

Nonetheless, we do say things are right or wrong. What do we mean by this if there are no moral facts? A non-cognitivist might answer that when a person says that something is morally good or bad, she is simply approving or disapproving of it. At its most extreme, this view was manifest in a theory called emotivism. On this view, moral statements are expressions of feeling which are neither right nor wrong. They can be compared to statements like 'Ugh! Not gooseberries!', which express reactions but cannot be said to be right or wrong. Ejaculations like 'ugh!' and 'hurrah!' are neither true nor false. On this view, moral error is impossible and moral disagreement futile. Just as it literally makes no sense to say 'you should like Gooseberries' or 'I was wrong when I didn't like peas', it does not make sense to make such statements about moral principles.

There are, however, several problems with this conception of ethics. First, it is possible to distinguish between what you dislike or disapprove of and what you think is morally wrong. For instance, you might approve of someone brutally murdering someone who tortures your family, even though on reflection you cannot morally justify it. Similarly, you might be disgusted by the idea of your grandmother marrying a 20-year-old without thinking her decision is morally wrong. But if morality is just an expression of what you approve of or like, such distinctions would be impossible.

The role of reason

Perhaps the greatest problem for non-cognitivism is that it seems to leave no room at all for reason and reflection. For example, non-cognitivism entails that moral error is impossible, since moral judgements are neither true nor false. One reason why this is a problem is that when we change our minds about moral issues, it often (but by no means always) is precisely because of rational reflection. People came to see that black slavery is wrong at least partly because they came to realise that there was no rational justification for the different treatment of people of different skin colour. Many people are troubled by the morality of abortion because they cannot see any rational principle that would draw a sharp dividing line between the early foetus and the new-born child. In both cases, when people change their minds about their moral stances, they see their previous one as being mistaken. But if non-cognitivism were true, it would not be possible to say that we used to hold incorrect moral principles.

This highlights the fact that reason does play a role in ethics. Although it is true that offering reasons why we don't like gooseberries is a fairly pointless activity, anyone who said that all students are evil and didn't offer a reason for this claim would be thought to be a little crazy.

As it is clear that thinking things through does change our moral principles, and that this process of thinking through actually seems to be central to good ethics, it seems that any credible non-cognitivist theory must find a place for rationality. Prescriptivism is one attempt to do just this.

Prescriptivism

Prescriptivism is a fairly recent moral theory, most closely associated with the work of Richard Hare. Prescriptivism has two key characteristics, one negative, one positive. The positive is that it views moral judgements as prescribing courses of actions. This means that if one accepts a moral judgement and can act upon it, one does so act. For example, consider the moral judgement, 'It is wrong to steal'. If one accepts this is true, then this judgement prescribes a course of action – not stealing. And if one genuinely accepts this moral judgement, one will not, in fact, steal. Prescriptivism is thus an *internalist* doctrine. That is to say, it claims that to make a moral judgement sincerely is to commit oneself to the action specified in the judgement, or to will that someone else do it.

The negative part is that moral judgements are not descriptive and can never be entailed by anything merely descriptive. A descriptive statement contrasts with a prescriptive one in that descriptive statements set out facts and can be true or false, whereas prescriptive statements set out a course of action and cannot be true or false. The command to do something can be obeyed or disobeyed, but it cannot be true or false.

Why can't prescriptive judgments be derived from descriptive ones? The answer is explained in terms of the so-called 'is/ought gap', which Hume discusses in his *Enquiry concerning the Principles of Morals* (1751). Hume pointed out that many people make the mistake in ethics of starting off talking about facts – things which *are* – and then talking about value – what *should be*. But they do so without justifying this shift from 'is' to 'ought'.

Hume's point is essentially a logical one. In a deductive argument, one can never derive a conclusion which contains an 'ought' unless there is at least one 'ought' in the premises. This 'ought' can be implied, but it has to be there somewhere. Consider this example:

> Fare-dodging on the train is the equivalent of theft.
> Theft is wrong.
> Therefore, one ought not to fare-dodge.

Here, the argument is not strictly valid. The conclusion only follows if we add the premise:

> One ought not to do what is wrong.

Of course, many people would say that this premise is implied by the premise 'Theft is wrong'. But it is important to realise that strictly speaking, the conclusion 'Therefore one ought not to fare-dodge' does not follow without it. Without this premise, one cannot get from the purely descriptive premises to the prescriptive conclusion.

To make this clearer, consider this argument.

> Torture causes great pain.
> Sleep deprivation is a form of torture.
> Therefore, one should not deprive people of sleep.

Here, the conclusion does not strictly follow from the premises. But nor is there even an implicit moral premise, such as 'torture is wrong'. Because the premises are merely descriptive, the prescriptive conclusion does not follow.

The is/ought gap is, then, at least on one reading, an uncontroversial point about the logic of moral arguments. Unless at least one premise contains a prescriptive element, one can never reach a prescriptive conclusion.

Prescriptivism accepts the is/ought gap and understands moral judgements to have a special prescriptive character which makes them fundamentally different from merely descriptive statements.

Such a view seems to run into a problem, however. If moral judgements are not descriptive, and therefore neither true nor false, how does one reason about them? This echoes the problem which faced emotivism. If ethics is just about preferences or feelings, what has reason got to do with it?

The distinctive feature of prescriptivism is its claim that this problem only appears to arise because we hold the false view that it is only possible to reason about descriptive claims. Prescriptivists show how this view is wrong simply by providing examples of how it is possible to reason about things that are not factual and analysing the rules which govern such forms of reasoning. For instance, 'Go to London now!' is neither true nor false, but that doesn't mean I can't reason about it. First, if someone utters inconsistent imperatives, it is reason that picks up on that inconsistency. It is clear that 'Stay here!' is inconsistent with 'Go to London now!' and spotting this inconsistency means applying rules of reasoning. So one way in which reasoning is important in ethics is that it is important for consistency.

Another role for reason is connected with the idea that any ethical principle must be universalisable. Universalisability has been acknowledged by many moral theorists as a key feature of ethical judgements. What it means is that to say something is right or wrong is to make a general claim that it is always right or wrong in relevantly similar circumstances. For example, if I say that it is wrong for you to torment your hamster, part of what it means to say it is wrong is that it would also be wrong for other people to torment other hamsters in similar situations. This is an instance of how any particular moral judgement – *that* is wrong – can be universalised to a related universal moral judgement – *all such acts* are wrong.

The importance of universalisability for ethics is apparent in the way in which we call people who do not universalise moral judgements hypocrites. For instance, a person who claims adultery is wrong but who commits adultery himself is called a hypocrite. This only makes sense if we assume that by saying 'adultery is wrong', they mean that rule to cover all cases of adultery. Hence, the idea that moral principles are in this sense universal seems integral to the very idea of a moral principle.

Universalisability does not imply crude generalising. A situation may include very specific features, such that no-one else would ever be in the same position, in which case no general rule can be inferred from it. But nonetheless, it is part of what it means to act wrongly in that case that anyone else in the same situation would be wrong to do the same.

As the examples of consistency and universalisability show, it does seem to be the case that there is plenty of room for reason to have a role in ethics, even if ethics is non-descriptive and hence non-factual. However, there are criticisms that could be laid at prescriptivism's door.

First, there is the problem of its internalism. Internalism claims that to say 'I ought to do X' is to commit oneself to doing X. But if that were true, surely it would be self-contradictory to say 'I ought to, but I don't'. Yet we say things like this all the time and we don't seem to be contradicting ourselves when we do.

Hare replies to this criticism by pointing out that the 'but' proves there is something wrong with saying this kind of thing. To say 'I ought to, but don't' is to acknowledge an inconsistency, which is to admit either that one doesn't sincerely think one ought to do the thing, or that there is some other reason holding you back, such as weakness of will (*akrasia*).

A second difficulty is that although prescriptivism gives reason a role in ethics, it is not clear that this role is sufficiently wide-ranging. For instance, what if I say everyone able to afford it ought to sacrifice a banana to the God of breakfast every Sunday morning? This principle does seem to be universalisable and it need not be inconsistent with any other moral beliefs. In that sense, it satisfies the rational constraints prescriptivism demands. But surely such a moral judgement is absurd and it must be possible to criticise its rationality. However, it is not clear that prescriptivism can tell us how rationality can be invoked to criticise this moral principle.

We have spent some time looking at prescriptivism as an attempt to develop a sophisticated non-cognitivist ethics. We have here, of course, merely scratched the surface of the debate. But we need to move on from meta-ethics to normative ethics, and theories of what we ought to do and not do.

Deontological and consequentialist ethics

Travelling in a hostile land divided by bitter civil war with 20 other innocent civilians, you are stopped by some local militia. They accuse you and your friends of being spies for the enemy. They threaten to execute all of you unless you prove that you are on their side by shooting a civilian they have captured from the enemy side, whose only crime is to be from a different ethnic group to that of the militia. Your choice is stark: take one innocent life yourself or allow someone else to take 21. What do you do?

There are at least two ways to think about this horrible moral dilemma. One is to say that you should do whatever has the best net consequences. Since one course of action will lead to the loss of 21 innocent lives and the other only one, and since there is no third option available, the morally right thing to do is to kill the innocent prisoner yourself. An ethic which reasons in this way is known as *consequentialist*, since it looks at the consequences of an action when judging its moral value.

A second way of thinking about this is that you have two choices of action. One choice involves you killing and the other does not. Killing is morally wrong, not killing is morally acceptable. Therefore, there is only one morally wrong choice you can make here, and that is to kill the innocent prisoner. So the moral thing to do is to refuse and face the consequences. An ethic which reasons in this way is known as *deontological* (from the Greek word *deon*, meaning duty).

The difference between the two approaches is stark in this particular example. In general, the difference is that the deontologist claims that certain acts are wrong in themselves, no matter what the consequences are. The consequentialist, on the other hand, claims that no acts are right or wrong in themselves, but only in virtue of the consequences they produce. So even cannibalism could be morally acceptable, if the consequences of it are good, as they might be when the survivors of a disaster can only stay alive long enough to escape or be rescued by eating human flesh.

The difference between the two views is perhaps best captured by looking at the different ways each one relates the rightness or wrongness of actions to the goodness or badness of situations. Consequentialism defines what is right in terms of the good. In other words, the right thing to do just is what produces the better outcome. For the deontologist, what is right and what is good are distinct. It may be right to do something which doesn't produce the best outcome, such as refusing to shoot the innocent prisoner, even though more people die as a result of your decision than otherwise would have done. In the same way, it might be wrong to do something which does produce the best outcome, such as going ahead and executing the prisoner.

The distinction can also be understood in terms of means and ends. For the consequentialist, the good should be obtained by all means

For example, consider the example of the innocent prisoner which we looked at above. Consequentialist and deontological approaches both offered very different solutions to the puzzle of what the right thing to do was. Both offered a pretty clear-cut solution. But this might strike us as very odd indeed. After all, what such hypothetical circumstances surely show more than anything is how agonising moral decisions can be. We should therefore be suspicious of any theory which offers a clear-cut, off-the-peg solution to such a dilemma.

How might virtue ethics offer a more plausible approach? First, it is unlikely that virtue ethics could provide any simple answer. Virtue ethics stresses that being good is a matter of character, and that character is something which is developed. It is about having certain dispositions and the wisdom to make good choices and judgements. It is not about being armed with a kind of moral calculus which allows you to measure any act against an ethical scale and read off whether it is right or wrong. This stress on character and judgement over rules and principles means that virtue ethics rarely generates automatic responses to ethical dilemmas.

Nevertheless, if virtue ethics is to provide a plausible alternative to consequentialism or deontology, it must have something to say on this matter. If we are to consider how we should act in such a situation, we should consider how a virtuous person would act. To do this, one needs to build up a picture of the virtuous person. She will be thoughtful of others as well as herself. She will be averse to causing harm and will try and benefit as many people as possible. She will try not to reward wickedness or do wrong herself. She will respect other people.

In making this list you will notice that it includes virtues associated with both deontology and consequentialism. The desire to avoid harm and to benefit as many people as possible sounds very much like consequentialism. But to respect others and avoid wrongdoing sounds much more like deontology. This reflects the fact that both consequentialism and deontology are based on important moral considerations. Their alleged error is to focus too narrowly on just a few, instead of realising that a good person takes all into account and has to make a judgement in each case about what is the right thing to do.

Virtue ethics can sound very appealing but it does face several objections. In particular, it is very hard to see how it can actually tell us what to do. In this example, for instance, it is clear to see what the good person would be like and what kinds of considerations they would base their decision on. But can the theory actually tell us what to do, or whether the person who chooses one way or the other has done the right thing?

There is also a whiff of circularity about the idea of the virtuous person. The right thing to do is what the virtuous person would do. But what is the virtuous person if it is not the person who does the right thing? It seems that if we try and discover what the good person is, we end up saying it is the person who acts well; but when we try to find out what acting well is, we have to say it is acting how the virtuous person does. We never seem to get to the root of what makes things right.

Perhaps the issue will become clearer when we look at how these three normative frameworks – deontology, consequentialism and virtue ethics – are fleshed out in more specific ethical theories.

Utilitarianism

Consequentialists say that one must do that which has the best consequences. But what are the best consequences? Utilitarians say that the morally right act is that which has the consequence of producing more 'utility' or usefulness. Only acts which benefit or harm somebody can be right or wrong.

The obvious next question is, in what way must our actions be useful for them to be good? In other words, what is utility? There are three main forms of utilitarianism, all of which answer this question differently. Classical or hedonic utilitarians say that utility is increasing the pleasure and reducing the pain of as many people as possible. Preference utilitarians say that utility is the satisfaction of the preferences of as many people as possible. Welfare utilitarians say that utility is improving the welfare of as many people as possible.

Classical utilitarianism is most closely associated with Jeremy Bentham (1748–1832) and John Stuart Mill (1806–1873). However, with its emphasis on pleasure or happiness as the highest good, many see it as taking too narrow a view of both what we want out of life and what we consider to be morally important. It is hard to see how acts of self-sacrifice, such as enduring torture to spare comrades, or giving our lives for others, can be described as the pursuit of pleasure. It is also clear, however, that these acts deserve our praise. The failings of this view are also made clear by the question, 'Would you rather be as you are, but unhappy, or reduced to the level of an imbecile and be happy for the rest of your life?' The mere fact that many would choose to be unhappy shows how we are not all the hedonists classical utilitarianism believes we are or should be.

Mill tried to answer this objection by distinguishing between the higher pleasures of the intellect and the lower pleasures of the body. The former are worth much more than the latter, so it is always preferable to at least be capable of enjoying such pleasure than being only capable of enjoying the simple pleasures of the flesh. The proof of this is that anyone who enjoyed both kinds of pleasure would always choose the higher over the lower. However, if what Mill really valued was pleasure and happiness, then how could he be so sure that a well-fed pig, for instance, does not enjoy more happiness than a miserable poet? If happiness really is the highest good, it is not obvious why so-called 'higher pleasures' are superior, or that a person who was acquainted with both would necessarily choose them.

Preference utilitarianism aims to avoid the shortcomings of classical utilitarianism by saying we should attempt to satisfy our preferences. This has the advantage of allowing us more individual choice. Thus, if people prefer to live as happy imbeciles then so be it, but it would be wrong to enforce this option on those who would not prefer such a life or force those who do prefer it to change their lifestyle.

However, this view too has problems. First, some things are good whether people desire them or not. For example, it would be good to relieve the suffering of a minority, even if the majority doesn't want to. Second, some things are bad even if people do desire them. A Nazi government could be one such example. Critics say that preference utilitarianism reduces morality to the level of a free-market economy, where 'good' and 'bad' are simply defined in terms of what people want. Surely, it is argued, not all that is good is desired, and not all that is desired is good.

Welfare utilitarians claim that what is useful is what best fulfils the interests of people. This has to be distinguished from what people desire. People don't always desire what is in their best interests, hence the old saying 'be careful what you wish for, you might just get it'. There is also the problem that people's desires and preferences vary enormously, and thus it is very difficult to act according to people's desires. It is far easier to know what in general is good for people. This means welfare utilitarianism also has the advantage of being a practical doctrine. However, one major disadvantage of this theory is that it seems to be very paternalistic. We should do what is good for people whether they want it or not.

One problem faced by all these versions of utilitarianism is that perhaps there is no single good. We want to be happy, we want to make our own choices and we want our welfare to be considered by others. If we decide that just one of these things is the highest good, we inevitably miss some things out. But if we can't define utility clearly, then we can't come up with a clear account of what the right moral action is.

Another problem faced by all versions of utilitarianism is whether, when judging the utility of an action, each action should be taken on its own merits, or whether acts should be judged according to their general effect on utility. For example, although murder will generally reduce utility, there are bound to be some cases where it will not. In such a case, is it still not right to spare the life of the innocent victim? Some utilitarians would argue that it is. Because it is impossible to calculate the consequences of individual actions, it is better to follow general rules about what best serves utility. If we try to judge each case on its merits, we will make more mistakes than if we follow rules. So utility is best served by following rules rather than making decisions on a case by case basis. This view is known as rule, as opposed to act, utilitarianism.

The problem with rule utilitarianism is that there will always seem to be some occasion where the breaking of a generally held rule would be the right thing to do. Consider, for example, murdering someone who is about to kill someone else, stealing in order to stay alive or lying in order to save a life. In order to follow the spirit of utilitarianism, surely in these circumstances the rule should be abandoned and utility be maximised. The rule utilitarian could try and get around this by making her rules more specific. For example, the rule could be: 'Tell the truth unless lying saves lives'. But then in order to cover all possible eventualities, the rule would have to be: 'Tell the truth except when not telling the truth would promote greater utility'. But this would just be act utilitarianism all over again, as it would in effect mean, 'Tell the truth when that promotes utility and lie when that promotes utility', which means 'Do whatever promotes utility'.

Another problem for all versions of utilitarianism is that it seems that they all have the potential to conflict with rights. The maximising of utility – be it for preferences, welfare or pleasure – may be best served if a minority's rights are trampled over. Utility might also be best served if all people with damaged kidneys, for example, could be given transplants with kidneys taken from healthy people, without their consent. If all we are concerned about is the final outcome, why should we in principle be concerned about rights?

Many utilitarians accept this challenge. Bentham called natural rights 'nonsense on stilts' and argued that rights are merely useful constructs (see Chapter 5 on political philosophy). In any case, they argue that no utilitarian theory will, in practice, conflict with what we take to be basic rights, since a society where such 'rights' are ignored could not be one with high utility.

Kantian ethics

The great German philosopher Immanuel Kant (1724–1804) developed the most famous version of deontological ethics. Central to Kant's ethics is the idea of the categorical imperative. An imperative is a command, of the kind 'don't eat that second slice of cream cake' or 'do not lie'. Imperatives can be hypothetical (or conditional) or categorical. A hypothetical imperative is where the command contains an explicit or implicit 'if' clause. For example, the command 'Don't eat that second slice of cream cake' is hypothetical when it is followed by or assumes something like 'if you want to keep to your diet'. In such an instance, the command not to eat the cake is not absolute – the command should be followed only if you want to achieve some further aim or goal. If you do go ahead and eat the cake, you will have done the wrong thing only in regard to the goal of sticking to your diet.

Categorical imperatives, on the other hand, do not have any 'ifs'. When 'Do not lie' is uttered as a categorical imperative, the idea is that lying is something you should not do just because it is wrong, not because following the command is merely a means to achieve an end.

It should be clear that only categorical imperatives belong to morality. If you eat the second piece of cream cake, you have not been a bad person, you've just failed to achieve a goal. Only when you act against a categorical imperative do you behave immorally.

The hallmark of a categorical imperative is its universalisability (see the section on prescriptivism above). That is to say, an imperative can only be categorical if one could will that everyone followed the command. For example, 'Always tell the truth' and 'Lie to get what you want' both look as though they could be categorical imperatives. But whereas it is possible to will that everyone told the truth, one cannot will that everyone lied to get what they wanted. This is not because it is physically or psychologically impossible to will such a thing. Rather, it is that if everyone followed the command, its purpose would be undermined. In a society where everyone lies to get what they want, trust is impossible. This means that lying is no longer effective. You can only lie to get what you want if people generally accept what people say as the truth. So if everyone lies to try and get what they want, the power of the lie to achieve this disappears. Thus, it would be in some sense irrational to will that everyone followed such a rule.

So, for Kant, moral rules are universalisable categorical imperatives. But the real question is, where do we get these categorical imperatives from? Kant's answer has at its root the idea that each of us is a rational agent and that each of us is able to will – to desire or choose – freely and autonomously. Moral rules are derived when we use our rationality to guide our wills. It works something like this.

First, we recognise that what we will can be in the form of a categorical or hypothetical imperative. We can will things for some end or purpose (hypothetically) or will them for their own sake (categorically). Only the latter are moral commands. Such commands are, as we have seen, universalisable. Kant's idea is that when we reflect on this, we will see that there are a number of rules which we should follow because it is rational to follow them and they are categorical and universalisable in nature.

The example of telling a lie may help to illustrate this. It is clear that the rule 'do not lie' is categorical in nature. It is universalisable since we could, and perhaps should, will that no-one ever lied. Kant's idea is that on reflection we will see that it is rational to follow this rule. Reason, detached from any self-interest, just has to recognise that as a universalisable categorical imperative, it is a rule it makes sense to follow. Importantly for Kant, our decision to follow it is based not on emotion or character, but merely the will's decision to follow the dictates of reason.

The centrality of the autonomous will in Kant's ethics is illustrated by another general rule which Kant takes to follow from his principles. This is the idea that one should always treat persons as ends and never as mere means to an end. This is, on the one hand, merely the logical consequence of the categorical imperative: we can consistently desire that people be treated always as beings with value in themselves, but not that we treat them as mere means to an end. But perhaps it is also indicative of the supreme importance Kant places on the idea that we are individual moral agents with the freedom to choose.

The main problem with Kant's ethics is that it seems one can understand and accept it and still not know what one should do. Kant himself came up with several prescriptions, the injunction never to tell a lie being one. But it seems that one could will any number of moral rules to be followed with consistency. The idea that reason is somehow able to determine which of these rules we should follow and which we should not seems rather optimistic.

Hume famously said that 'reason is the slave of the passions', by which he meant reason alone can never provide us with a motivation to act, it can only help guide us to achieve what we desire. This directly contradicts Kant's view that reason can provide us with motives to act. If Hume is right, Kant's ethics is doomed.

It is true of this whole book that the issues discussed have depths we can merely skim the surface of. But this is particularly true of Kant. His arguments on this topic are difficult and require a close and detailed study to really comprehend and assess. This means that they can appear weaker in précis than alternatives which, on closer examination, are no stronger at all.

Aristotelian ethics

Aristotle (384–322 BCE) was the father of virtue ethics. When it came to putting flesh on these moral bones and providing us with an actual guide to life, Aristotle's key idea was that of the golden mean.

In mathematics, the mean is the average of a series of two or more numbers. So, for example, the mean of two and six is four. Aristotle borrows this idea and applies it to the virtues, although it should be stressed that Aristotle's mean is not something that can be calculated with mathematical precision.

In ethics, the mean is the ideal point which lies between two extremes. For example, many consider courage to be a virtue. Typically, we think of courage to be a virtue, and the vice of cowardice to be its opposite. But on Aristotle's view, courage is actually the ideal that lies between two extremes – cowardice at one end and rashness at the other. Rashness is a kind of excess of courage, while cowardice is a deficiency of it.

The same model applies to all the other virtues. Honesty is a virtue of which dishonesty is a deficiency and something like tactlessness is the excess. Helpfulness is a virtue of which unhelpfulness is the deficiency and servility the excess. Modesty is a virtue of which reticence is the excess and boastfulness the deficiency.

The mean provides a principle which helps us to modify our characters in order to achieve what Aristotle called *Eudaimonia*, which means flourishing. The problem is that the doctrine of the mean does not prescribe exactly what the ideal between the two extremes is, it just tells us virtue is to be found there. This is consistent with Aristotle's view that ethics is not a precise science and judgement is required to get things right. The doctrine of the mean points us in the right direction, but it doesn't give us a simple list of things we have to do in order to live well.

Animal rights

So far we have looked at issues in meta-ethics and normative ethics. Finally, we can turn to where the real 'action' is – applied ethics. What people most want to know about in ethics is what we should actually do. Applied ethics is about considering real ethical dilemmas and applying ethical principles to them. Here, we will look at three issues and consider just a few ways in which we can argue about them.

The issue of animal rights is one such hotly contested area in ethics. While millions of people routinely eat factory-farmed animals, many others refuse to do so, seeing it as barbaric and cruel. Back in the nineteenth century, Jeremy Bentham made the case for treating animals better when he said, 'The question is not, Can they *reason*? nor Can they *talk*? but, Can they *suffer*?' The fact that animals do suffer has been at the basis of many arguments for animal rights ever since.

However, before going on, it should be pointed out that the phrase 'animal rights' may not be helpful. People who object to eating meat, for instance, may do so, not because they feel animals have rights, but just because they think there is something wrong about causing them to suffer. The idea of a 'right' is very specific and one should refrain from using the word unless one is talking about rights specifically.

Returning to the issue at hand, a typical argument for the better treatment of animals runs something like this:

Animals feel pain.
No innocent being should have pain inflicted on it unnecessarily.
Therefore, animals should not have pain inflicted on them unnecessarily.

This argument is valid in that, if the first two premises are true, the conclusion necessarily follows. In assessing the argument, we therefore need to consider whether the premises are true and, if they are, what follows from the conclusion.

As regards the first premise, one may ask, 'How do we know that animals feel pain?' The problem with this question is that it seems we can never know for sure that *any* living creature feels pain, including other human beings. However, by observing the behaviour of animals, and noting the basic similarities between the nervous systems of animals and humans, we can be much more sure that they do feel pain than that they don't. To demand more certainty than this would seem to be inappropriate, as we don't demand this certainty with fellow humans. Hence, the first premise does seem to be secure.

The second premise is deliberately worded with care. It contains the word 'innocent' because it would not be wrong to cause, for example, an attacker pain if that were our only means of defence. It contains the word 'unnecessary' because sometimes pain is required for a greater good. A dentist does not do something morally wrong when she hurts us administering an injection of anaesthetic.

This premise has an intuitive appeal. Surely, if we could choose between a world with a certain amount of pain and a world with twice this amount of pain, with no further benefit to the world with more pain, we would choose the first world. Unnecessary pain is unequivocally bad, and to ask why is to ask an inappropriate question. If we accept this, then not to count animal pain would seem arbitrary and unfair. The philosopher Richard Ryder calls this disregard of animals purely because they are not human 'speciesism'. Just as it is wrong not to take account of people's interests purely because of their race, sex or skin colour, so it would be wrong not to take account of an animal's interests purely on the grounds of species.

Against the second premise, it could be argued that pain itself is neither good nor bad and it is thus neither right nor wrong to cause it. This may seem implausible, but one could distinguish between pain and suffering. Only animals with highly developed consciousness can truly suffer, it is argued. Without this, the feeling of pain is merely transitory, a reflex response by the body. It is nonsense to talk of pain being bad for a goldfish. The goldfish merely feels the pain and then forgets about it. With humans, though, we dread and remember pain, and this is what makes it so intolerable in excess.

Against this objection, two points could be raised. First, surely some animals do suffer as well as feel pain. Given the difficulty of drawing a line between these two so-called 'different states', it is better to err on the side of caution, and not cause pain to any animal. Second, even if the distinction is a good one, it is still hard to see how this makes the causing of 'mere' pain a matter of indifference.

A further objection to the premise is that the idea of unnecessary pain makes it too vague. Given that all pains are not equal (compare a pinprick with severe nausea), isn't a bit of animal pain a small price to pay for the pleasure and nutrients given to humans? Animal pain that we cause is not unnecessary: it serves our interests.

But in modern societies, it is hard to see how the causing of pain in hunting and farming is necessary. We don't need meat to live. In fact, some studies suggest vegetarians live longer than their carnivorous contemporaries. So it's hard to see how such pain is necessary, on any definition of the word.

What if we accepted this argument as valid and sound? Well, it would be enough to show that we should grant animals something like rights, because it argues for the moral need to take into account the interests of animals. But how far would these rights extend? In the case of vivisection (animal testing) for cosmetics, which causes much pain and is clearly unnecessary (we have enough safe cosmetic ingredients for even the most demanding of faces), this would be deemed morally unacceptable. In the case of vivisection for medical purposes, we would have to balance out the benefits gained by eliminating the suffering of sick humans against the suffering inflicted on the animals experimented on. This is very difficult, because we would have to compare the pain and suffering of many different species.

In a surprising way, the argument above may actually support humane farming. Though factory-farmed animals certainly suffer unnecessary pain, humanely reared animals probably live a life more pain free than they would in the wild. And if death came easily, there would seem to be no objection, with this argument, to eating meat. Hunting is complicated, because, on the one hand, the animal lives a normal life before it is killed. So we would need to think about how death by hunting generally compares to death by natural causes, which includes, of course, being killed by other animals who may claw and chew a creature to death much more painfully than a bullet.

Abortion

Perhaps the best way to approach this issue is to consider two arguments against abortion, as set out (and subsequently criticised) by Peter Singer in *Practical Ethics* (1979). All we can do here is just sketch out the key debating points in the argument. There are two versions, one of which considers innocent human beings, the other of which considers potential human beings:

> It is wrong to kill an innocent/potential human being.
> A human foetus is an innocent/potential human being.
> Therefore, it is wrong to kill a human foetus.

This argument alone throws up enough questions to ensure a lifetime of debate. Perhaps its most contentious point is the second premise. Is it true that a foetus is a human being?

The question of when a foetus becomes a human being is a difficult one. What is clear is that the development of the foetus is gradual and there is no 'magic moment' when it becomes a full human being. However, perhaps this should not concern us as much as it often does. After all, there is no 'magic moment' on the colour spectrum when yellow becomes green, but yellow and green are still different. In the same way, the fact that there is no clear boundary between foetus and fully developed human does not mean there is no distinction at all.

Even so, many problems remain. Some argue that the foetus is not a life in its own right, it is just a part of the mother. The plausibility of this depends very much on what stage of the pregnancy one is talking about. When the foetus is viable (able to survive outside the womb), it no longer seems plausible to say that the foetus is just a part of the mother.

Another issue regards the question of whether the significant factor is species membership or personhood. The foetus could be considered as a member of the species *homo sapiens* from an early age. But is this what makes its life valuable? Many believe that what we really value about human life is the fact that we are persons: independent, thinking, feeling beings with a sense of self. This is what makes it wrong to kill a human, not the fact that it belongs to a certain species. If we met a pig that had these human capabilities, it would be as wrong to kill it as it would be to kill a human. On this argument, the crucial point is not whether the foetus is a human, but whether it is a person, and until it has reached a certain level of development it cannot be said to be a person in this sense.

So a central issue here is the actual status of the foetus. The argument against abortion set out above can be challenged if we question the status granted to the foetus in the second premise.

The first premise can also be attacked. Is it always wrong to kill a human being? On one version of the argument, it is stated that it is wrong to kill a potential human being. However, we don't in general grant the same rights to a potential something as to an actual something. In the United States, everyone is a potential president, but only the actual president has the rights and privileges of his office. So if the foetus is only a potential human or person, rather than an actual one, we may not agree that it is necessarily wrong to kill it. The value of a potential life cannot be assumed to be the same as that of an actual life.

More generally, we might ask whether the value of a life depends upon how well developed a being's capacities for thought, pain, pleasure and so on are. Even if we grant that a foetus is a human being; until it can feel or think, is it really as wrong to kill it as it is to kill a thinking, feeling creature? As Peter Singer controversially puts it, why do some people think it is so terrible to kill what is little more than a cluster of developing cells when they think it merely regrettable to kill an unwanted adult dog, which has feelings and possibly even thoughts?

Euthanasia

Euthanasia is another controversial topic in ethics. Euthanasia is the providing of an easy and painless death. It can be voluntary, involuntary or non-voluntary. Involuntary euthanasia is killing against the wishes of the person being killed. It is straightforwardly murder and is not a form of euthanasia that is widely discussed in applied ethics. Non-voluntary euthanasia is killing where the person being killed is unable to give consent. For example, if someone is in an irreversible coma, we might think it right to end their life. But we cannot ask them permission to do so.

Perhaps the most pressing issues surround voluntary euthanasia. This is where people, often suffering with a painful, terminal illness, want the help of doctors to end their life before it becomes intolerable. This is often called assisted suicide, because these are cases where the person involved would commit suicide if they had the means to do so painlessly. But usually the help of doctors is required to ensure painless and easy death, so suicide is not an option.

Here, one way to argue is to start from the assumption that we have the right to make major life decisions for ourselves and seek to place the burden of proof on those who say this doesn't apply in euthanasia. Set out formally, the argument would look something like this:

> Human beings have the right to make major life decisions for themselves.
> The decision to end one's life is a major life decision.
> Therefore, human beings have the right to make the decision to end their own lives.

One might think this argument is inadequate because euthanasia requires the help of another person. But while it does not establish the right to demand that someone help you end your life, it does seem enough to establish your right to ask and be helped if someone chooses to help. In general, if one has a right to do something, one also has a right to be helped voluntarily to do that if one cannot achieve it oneself.

How might someone attack this argument? The best route in would be to question the first premise. Maybe we don't have the right to make decisions about all major life choices, and life and death is one such exception to this rule. It might be argued that life is sacred, and that it is always wrong to take it. Therefore, it is as wrong to take one's own life as it is to take the life of another and so this is one area of life where we do not have the right to choose for ourselves.

However, we do not generally think life is sacred in this way. Soldiers will shoot colleagues on the battlefield, for example, if they see that they are in pain and have no hope of being saved. We put down animals that are suffering rather than see them continue to suffer. Anyone who approves of abortion or meat eating also thinks that certain types of life are not sacred. The key question here, then, is, when must life be preserved and when is it acceptable or preferable to end it?

Approaches to applied ethics

These short discussions are just examples of how we might approach moral issues. There are a few general features about them worth noting. First, applied ethics is sometimes described as applying normative theories to actual issues. This is certainly one way of going about it and we could have simply tried to apply utilitarianism, Kantian or Aristotelian ethics to the issues of animal welfare, abortion and euthanasia. For example, applying utilitarianism to abortion, we could ask: Is the general happiness best served by abortion? Should happiness be maximised or should only the happiness of already existing people be maximised? If the bringing of new life increases happiness, then can we not produce the same or a greater amount of happiness by having an abortion and having another child at a different, more suitable time? This is certainly one approach and we would encourage the reader to think about how one might apply the normative theories we have looked at to specific issues. But what the short discussions of the three topics have made clear, we hope, is that there can be much fruitful discussion in applied ethics which is not about simply applying a normative theory. Often, we can make great progress just by setting out the basic objections or arguments in support of ethical stances and closely examining them. This is very important, for if applied ethics were just about applying normative theories, agreement among people who disagree about normative theories would be much harder to achieve.

A second general point is that discussions in applied ethics often confuse what is legal and what is moral. The two realms are distinct, though hopefully related. Applied ethics is about deciding what is right or wrong. We may decide that something is right which is currently illegal, or something is wrong which is currently legal.

Conclusion

Moral philosophy is an exciting field of philosophy. It is where the real-life application of philosophy is most apparent. But at the same time, to do it properly one needs to spend a lot of time considering issues of meta-ethics and normative moral theory which take one far from the concerns of everyday moral choices. What one needs to remember is that the concerns of meta-ethics, normative ethics and applied ethics are not absolutely distinct. The boundaries between these three parts of the subject are fluid. But at the same time, it is not always necessary to call upon the resources of all three. One does not need to have a complete meta-ethical and normative framework in place before one can address issues of practical ethics. Sometimes good arguments and sound reasoning are enough.

Summary

Ethics is concerned with the issue of how we ought to live, not in order to achieve a particular goal, but in order to live a **good** life in general.

At the most abstract level, meta-ethics is about the general nature of morality. Moral realists believe that moral judgements express truths which exist independently of humanity. Cognitivists add that these truths can be known. Non-realists believe that moral judgements do not have this objective existence. It follows that they are **non-cognitivists**, as these moral truths cannot be known since they do not exist. A simple non-cognitivist position, such as emotivism, holds that moral judge-ments are no more than an expression of an opinion or a taste. More sophisticated non-cognitivist positions, such as prescriptivism, hold that although moral judgements are neither true nor false, it is nonethe-less possible to reason about them and disagree about matters of ethics on rational grounds.

Normative ethical theories can be deontological, consequentialist or virtue-based. Deontologists hold that acts are right or wrong depend-ing on the nature of the act itself, not because of its consequences. Consequentialists argue, to the contrary, that things are only wrong if they cause harm and right if they make things better. Proponents of virtue ethics argue that morality has its basis in the character of the moral agent, not in an analysis of the right or wrong of particular actions.

Utilitarianism is a normative consequentialist ethic which holds that acts are right if they increase utility and wrong if they decrease it. Utility can be understood as happiness, the ability to select either for what one prefers or for one's welfare.

Kantian ethics is a deontological ethic. It holds that we should only follow moral rules which we can consistently will to hold as **universal** rules. To act morally we have to act out of a pure will to follow morality and not out of any other motive or just habit.

Aristotelian ethics is a virtue ethic. It holds that the good person develops virtues which lie at a mid-point or 'mean' between two extremes. For example, generosity is the mean between meanness and profligacy.

When we discuss particular issues in ethics, we move from normative to **applied ethics**. One normative question is how we should treat animals and whether their capacity to feel pain grants them rights. Another is the issue of abortion, and whether it is ever right to kill a foetus. A third is the issue of euthanasia and whether it is permissible to help someone take their own life.

Glossary

Acts–omissions The distinction between things we do which bring about a certain consequence and things we do not do, with the same consequence.

Akrasia Weakness of will, when we do something we know to be wrong.

Applied ethics The area of ethics concerned with the rights and wrongs of particular issues.

Good Good and bad describe states of affairs or persons, in contrast to right and wrong which describe the morality of actions.

Internalism The theory that if one believes something to be wrong, one is necessarily motivated not to do it.

Is/ought gap The impossibility of deducing matters of value from matters of fact. Also known as the fact–value distinction.

Meta-ethics The area of ethics concerned with the general nature of morality.

Non-cognitivism The view that moral truths cannot be known, because there are no moral truths independent of persons.

Normative ethics The area of ethics concerned with theories of right and wrong.

Relativism The idea that there are no universal moral truths and that right and wrong are always relative to a society, group or individual.

Universalisability The feature of moral judgements that they apply to everyone at all times equally.

Further reading

In the companion volume to this book, *Philosophy: Key Texts*, we look at three books which focus on ethics: Sartre's *Existentialism and Humanism*, Plato's *Republic*, which presents a form of moral realism, and J. S. Mill's *On Liberty*, which sets out Mill's development of Bentham's classic utilitarianism. All are very accessible, interesting works.

Other classic texts worth reading include Hume's *An Enquiry concerning the Principles of Morals*, which is a brilliant early non-cognitivist work; Kant's *Groundwork of the Metaphysics of Morals*, a difficult but rewarding exposition of a deontological ethic; and Mills's *Utilitarianism*, the classic exposition of the eponymous theory.

Some accessible twentieth-century texts include *Writings on an Ethical Life* by the utilitarian Peter Singer (Fourth Estate); *Moral Luck* by Bernard Williams (Cambridge University Press); and, for a more demanding read, *Reasons and Persons* by Derek Parfit (Oxford University Press).

A Companion to Ethics, edited by Peter Singer (Blackwell), is a superb collection of short essays on a broad range of ethical issues. *Being Good* by Simon Blackburn (Oxford University Press) is one of the best short introductions to ethics.

3
Philosophy of Mind

What is the philosophy of mind?

The universe contains many amazing things. At the smallest level there are inconceivably small particles with exotic names such as quarks and neutrinos. These form the basic building blocks of atoms such as hydrogen and nitrogen. From these atoms the whole material world is formed, from tiny organisms such as amoeba, to large mammals such as elephants. There are mountains, oceans and forests of infinite variety.

The earth itself is only one planet in one solar system. Our sun is inconceivably hot, planets such as Jupiter inconceivably large. And our solar system is itself just one small corner of the universe, an unfathomably vast, expanding cradle of space and time.

We understand more about the universe than ever before. We understand it thanks to the growth of knowledge in the physical sciences. All I have described so far is explained within the terms of science, with reference to the behaviour of physical matter. But one thing does not seem to be included in this picture. Perhaps ironically, perhaps tellingly, the one thing physical science does not seem to be able to explain is what makes its own explanations possible: the existence of minds. It is our minds which have enabled us to understand the universe as much as we do, yet arguably this understanding has not extended to the subject of that understanding: human consciousness.

The problem of how the existence of minds fits into our understanding of the world is central to the philosophy of mind. In particular, it has led to one key question which is still unresolved: the so-called mind–body problem. This is the problem of how the mental is related to the physical, and in particular, how our minds, our thoughts, our feelings and sensations are related to our bodies, matter, atoms and so on. Although there are other problems in the philosophy of mind, such as the problem of other minds, the possibility of unconscious mental states and personal identity, the mind–body problem is by far and away the dominant issue in the field. For that reason, we will first look at various solutions to the mind–body problem: dualism, behaviourism, physicalism and functionalism. We'll also consider the possibility that consciousness is a basic property of matter, and the opposite approach – that mental properties should be 'eliminated' from our vocabulary.

But before we begin, a word of caution. Most solutions to the mind–body problem offer an answer to the question of what mind is, which is supposed to make its relationship to body explicable. So we get a statement, 'Mind is X'. The problem is that not all statements of the form 'X is Y' are identity statements, and not all identity statements appear to mean precisely the same thing.

For example, consider these statements, which are all of the form X is Y:

1. Gary Parry is the Prime Minister of Ruritania.
2. Money is the root of all evil.
3. A noun is a word which labels a thing or an idea.
4. Dough is flour, yeast and water.
5. A cat is a feline.
6. Bill Stickers is innocent.
7. Water is H_2O.

We can discern several different usages of 'is' here. One is the 'is' of identity. In such sentences, 'is' can be replaced by 'is the same as' without any loss of meaning. There is also the 'is' of definition. In addition, there is the 'is' of predication where 'is' introduces a description of some kind. One may be able to discern other ways of describing the function of the verb 'to be' in these sentences. We will leave it to the reader to ponder which usage of 'is' occurs in each sentence. We expect you will find that it is less obvious which is the best way to describe each use of 'is' than you would at first think it is.

We will be considering the significance of the different ways in which 'mind is X' can be understood as we go along. At this stage, it is important simply to note that there is an ambiguity in saying 'mind is X'. The problem we will see is that when different theorists claim mind is such and such and others disagree, they're not always using 'is' in the same way.

Dualism

One theory of mind with a long history is dualism. Dualism comes in various forms, and we will be considering the most prominent, substance dualism (hereafter, simply dualism). Dualism is the view that mind and matter are two different kinds of 'stuff'. Matter is what the physical sciences deal with and is the stuff out of which all the things in the universe mentioned at the start of this chapter are made. Mind, however, is a different kind of substance which is not the subject of physical science, but which nonetheless exists within conscious beings such as ourselves.

To see why some people believe dualism is true, it is necessary to consider the metaphysics of identity. The classic principles of identity are, first, Leibniz's Law, after the philosopher who wrote it, and, second, the principle of the identity of indiscernibles. They say:

1. *Leibniz's Law.* If A is identical to B, then any property of A is a property of B, or whatever is true of A is true of B.
2. *The principle of the identity of indiscernibles.* If A and B are identical in all respects, then they are identical objects, i.e., one and the same object.

If identity is understood in these ways – and philosophers generally agree that identity should be understood along these lines – then if one thing is identical with another, both must occupy the same time and space and have identical properties. This seems to be true. If John is blind and Smith can see, Smith can't be John. Nor can Smith be John if Smith is now in Lanzarote and John is in Huddersfield. But if all that is true of John is true of Smith, they must be the same person.

One must be careful to note here that the properties which identical objects share must include spacio–temporal location – where they are in time and space. If two things are in different places but have all other properties the same, they are only *qualitatively* identical, not *quantitatively* or *numerically* identical. So, two billiard balls off the same production line are only qualitatively identical. Lewis Carroll and Charles Lutwidge Dodgson, however, are quantitatively identical. It is the latter form of identity which is the subject of Leibniz's Law and which concerns us here.

The simplest argument for dualism is based simply on these principles of identity. The argument starts by looking at the properties of mind and matter, which includes our physical bodies.

When we consider the properties of matter, we could count among them the fact that matter exists in definite moments of time and space. You can always say where and when a bit of matter is, to the nanometre, if you have precise enough equipment. (This may not be true of the very smallest level – the level of quantum physics – but since quantum theory is very much cutting-edge science and not yet properly understood even by specialists in the field, we should not be too hasty in jumping to conclusions on the basis of its findings so far.) Another feature of matter is that it is in principle observable by all. With a powerful enough microscope, one could see even the smallest particles. Finally, matter is subject to the laws of physics and, except at the level of its most elementary particles, is always divisible.

When you turn now to mind, you find that it doesn't seem to fit the same description. A thought cannot be located in space and time in the same way as a particle or object can. It just doesn't seem to make sense to say that a thought occurred three inches behind my nose, for example. Nor are minds in principle observable by anyone. You cannot 'look into my mind' in anything other than a figurative sense. Thoughts, feelings and sensations do not seem to be suitable subjects for the laws of physics – it is not gravity that brings our thoughts down to earth. Mind also seems to be essentially indivisible. My consciousness cannot be split up into infinitely small parts – it forms a whole.

Mind also seems to have a special feature for us which matter doesn't. I can be in error about features of the external world. But I cannot be in error about the state of my own mind. If I think I can see a yellow canary, I could be mistaken that there is a canary, but not that I am having a visual experience that seems to be of a canary.

We can set out these differences between the properties of mind and matter and see how they starkly contrast with one another.

Mind	Body/Matter
Exists in time, but not in space	Exists in space and time
Private, i.e. is only directly observable by the person who has the mind	Is directly observable by all
Is not subject to laws of physics	Is subject to laws of physics
We cannot be in error about states of our minds	We can be in error about states of the physical world
Cannot be divided	Can be divided

If this is a genuine set of differences, we can easily apply Leibniz's Law to produce the following argument:

1. If mind is identical to matter, then mind must have all the same properties as matter.
2. Mind has different properties to matter (see table).
3. Therefore, mind is not identical to matter.

What then is mind? Given that matter is a kind of substance, it seems natural to suppose that mind must be some other kind of substance. Hence, we reach the conclusion of dualism: that there are two types of substance in the world: mind and matter. Dualism is a view that has dominated the thinking of mankind for centuries, and is central to many religious conceptions of persons. Such is its acceptance that Gilbert Ryle, writing after the Second World War, dubbed it 'the Official Doctrine'.

The merits of dualism are that it fits in with our intuitive views about the mind, and the argument for it is straightforward. It has proved to be a very resilient view, and despite the rise of physicalism and naturalistic accounts of human nature, many, if not most, people still subscribe to it. But it is also perhaps the most criticised view in the philosophy of mind.

Arguments against dualism

One major difficulty with dualism is the problem of interaction. We have an idea of how matter affects matter. As they are fundamentally the same kind of substance, any two bits of matter can interact with one another. But how can mind interact with matter if they are fundamentally different types of thing? If mind is not in space, how can it affect or be affected by things in space? How can a thing without mass move a thing with mass?

Mind and body clearly do interact, and that interaction is at least sometimes causal in nature. My decisions seem to be able to cause my arm to move. Physical objects can make me think, or give me perceptions. But the only way we can understand causation is on the principle that like affects like. If mind is not at all like matter, the possibility of interaction seems to disappear.

One reply would be that if the argument for dualism is good and interaction is a fact, it must be true that mind and matter can interact. Just because we can't understand how they interact doesn't mean dualism is wrong. We should not use our lack of understanding to criticise dualism. What is more, why should we assume that all forms of interaction must fit the model of physical causation? Isn't that just a bias we have in favour of our most successful theories? Just because the physical sciences have explained a lot, it doesn't mean they explain everything. You could even argue that we have not explained physical causation at all. All we have done is found the laws that govern causation. But we don't know why things should cause other things to happen at all.

The interaction problem identifies a puzzle in dualism; it does not attack the argument for it. Other criticisms are directed at the argument itself. A popular one is based on a logical mistake called the masked man fallacy. Here's an example of the fallacy at work. I know who John is, but at a party I see a masked man, and I don't know who he is. Under Leibniz's Law, if John is identical to the masked man then everything which is true of John must be true of the masked man. But it is true of the masked man that I don't know who he is and it is true of John that I do know who he is. So John can't be the masked man.

This is clearly absurd. There is nothing in this situation which rules out John being the masked man. So is Leibniz's Law wrong? Not at all. The fallacy hinges on the fact that I may know X under one description, but not under another description. Facts like these are irrelevant to what is really true of the thing itself. What I know about John and the masked man are thus not real properties of either of them. They say something about me, not them.

What this teaches us is that what we believe or know about an object can neither be considered to be properties of that object nor things which can be true of that object, at least for the purposes of identity statements. It is not a real property of a thing that I know, perceive or believe something about it. So long as we don't make the mistake of counting these truths among the real properties of a thing, Leibniz's Law holds.

How does this apply to the argument for dualism? The argument for dualism depends upon the fact that mind and matter have different properties. But if we look back at our list, how many of these are genuine properties of mind and matter, and how many are more accurately described as features of how we think about or perceive them? For instance, it may be false that minds are not in space. It may just be that we don't perceive them spatially. In fact, in some sense minds do seem to be in time and space. I think mine's somewhere behind my eyes right now! Where's yours?

Similar doubts can be cast on all the other apparent real differences between mind and body. The fact that minds are private is simply a result of the different perspectives we have on minds and matter, not a result of the nature of minds. Telepathic people would not think minds were private, so if telepathy is even conceivable, mind is not necessarily private.

The fact that we cannot be wrong about states of our own minds, but can be wrong about matter clearly concerns what we know about mind and matter, not how they actually are. So this may not be a real difference in properties. (It is also possible to argue that we just can be wrong about the states of our minds. We may think we feel righteous indignation when we really feel jealousy, for example.)

Each set of apparently different properties can be treated in a similar way. Of course, it is a matter of debate whether any of these are real properties or not. You may still think some are. But the case has to be made in the light of the lessons of the masked-man fallacy.

One of the most powerful arguments against dualism is found in Gilbert Ryle's classic *The Concept of Mind* (1949). Ryle believed that the argument for dualism rests upon what he calls a category mistake. A category mistake is where you put something under one category when it should come under another. Historically, there have been two main philosophical categories: substance (stuff) and attribute (size, shape, colour and other characteristics described by adjectives). Even within each category there are different sub-categories. Not all nouns refer to things in the same way. For example, if you want to see Oxford University, I have to show you all the different colleges and buildings which make up the University. Although the University is clearly not any one of these things, nor is it another thing additional to all these parts. The University is not in the same category of existence as all the individual institutions that make up the University. Another of Ryle's examples is of the foreigner who watches a cricket match, and sees who bowls, bats and fields, but doesn't see who contributes the team spirit. Contributing team spirit is simply not the same kind of thing as fulfilling a single function. It is the difference between doing an action and the way you do an action.

The problem with the argument for dualism is that it says mind is not the same as matter and concludes that it must be a different kind of substance to matter. But isn't it more correct to conclude that the mind just isn't a substance at all? Calling it a substance is simply to put it into the wrong category. Just because the mind cannot be described as physical stuff that doesn't mean it has to be described as some other kind of stuff.

If we look back at the argument for dualism, we can see that the conclusion was just that mind is not the same as matter. Interpreting this as meaning that mind and matter are two different substances required an extra step. This step is not taken by a family of positions, variously known as property dualism, neutral monism or double (or dual) aspect theory. These positions all differ subtly from each other, and confusingly are not even consistently described by different philosophers. Nonetheless, what they all have in common is the claim that mind and matter are two different attributes of one substance. In other words, there are not two 'stuffs' – mind and matter – but one stuff which has mental and physical properties. On some accounts (such as neutral monism and Spinoza's double aspect theory) this basic 'stuff' itself is 'neutral': neither physical nor mental, but having both sets of properties. Neither of these properties is more fundamental than the other and neither can be explained in terms of the other. Some other versions of property dualism maintain that the basic stuff is physical, but that it also has mental properties which cannot be described or explained in physical terms. We will return to this view shortly.

Neutral monism is attractive as it preserves the intuitive difference between mind and matter without leading to the implausibilities of substance dualism. But it is not without its own difficulties. One is that mind seems to be a property of relatively few things in the universe. If so, then we must account for the fact that mental properties are not universal, but seem to only be the properties of certain types of matter – namely, brains. Otherwise, we are forced to accept the view that everything has both mental and physical properties, even stones. This view is known as panpsychism. But it is very hard to even make sense of the idea that a stone could have mental properties. So we either have to accept the implausible idea that everything has mental properties, or account for the fact that although some things have both mental and physical properties, most have only physical ones.

Arguments about dualism may be inconclusive. But when deciding whether to accept it as true, we don't only need to consider these arguments. We also need to consider rival views and how plausible they are. So we need to move on to examine a few of them.

Behaviourism

The picture dualism paints of the private self, hidden within the public body, seems to lead us to an insoluble problem. Mental events are supposed to be by their very nature private, only directly observable by the person who has them, whereas physical events are said to be public. But if mental events are indeed private, then how can we meaningfully talk about them or know other people have them? (See the section on other minds.) Dualism creates two worlds – the inner and the outer – and leaves unexplained the link between them.

Behaviourism attempts to solve this problem by claiming that mental concepts do not refer to private, inner events at all, but to public events. In other words, it defines psychological functioning in terms of observed behaviour. We do not need to talk about what goes on 'inside our heads' at all. All we need talk about is behaviour. By behaviour we should mean any publicly observable event, be it behaviour in the ordinary sense of the word or in the sense of the physical behaviour of matter.

Behaviourism comes in two main varieties and varying strengths. Methodological behaviourism belongs in psychology, and is basically a means of doing psychology solely based on observation of behaviour (rather than relying on introspection), with the aim of making the discipline more scientific. The major philosophical variety is logical behaviourism, which claims that everything mental is either a behavioural state, or a disposition to behave in a certain way. So, for example, to be in pain is to be unable to comfortably use the part of the body in pain, to tend to grimace, bite your lip or scream if prodded and so on. To be impatient is to tend to act in an impatient way more often than is usual.

Behaviourism often appears barmy, because it seems to talk about mental states as if they didn't exist. To talk of pain without talking about the sensation one feels seems to miss the point. But behaviourists do not all deny we have such sensations. Weak behaviourists claim that although psychological concepts refer to behaviour that does not mean that there are no such things as inner sensations. It is just that they have no part to play in the meaning of mental terms. Only strong behaviourists claim there are no such things as sensations and consciousness. This view seems to require us to 'feign anaesthesia'.

If you think behaviourism is crazy, ask yourself this: could you ascribe a mental life to someone on anything other than behavioural grounds? If the answer is no, you are beginning to see the appeal of behaviourism. If all we need to know to ascribe a mind to someone is behavioural information, then why should we believe that mental concepts refer to something else unconnected with behaviour?

We have seen what behaviourism is, but not arguments for it. One argument takes up Ryle's allegation that dualists made a category mistake by placing the mental under the category of substance. So what is the right category for the mental? Ryle thought that the mental is a complexity of performances, in other words, of behaviours. Most of *The Concept of Mind* is spent accounting for every mental occurrence under the sun in terms of behaviour. For example, 'to know something' is not to be in possession of some hidden idea, or an inner piece of knowledge, but to be able to speak correctly about the thing, recognise it when you see it, tell it from a hawk or a handsaw and so on. Ryle also distinguishes between occurrences, which are individual events, and dispositions, which are tendencies to perform such occurrences. For example, saying something clever is an occurrence, and being clever is the disposition to perform many such occurrences. In neither case is there a need to talk about the inner self or soul.

Ryle's argument is not a deductive, but an inductive one. He claims dualism leads to intractable difficulties and it mistakenly takes mind to be a substance. That is his negative case against dualism. His positive case is simply that behaviourism provides an alternative 'one-world theory', which is preferable to the two worlds of dualism. This theory not only makes the mental explicable, but it also accounts for how we are able to know that others think and to explain our mental lives in the first place. We can do these things because the mental is as public as the local library.

A second route to behaviourism comes from logical positivism. The logical positivists were a collection of early twentieth-century philosophers who thought too much philosophy was airy nonsense. They sought to distinguish sense from nonsense and thought they had found a way of so doing in the *principle of verification*. This is the principle that statements are only meaningful if they can be verified either (directly or indirectly) by sense experiences or by their logical relation to other words and concepts. The former is the way matters of fact are settled and the latter matters of logic. So, for example, 'The world is controlled by undetectable green Martians' is meaningless because nothing could count as evidence for or against it, whilst 'Tony Blair is a weatherman' is meaningful, though untrue, because we know what would have to be the case for it to be true and it isn't the case. The logical positivists hoped that this principle would help rid philosophy of all nonsense.

How does this lead to behaviourism? Well, what would count as evidence for a person being in a mental state such as pain? Here's a list: they say they are; they roll around on the floor; C-fibres are stimulated in their brains; they don't want to play rugby; they have a knife sticking out of their knee. You can think of many more. The point is, 'they are feeling a sensation' doesn't come into it. It can't count as evidence because if it exists, it's unobservable. So, there may be inner sensations, but they have no role to play in the meaning of mental concepts. The only way of talking about the mental which makes sense turns out to be talk about behaviour.

Behaviourism has its attractions, most notably in the way in which it demystifies the mind. It makes it clear just how it is we are able to talk about the mind, because it destroys that idea of the mind as private and inner – what Ryle called 'the pernicious myth of the ghost in the machine'.

It also provides us with a test for consciousness: If something behaves like a thinking thing, it is a thinking thing. Since our mental vocabulary refers only to behaviour, if a machine or another being behaves in a way consistent with consciousness, we must say it is conscious. We cannot demand it behaves in the right way and in addition is conscious, as there is simply nothing additional to behaviour which constitutes consciousness. We believe other people are conscious because of their behaviour. Therefore, we would also have to attribute consciousness to robots or aliens if they behaved in the appropriate way. Otherwise, we would be demanding a standard of proof not only higher than the one we apply to ourselves, but also arguably higher than it is possible to meet. For what other test of consciousness is there than behaviour?

Arguments against behaviourism

Many people claim behaviourism fails because it leaves out the defining feature of mind: *qualia*. Qualia are the ways things feel or appear to us. In Thomas Nagel's phrase, there is 'something it is like' to feel pain or to see a colour, and this is not accounted for by behaviourists.

One obvious reply to this is that a weak behaviourist would not deny qualia exist, but would only claim they have no part to play in the meaning of 'mind'. This may not be an adequate response. First, how can the defining feature of a thing not be essential to what that thing means? This seems a contradiction. Second, surely the behaviourist would have to claim that the very term qualia was meaningless or irrelevant. For example, the logical positivist would view the claim that there are such things as qualia as unverifiable, and thus meaningless nonsense we should not discuss. Hence, the behaviourist must insist that we cannot talk about the one thing that seems essential to mind, which is hard to swallow.

But it's worse than this. Is there any logical contradiction in imagining a mental state with no behavioural manifestations? Surely not. What are the behavioural manifestations of imagining a square, or dreaming whilst in a coma? The behaviourist could just bite the bullet and say a mental event without a behavioural manifestation is impossible, but they would have to give some pretty good reasons to persuade us this is true given the apparently obvious counter-examples.

One objection which is less persuasive is that behaviourism would not be able to draw a distinction between, for example, acting being in pain and actually being in pain. In fact, the behaviourist can account for that difference. If a person is acting being in pain, there are circumstances in which the truth would out, where they would behave in a way inconsistent with their really being in pain. To say someone is in pain is not just to say something about their actual behaviour, but how they would behave in other circumstances. We may not be able to actually trip someone up, but this only shows they are good actors, not that they are in pain.

Apart from these general objections to behaviourism, we can also criticise the particular arguments which are used to establish it. As concerns Ryle's argument, it is enough to point out that, although he may be right to say the dualists have put mind in the wrong category, he may have also been wrong to characterise it in terms of behaviour. Given the difficulties such a categorisation makes, as shown above, this may seem a fair criticism.

The logical positivist's main problem is that the principle of verification is a very dubious one. The main reason for saying this is that the principle itself is not verifiable, so by its own criteria it is meaningless! Hence, it can be shown to be self-defeating. Second, how far can we stretch the idea that something need only be verifiable in principle? Although it seems true that we can't verify statements concerning private mental events, that seems to be a contingent not a necessary fact. Were we telepathic – and this seems a logical possibility – we could observe other minds as easily as we could other bodies, and so verification would be possible. This seems consistent with the claim that meaningful statements are in principle verifiable.

The behaviourists certainly seem to have hit upon something when they say talk of the mental is based on behaviour, but perhaps they go too far when they claim the mental is nothing but behaviour. Even if we reject behaviourism, we should thank it for reminding us of how much of what we say about 'the private' is in fact perfectly explicable in terms of 'the public'.

Physicalism

Physicalists claim that mind is brain and they support this claim by arguing that it is an empirical hypothesis for which there is overwhelming evidence. Supporters of this theory have thus to do two things: First, show the evidence that supports it and, second, show that the philosophical barriers to accepting the theory are illusory.

First, the evidence. Exhibit A is simply the huge problems caused by supposing there are two substances in the world: mind and matter. Dualists have never given a convincing explanation of how they interact. What's more, there is no reason why postulating a second substance – mind – makes the existence of mental states any easier to understand. What is puzzling is how any kind of substance can be conscious. Simply postulating a mental substance *that* is conscious does not address the hard question of *how* it could be so. Given that there is nothing to gain from claiming there is a mental substance, and quite a lot to lose, applying the principle of Ockham's Razor (that we should not postulate the existence of more entities than is necessary), we should accept a monist view that there is only one substance: matter. And so our minds also must be made of matter.

Exhibit B is also based on Ockham's Razor, but focuses on the successes of science rather than the failures of dualism. As J. J. C. Smart put it, it just seems inconceivable that everything in the universe is made up of complex arrangements of physical matter and is explicable in scientific terms – except minds. The principle of Ockham's Razor suggests that, if possible, we should account for the universe in terms of only one type of entity, and considering that we can explain so much physically, it would be more natural to consider the mind as physical than it would to suggest the world is mental.

Exhibit C moves from science's general success to particular findings about the mind. Experiments show that mind and brain are intimately connected. We could believe that there is simply a correlation between the mental and the physical. But then, how would this correlation be explained? Again, isn't it simpler and easier to say that in place of a correlation, there is in fact an identity between mind and body? The reason why C-fibres fire in my brain when I feel pain is not because pain and C-fibres are correlated, but because C-fibre stimulation and pain are the same thing. Consider this analogy: you don't have to be Sherlock Holmes to work out that if everywhere the 44th president of the United States is, Barack Obama is there too, to realise that Barack Obama is the forty-fourth president of the United States .

The problem for physicalism is that there seem to be many philosophical barriers to accepting the theory. One is that because we can
conceive of artificial intelligence and aliens with minds, mind cannot
be the same thing as brain. This is because neither computers nor aliens
would have brains, as 'brain' refers to a bit of earth biology. This is not
a fatal objection, because physicalism does not claim that the identity
is necessary, but contingent. Minds could conceivably be other things,
but in our case they are brains. So when physicalism claims minds are
brains, it does not deny that they could have been, or elsewhere could
be, other things. That mind happens to be brain is a contingent truth,
just as the fact that Obama is the forty-fourth President of the United
States is contingent.

Some argue that mind can't be brain, because the meaning of the
words are completely different. If mind was brain, they would mean the
same thing, but as we have known what mind is for centuries without
knowing it is brain, this is impossible. But saying that a mental state
is identical with a brain state does not mean that 'brain' and 'mind'
mean the same thing. Consider the example of how lightning is identical with an electrical discharge. This does not mean that 'lightning'
and 'electrical discharge' mean the same thing. We have to distinguish
the *extension* and *intension* of a noun. The extension of a noun is those
things which the noun applies to. The extension of the word 'tiger' is
all the tigers that there are. However, the intension of a noun is the
definitional meaning the word has. The definitional meaning of the
word 'tiger' is something like, 'a particular kind of feline indigenous
to India'. Although 'lightning' and 'electrical discharge' do not have
the same intension, they do have the same extension. It is the extension of the nouns which is held to be identical. So it is with mind
and body.

For similar reasons, the objection that mind and brain are logically
distinct (i.e., you can't deduce facts about one from facts about the
other) doesn't hold water. J. J. C. Smart also claims that the logics of
mind statements and body statements are distinct. Using his analogy, a
nation is identical with its citizens, but the logics of nation statements
and citizen statements are different. You can't directly translate facts
about one to the other, but that does not mean that nations are anything
over and above their citizens.

To sum up, in philosophical jargon, mind and brain may mean
different things (be semantically distinct) and not be logically equivalent (be logically distinct), but still be the same thing (ontologically
identical).

However, these logical and semantic objections do not exhaust physicalism's difficulties. The most serious are yet to come. The starting point is that it seems we cannot deny that there are irreducible mental properties. By this we mean that there are features of the mental, in particular qualia, which cannot be explained in physical terms. 'What it is like' to have a mind is not part of physics, but it is an essential part of the mental. So, if physicalism is to be credible, it must allow space for qualia and consciousness. Many have argued that it cannot do so, because the claim that mind just is matter is shattered as soon as you accept that there are mental properties, as matter can only have physical properties. Hence, physicalism seems to miss something out. But despite the doubts, physicalism has got to be on to something. The link between mind and brain is not just close, it's intimate. The claim that there can be no thought without brain activity is as sound a scientific claim as any. But there do seem to be real, insurmountable problems with drawing the conclusion from this that mind is identical to brain.

There are some possible solutions to this, which we'll consider shortly, but first we shall look at what is still a very popular and well-known philosophical view of the mind: functionalism.

Functionalism

Philosophy is often criticised for its lack of progress, but there has at least been development in the philosophy of mind, and we can see functionalism as a theory which learns from past theories and their mistakes. If we survey dualism, behaviourism and physicalism, what could we actually agree about? Here's a suggested list:

> The lesson of dualism is that the claim that mind and brain are distinct substances is misguided and wrong.
>
> The lesson of behaviourism is that the basis of our understanding of mind is what is publicly observable.
>
> The lesson of physicalism is that, given what we have found out, we must find a place for brain in our discussion of the mind.
>
> And a general lesson is that we must not leave out consciousness or qualia from our account of mind.

Functionalism builds on these insights and adds one of its own: given that artificial intelligence appears to be a real possibility, our concept of mind must provide us with a means of detecting minds in things other than ourselves. Functionalism can trace its roots back to mathematician

Alan Turing's famous test. The Turing Test is a way of seeing whether a machine can think or not. If it is able to produce outputs in response to inputs which are indistinguishable from those of a person, then it is intelligent. Hence, a thing has a mind if it is able to produce 'intelligent' outputs. This, in a nutshell, is functionalism.

Functionalists believe this theory meets all the criteria of a credible theory of mind. First, it does not require a special, mental substance. Second, it bases the concept of mind on what is public, observable and within our own experience. Third, it gives a role to brain. It is clearly because we have brains that we are able to produce intelligent outputs, so even if it is not true that mind is brain, the fact that we have a mind is largely, if not entirely, down to our having brains. Fourth, it gives us a test for the having of a mind that we can apply equally to humans and other beings or machines. The problem of other minds is thus dissolved. Fifth, it allows room for qualia and consciousness, because it doesn't tell us everything about the nature of a particular mind, it only says what a system must do to have a mind. The test for having a mind is functioning, but then the mind in question may have other features as well, such as sensations.

Functionalism is often confused with behaviourism. But there is one important difference. The behaviourist says mind is no more than behaviour. Being in a mental state is being in a behavioural state. Functionalists, however, do not say a mind is the inputs and outputs, but rather that the mind is what receives inputs and produces outputs. Because any number of things may be able to function in such a way, and they may all have different internal structures, there is scope for different kinds of minds. The qualia of our minds are thus just a feature of our minds, rather than an essential feature of minds.

Functionalism flourished for a while, but there is one major objection against it. Searle's famous Chinese room argument is a powerful critique of functionalism. (It also works against behaviourism, arguably even better.) His argument is aimed at destroying the main claim of functionalism that anything that has the appropriate input–output relations has a mind.

Searle's objection can be summed up in a sentence: it is a consequence of functionalism that if we could arrange a load of beer cans to accept inputs and produce outputs in the right way, then according to the functionalist it would have a mind. Searle thinks this is absurd, but this is not much of an argument, because the functionalist would be happy to accept this consequence, and would simply ask why Searle is so threatened by the idea of thinking beer cans.

Much depends here on what is meant by 'think'. There is a weak sense of think, which simply means to be able to work things out, process information and so on. In this sense, you could say – and Searle himself admits this – that even pocket calculators think, just not about very much. The kind of thinking humans do, however, involves some kind of conscious understanding of what we are thinking about. That is the sense of 'think' in this current discussion and is the one Searle denies to the beer cans.

Searle can back up his vivid beer can objection with an argument. It does not show that a computer could not think, or that artificial intelligence is impossible, but that a digital computer (the kind of computer we currently have) could never think, and his explanation of why it couldn't raises serious problems for the functionalist.

The argument hinges on the difference between semantics and syntax. Syntax concerns the formal rules for the construction of sentences in language, whilst semantics concerns meaning. A computer is a purely syntactical system. It follows rules but that is all it does. Searle argues that it is impossible for a purely syntactical system ever to also have semantics, that is to say, meaning. His argument for this is simple.

Imagine a room, in which there is a man, a guidebook and a lot of Chinese characters. A series of Chinese characters are sent into the room. The man inside then looks through his guidebook, follows instructions to arrange other Chinese symbols into sequences and then passes these out of the room. Unbeknown to the man, who has no knowledge of Chinese, the symbols he receives are questions, and those he sends out are answers. It is clear that the Chinese room is functioning like a system which understands Chinese. It is also clear that no understanding of Chinese is required at any stage of the process. It is also clear that there is no way in which, from this process alone, the man can come to understand what the Chinese symbols mean. This demonstrates that functioning is not a sufficient criterion for having a mind because semantics cannot arise in a purely syntactical system. A digital computer, as it is basically a syntactical system which operates merely by manipulating symbols according to set rules, is thus just like the Chinese room, and so it is clear that a digital computer could not think, as thinking requires semantics.

One objection to this argument is that, although it is true that the man in the room doesn't understand Chinese, the system as a whole – man, book, symbols and room – does. It could be argued that the brain is like this. One cannot point to a part of the brain which understands, but nonetheless, the brain as a whole does.

Searle rejects this objection. The basic point still stands – the system as a whole is a syntactical one, and one cannot get from syntax to semantics. To suppose otherwise is merely to presume functionalism. There is no other good reason to say that the room as a whole thinks.

A further objection is that if the room were not a room, but a kind of robot interacting with the world, then it would think. Searle is not convinced. It just doesn't seem relevant to the question how sophisticated, mobile or interactive the system is. If it works on pure syntax, no matter how much we get it to function like a thinking thing, it won't be a thinking thing.

Searle's argument is a strong one, but it raises several questions. First, what grounds other than functioning do we have to go on in order to decide whether a system is conscious or not? Searle may not be able to provide a positive answer to this, but he could maintain that if we know a system is only syntactical, we can know it doesn't think. In other cases, we simply may not be able to say.

Second, isn't it possible that semantics is an *emergent property*? In other words, could it not be true that consciousness begins to arise as a result of increasing sophistication in a syntactical system? If not, from where does consciousness arise? Searle need not answer this second question, but his argument certainly seems to rule out the first possibility without any real justification.

One further difficulty is simply that functionalism cannot distinguish between a system which simulates thought and one that produces it. Surely, there must actually be a difference between the two, but functionalism doesn't account for it.

Non-reductive materialism and epiphenomenalism

Given the problems with functionalism, and other forms of materialism, it may be that the problem lies in the general attempt of trying to explain the mental in terms of physical processes. This approach is known as 'reductionism': the project of 'reducing' one kind of phenomenon (in this case the mental) to another, more fundamental one (in this case, matter). Incidentally, functionalism need not be a materialist theory – whatever functions as a mind is a mind, even 'immaterial' things – if that were possible. However, it is usually utilised by physicalists. Perhaps, there is just something *irreducible* about mental experience. In this case, the earlier discussion of *qualia* – that there is 'something it is like' to have mental experiences – suggests that the attempt to model all aspects of the mind from 'outside' – a 'third-person' perspective – is ultimately misguided. Perhaps the subjective cannot be reduced to the objective.

One solution here would be to allow the existence of irreducible mental properties, but still claim that mind is brain. This position is known as *non-reductive materialism*. This need not lead us back to substance dualism (and all its problems), but can simply be a form of materialism that acknowledges that mind is a distinct *property* of matter. So, we may talk of brain states or neurons, or we may talk of perceptions or ideas, but we should not confuse the two, or assume that a complete physical description of the world will include facts about what it is like to have conscious experience. Such an approach is a variety of what we earlier called *property dualism*, in that it proposes the existence of one type of stuff which has two distinct properties. This is distinct from both dual aspect theory and neutral monism, which state that there is one kind of stuff which has both physical and mental properties, but which should not be identified with either. However, non-reductive materialism assumes that both mental and physical phenomena are properties of one underlying *physical* stuff.

The good thing about this view is that it would seem not to turn us into zombies or robots. We have thoughts and feelings, and there is 'something it is like' to be us. However, there is also a problem: if mind and matter are distinct, then what exactly *is* mind? As we saw, the problem with traditional or *substance* dualism is that it makes mental 'stuff' a mysterious, ghostly entity, something which science cannot account for. The way non-reductive materialism gets around this is to introduce the notion of *supervenience*. An often used example is that of the fluidity of water. At the molecular level, water is made up of molecules, just as other physical things are. However, our everyday experience of water presents something slippery, wet and fluid. How can we match up these two aspects? There is no mystery, the physicist points out, the fluidity of water is merely caused by the behaviour of the molecules: independently, the molecules are single, solid entities; but together, they are *fluid*. Thus, we can say that the property of 'fluidity' is not possessed by any single molecule, but *supervenes* on their behaviour as a whole. Supervenience is therefore simply a term to describe this type of relationship between the 'lower' and 'higher' level properties of physical things. In a sense, whilst high-level properties (fluidity) can be *explained* by low-level physical properties (molecular behaviour), they cannot be *reduced* to it. Fluidity is something which *emerges* from low-level physical properties. In these terms, applied to the philosophy of mind, we may say that consciousness is an emergent property which supervenes on physical brain states.

Emergence is an interesting concept, which can be applied to all manner of things: the behaviour of an ant colony, the way a city develops. So, just as no-one tells each individual ant or citizen how to behave so as to produce an overall order or pattern, one will nonetheless simply 'emerge'. And so with the brain: no one brain cell is conscious, but together the cells produce consciousness. But whilst this model may work for insects or cities, we may argue that consciousness is a special case, for the interaction of brain cells together produce physical brain states. This is fine if the mind *is* the brain, but as we've seen with behaviourism and physicalism, there are problems with the idea that mental events can be reduced to either potential behaviour or brain states without loss – and this is something that non-reductive materialism wants to deny anyway. Unlike water and fluidity, or individual ants and the functioning of the colony, the gap between brain states and consciousness is arguably of a different kind. The difference between the behaviour of individual neurons and overall brain states is *quantitative*, involving number and dimension; but the difference between a brain state and a mental state is *qualitative*. The analogy with ants and colonies therefore breaks down.

This said, non-reductive materialism remains a viable path for those who wish to retain our common-sense notions of what it is like to be conscious. Some version of it is held by John Searle, who argues that the brain causes consciousness, but that subjective mental states are an irreducible fact about the world. Searle has taken a lot of criticism for his position, for his account seems to stop short of clarifying how mind relates to brain – in fact, he admits that it remains a mystery (though it may not always do so, as science and philosophy progress). However, there are problems.

If consciousness is a non-reducible property of matter, then what role does it play in our actions and decision making? Some worry that the answer is 'none at all'. If mental features can be explained as merely the way in which brain appears to us, as a kind of by-product, then they are arguably ineffectual – a sort of 'smoke' produced by the machine, as it has been described. That's not how it feels to us, of course. We feel that it is because of our conscious thoughts that we act. It is our decisions which cause action. But physicalism seems to undermine this. It claims brain processes cause action, and the feeling of making a decision has nothing to do with it. As Searle put it, it is as though the froth on the sea were to think, 'gee, pulling these waves back and forth is really hard work!', where froth is to consciousness what sea is to brain. This seems to make consciousness an *epiphenomenon*, that is, a phenomenon which just 'sits' above brain without causing any of what goes on.

Few are willing to embrace epiphenomenalism, as it seems to deny many of the most basic beliefs we have about ourselves. Most obviously, it undermines our feeling that we are free. If consciousness is just an epiphenomenon, then our conscious thoughts and decisions are not causing our actions, and so we would seem not to be free. But the fact that a theory has a disturbing consequence is not a good objection to it. Many philosophers agree that we are not free.

Another objection is that if mind is an epiphenomenon, then why does it exist? Why would we have been given or evolved consciousness if it has no part to play in our lives? Whether you're a determinist or not, surely consciousness must have a role.

One reply would be to say that thoughts do play a part in the causal story, because thoughts are just brain events, and these cause actions. But this isn't good enough, because it doesn't give the conscious feature of brain events a role to play. In fact, it is very hard to see how a physicalist could say that consciousness – an irreducible mental property – has a role in causation if mind is just a physical thing, a brain.

As you can see, the problems faced in trying to be true to both our scientific understanding of the world *and* our common-sense personal perspective are considerable. If conscious experience plays any genuine causal role, then surely it must be physical (in order to interact with matter); if not, then it is a mere epiphenomenon, and our conscious control over our actions and decisions is an illusion. Given this tension between science and common sense, some philosophers take a more radical view. In fact, they think that we should eliminate common sense altogether.

Eliminativism

Associated with such philosophers as Patricia and Paul Churchland, *eliminative materialism* attempts to do away with the central objections to reductive explanations of the mind by simply considering our common assumptions to be false. We think we have mental states, thoughts and perceptions, desires and so on, but really we are mistaken. The fact that certain C-fibres in your brain firing is not equivalent to the thought that 'I am in pain' (or whatever) is not a problem, because the mental aspect can simply be discarded. Just as science has shown many of our so-called 'folk beliefs' to be false – the god who makes the volcano erupt, the fairy who curdles the milk and so on – so the terms of neuroscience will one day replace our 'folk psychology'. Ascriptions of mental states are therefore simply mistaken – 'she is happy', 'he is worrying about the weather' – such things are the equivalent of sentimental talk about animals ('the dog is looking forward to his birthday'), or even the loose way we sometimes view inanimate objects as having personalities or traits ('the car is a bit lazy today'). All common talk of minds, thoughts and feelings, persons and so on, is therefore – at best – a loose and convenient way of speaking, and – at worst – misleading and false. Let's just get rid of it, and replace it with the proper terminology.

There are degrees of eliminativism. For instance, Daniel Dennett is eliminative concerning the existence of qualia – he believes they simply don't exist. We are deluding ourselves. As Searle has pointed out, this basically amounts to denying the notion that we are subjectively conscious. We are mistaken that 'there is something it is like' to be me. Consciousness is an illusion. But to have an illusion, Searle argues, is to have a qualitative experience. I can be mistaken about the nature of my perception – that a scarecrow is a person, that someone I see at a distance is my friend Dave – but I cannot be mistaken about having a perception. What would such a mistake entail? This is not to say that our everyday consciousness does not involve all sorts of mistakes and assumptions – it certainly does. We distort memories, misinterpret perceptions, even perhaps create a unified self out of scraps of experience – to contradict Descartes, there may be no unified 'I' at all. However, to be deceived about qualia would seem to push the possibility of deception too far.

But the general problem with the eliminative position is that, faced with the ongoing difficulties of accounting for mind and consciousness, it just seems to give up. So, whilst it might be desirable to resolve these difficulties, we may argue that 'eliminating' the things that it is difficult to explain is a bit of a drastic move.

*   *   *

All of the various approaches to the nature of the mind have their problems. Versions of functionalism remain the most popular in Anglo-American philosophy departments, but there is no winner in this race yet. The philosophy of mind is a very active area in philosophy and increasingly philosophers are trying to solve the mind–body problem in an interdisciplinary way, working with neurologists and psychologists.

There is more to philosophy of mind, however, than the range of theories concerning the nature of the mind and its relationship to the body. Another key issue is the problem of other minds.

Other minds

Put in its strongest form, the problem of other minds is: 'How can we know whether other beings have minds?' However, given that it seems impossible to prove that other people have minds, but we do believe that they have, a more modest question is: 'How can we justify our statements and beliefs about other minds?'

Why is there a problem about other minds at all? What seems to make them 'unknowable'? Our knowledge extends to everything which is part of the perceptible world. But how things appear to others, how things feel and so on (what Russell calls the 'qualitative character' of the world), is not included in this arena of knowledge. Therefore, it seems that we can know only the objective facts about other people and nothing of how the world appears to them or of the character of their thought.

It is also widely believed that people's thoughts and sensations are necessarily private, that they just cannot be inspected by others. If this is true, then it is clear that only the person who has the thoughts and sensations can directly observe them.

Strong physicalism could resolve this problem. If, say, a pain were a brain process, then observing the brain process would be observing a pain. However, we would still not be able to observe the *qualitative character* of the pain. This would remain private. And as the mind–brain identity is contingent, there is always the possibility that any particular brain state is not the mind state it was thought to be.

There are several interesting arguments about the problem of other minds in the writings of Bertrand Russell and A. J. Ayer. Russell put forward one solution to the problem: the argument from analogy. Because other people's behaviour resembles our own, and our behaviour is accompanied by mental processes, we assume that other people also have these processes. For example, if I report a pain, it is because I have a certain unpleasant experience. If someone else reports a pain, I assume that they too are having an unpleasant experience.

As it stands the argument is weak. As Ayer explains: if I lived in a society where no-one ever appeared naked, and I had a hidden birthmark, I would not be justified in assuming that everyone else had a similar birthmark. Similarly, to generalise from only my own case that other people also have thoughts is not a justifiable inference.

Ayer also rejects a behaviour-based version of the analogy argument. We learn what words like 'pain' mean by observing the behaviour of others. Hence, our justification for attributing pain to them simply comes from the fact that their behaviour exemplifies what pain means. In this way, 'pain' doesn't refer to a particular type of inner sensation at all. Rather, pain is *whatever* causes a certain type of behaviour. And so if that behaviour is present, then pain must also be present, as pain is simply the cause of the behaviour. In this way, the problem of other minds is dissolved.

Ayer argues that this is wrong, because he sees no reason to suppose that the meaning of words should be strictly determined by the way in which they were learned. In other words, just because we learn what mind-words mean by observing behaviour, it doesn't mean that the meanings of these words are exhausted by what can be observed in behaviour. The mistake here is to confuse the method of learning a word with its actual meaning. I might learn what a tiger is by seeing photos, for example, but it doesn't follow that 'tiger' means 'photo of a tiger'. In the same way, it doesn't follow from the fact that we learn about mental concepts from behaviour that the manifestation of certain kinds of behaviours ensures that which the mental concepts refer to are present.

The argument from analogy refuses to go away, however. It just gets more complex. Russell argued that the general form of the argument from analogy is that we observe in ourselves that 'A causes B', where A is a mental occurrence and B a physical occurrence. For instance, a mental occurrence such as the sensation of pain causes a physical shriek. However, we sometimes observe in others a B (for example, a shriek) when we do not observe an A (for example, a painful sensation). In these cases, we simply assume that there is an A which is the cause of B, only we can't observe it. (Consider how when we see the magician David Copperfield 'flying', we assume there is a string causing this action, even though we cannot see it.)

However, to justify this inference, we need to know that *only* A causes B, or that most Bs are caused by As. If not, then it is more than possible that the observed physical occurrence is caused by an unobserved, but not mental occurrence. Even though we are still only generalising from our own cases, we do in fact make this assumption.

Ayer, however, is not convinced. That A causes B in us is still a very flimsy basis on which to infer that this is true of everyone else. Russell may have explained what the assumptions are that govern our belief in other minds very well, but he is still only describing an assumption, not providing an argument.

Is there no solution to the problem of other minds, then? Ayer thinks there is and endorses that of Hilary Putnam. Putnam argues that the belief that other people have minds like mine is justified because it explains human behaviour. What is more, there is no other rival theory which explains human behaviour so well. The postulate of other minds is part of a wider theory (not a scientific theory, but a practical theory) which accounts for the behaviour of people by attributing conscious thoughts to them. This theory just has no credible rival. Put simply, we are justified in believing in other minds because no rival theory even gets close to explaining why other people behave as they do.

The problem with the problem of other minds is that, like all sceptical problems, it is impossible to prove beyond all doubt that other people do have minds. It is always possible that we are wrong to ascribe minds to others (see Chapter 1 on the theory of knowledge). The way out of the problem may be to accept that a full proof is just unattainable and demanding one is inappropriate. As Aristotle once said: 'It is the mark of the trained mind never to expect more precision in the treatment of any subject than the nature of that subject permits.'

Personal identity

Minds matter to us because having a mind is the hallmark of being a person. This is why the puzzle of mind is so important to the issue of personal identity. The philosophical problem of personal identity can be expressed in the question: 'What are the necessary and sufficient conditions for a person A at one time being the same person as person B at another time?'

The arguments of the dualists, and René Descartes in particular, favoured the view that continuity of the self depends on the continuity of a mental substance or soul. It follows from the arguments for dualism that a person's essence is an indivisible, immaterial thinking thing. As this is the essence of a person, it seems clear that this and this alone is required for a person to continue to exist.

All the objections given against dualism also apply against this view of personal identity. But there is one crucial objection offered by Locke which aims to show that, even if dualism is true, personal identity doesn't depend on the continued existence of the soul. He offers a thought experiment:

Let anyone reflect upon himself and conclude that he has in himself an immaterial spirit, which is that which thinks in him and in the constant change of his body keeps him the same. Let him also suppose it to be the same soul that was in Nestor or Thersites at the siege of Troy, but he now having no consciousness of any of the actions either of Nestor or Thersites, does he or can he conceive himself to be the same person with either of them? Can he be concerned in either of their actions, attribute them to himself, or think of them as his own, more than the actions of any other men that ever existed?

(An Essay concerning Human Understanding, Book 2)

Locke's point is simple. He invites us to imagine that we share the same soul as a person who previously existed. This is entirely possible, if dualism is true. But if we don't remember what that person did, and if their plans are not our plans, in other words, if there is no mental link between us and them, we can't be them, even though we have the same soul.

This is not so much an argument as a way of making some key intuitions about persons clear to us. If Locke is right, the continued existence of the soul, even if it exists, is not a sufficient condition for personal identity over time. Further, it suggests that the key factor in personal identity is continuity of consciousness. This is the key idea of the theory of personal identity known as psychological reductionism.

We are all familiar with the fantasy idea of waking up in another person's body, or being 'beamed up', *Star Trek* style. What is it about these fantasies that convince us that the person who wakes up in another body or on Mars is us? It is the fact that the person would think they were us, that they would have the same personality, plans and memories as us.

The most prominent contemporary proponent of this theory is Derek Parfit. He offers a compelling thought experiment to demonstrate the point in which he imagines what it is like to be teletransported across space to Mars. This process may involve destroying the original body and creating a new one from different matter. Even though the Parfit on Mars has a body that shares not a single cell with the Parfit on Earth, and certainly hasn't got the same soul, it seems right to say that Parfit has made the journey to Mars. This is because there is what Parfit calls psychological connectedness and continuity between Earth-Parfit and Mars-Parfit. This view is hence called psychological reductionism because it reduces all the factors that normally accompany survival, especially bodily continuity, down to what it considers essential – psychological continuity.

Locke's version of the thesis came under attack because it was thought (wrongly) that his only criterion for personal identity is continuity of memory. In other words:

> Peter 1 on 1/1/97 is the same person as Peter 2 on 2/1/97 if and only if Peter 2 remembers enough of Peter 1's experiences.

We say *enough* of Peter 1's experiences because we do not expect someone to remember everything over time. As this stands this is neither sufficient nor necessary for personal identity. It is not sufficient because if it were possible that another person could, through mind-reading, come to be aware of all your memories, they would clearly not then be you. It is not necessary for a more subtle reason. It is a law of logic that:

> If $X = Y$ and $X = Z$ then $Y = Z$

For example, if the teacher is Bertie and the teacher is an axe murderer, then Bertie is an axe murderer. Consider what happens when we apply this principle of logic and the memory criterion for personal identity to a case like this one, based on an argument by Thomas Reid:

> There is a young boy (YB) who stole some apples, who grew up to be a soldier (S) who saved a comrade, who grew up to be an old major (OM). The wartime hero remembered stealing the apples. The old major has forgotten about his wartime exploits but remembers stealing the apples.

What would the memory criterion say about this? It would say that YB is S, and that YB is OM, because there are memory connections between them. But then it would say S is not OM, because there are no memory connections between them. But this contradicts the law of logic stated above: If $YB = S$ and $YB = OM$ then $S = OM$. Because the memory criterion denies $S = OM$, which is surely true, the memory criterion must be wrong.

That is not the end of the road for psychological reductionists, though. They tend to say that memory alone is not enough: there also have to be connections of intention, personality, dispositions, preferences and so on. Of course, these factors all change over time, but as long as there is an evolving change, without sudden, drastic change, then there is psychological continuity and hence personal identity.

The real problem for this view comes in a continuation to the Mars story started above. Parfit imagines entering the teletransporter one day, only to find that he has been 'sent' to Mars, but not destroyed on Earth. There is now both an Earth-Parfit and Mars-Parfit. In this case, the person on Mars is psychologically continuous with the person on Earth, but he is clearly not that person, as the Earth person is still on Earth. He is best described as a clone. But if he is a clone in this situation, and he would be no different if the Earth person *had* been destroyed, then he must be a clone whatever happens. So it seems that psychological continuity is not enough for personal identity. It may simply result in a clone.

Such worries have led some people to think that the whole debate has gone horribly wrong. What we have failed to recognise, they say, is that we are essentially animals. Sure, you can have psychological continuity, and some people wouldn't want to go on living without it, but if we're talking about identity, the only thing that is necessary and sufficient is continuity of bodily existence. This view is known as animalism.

This view requires an immediate modification. We know people can continue to live with transplanted and synthetic organs and limbs. So what if we could be entirely replaced by such body parts? Isn't this compatible with survival? Because of this, most defenders of this view would say that the crucial organ is the brain, as this controls thought. Everything else could be replaced, but not the brain.

However, if they admit that the brain is vital because it carries consciousness, why not admit that consciousness is what is important, not the brain which just happens to be the carrier of consciousness? This would lead back to psychological reductionism. A second problem is to ask why the brain can't be replaced by synthetic parts anyway. Why is it okay to transplant hearts and legs, but not okay to transplant brains? So long as the brain was able to continue a person's mental life, what's the problem?

This is a long-running and difficult debate where people have strong gut instincts. All the views considered have something going for them, but all seem to have something wrong too. Perhaps the problem lies in a confusion over the question. Is the issue a factual one concerning identity, or is it a question of value, concerning what we would consider to be an acceptable future? If it is the former, then maybe it should be answered in the same way as we answer questions about other organisms, and so the animalist would be going along the right lines. If it is the latter, then perhaps a mixed view, with key elements of the psychological reductionist position is more fruitful. How you decide will perhaps reveal a lot about what you value in your own existence.

Personhood

Aside from the problem of when a person is the same individual (or not), there is the related problem of what a person actually is. Since, in society, persons generally have greater rights and responsibilities than non-persons, the notion of *personhood* is very important. We don't expect a dog to behave morally, and someone who needlessly kills a dog will not be tried for murder or manslaughter, but – if at all – for the lesser crime of animal cruelty. To restrict someone's freedom unjustly is generally illegal, but we may take someone's liberty away if they pose a danger to others – if they lose their rationality, perhaps. Being a person is therefore very much tied up with possessing certain features which enable you to perform certain social roles, and may also determine how an individual is treated.

So, what are commonly taken to be the essential features of personhood? First, as philosophers as diverse as Descartes and Locke agreed, we might say that a person is a 'thinking thing'. This means that each individual is a conscious subject, aware of him or herself. This not only means having experience, but being a self-aware 'I' with a history that changes over time, that possesses beliefs and goals, that can reflect upon its character and nature, and so on. As Descartes would also argue, such a self must be rational. This has traditionally been a key distinguishing feature between animals and humans: dogs may have goals or beliefs (in a certain sense) but they may not be able to consciously evaluate these – to say, for instance, 'I think I'll cut back on raiding the bins as it doesn't seem to be going down too well with the owners.' But, some argue, humans are *rational* animals, able to analyse and predict, to formulate plans or look for meaning. Thought is also linked to language, and the ability to communicate. Once again, Descartes saw animal communication as merely a sequence of expressive noises, devoid of true meaning. Part of what distinguishes persons from non-persons is therefore the use of written signs, symbols and sounds to communicate mental content (which Descartes thought animals lacked).

As you can see, the above aspects of personhood are closely allied with the psychological approach to personal identity. But the physical also plays a part. Descartes may have considered human beings to be essentially the mind (or soul), but, in line with the animalist or physiological view of personal identity, many would argue that the physical body is equally essential, as it determines our separateness and provides each of us with a unique point of view. Our physical characteristics and traits may also determine how we feel about ourselves, and will influence how others see us and the part we play in society. Humans are, many would argue, by virtue of their biological nature, social beings. As Aristotle put it, only animals or gods have no need of society.

Finally, bringing together all these aspects, is the idea that persons are the bearers of rights. Kant, for instance, linked rationality to moral responsibility. Since we are guided by reason, we are rationally bound to perform actions which do not infringe on the rights of others. But, of course, we are not literally constrained – we are not rational robots – but choose (or not) to follow the voice of reason. Perhaps our most distinguishing feature is therefore arguably our freedom. As existentialists would argue, it is the one thing we cannot give away; in Sartre's words, 'we are condemned to be free'.

Perhaps few would deny that the above list of features – or something like them – constitute our most common notion of what a person is. However, there are a wide range of problems that such a list generates. First, it is an ideal that not every human will meet. Even the best of us are not always fully conscious, rational, autonomous individuals. Perhaps, then, we should say that what is important is our *capacity* to behave as such. But even here there are problems. A foetus, for example, does not yet possess the capacity for rationality or autonomy, and is therefore perhaps not a rights bearer – which is one argument for permitting abortion. Or, even when born, due to some congenital defect an individual may never develop those features. And what about the Alzheimer sufferer, for instance? Should these individuals be treated as non-persons because they appear to have lost certain features of personhood?

Another problem concerns the possibility that such features are not exclusive to human beings. Peter Singer, for example, has argued that some of the higher mammals – dogs, monkeys, apes – do indeed meet the conditions for personhood. Studies have shown the capacity for human-like language and communication in dolphins and chimpanzees, among other creatures, and there is even some evidence that they have a sense of self. In experiments, numerous animals – elephants, chimps, dolphins, even magpies – have been seen to recognise themselves in a mirror, which some might take as a sign that they have a concept of self. If so, then we are wrong to treat such creatures as non-persons, or to think that personhood is a strictly human feature.

We may extend this objection in a more radical direction if we consider the possibility of artificial intelligence. As we've seen, given the problems with dualism, and the general notion of an immaterial soul, physicalism proposes that the mind is a purely material entity. If so, then it is possible that technology may one day evolve to a point where computers are not only intelligent, but conscious – and in effect, persons. This would cause all sorts of problems, not only morally – how we treat 'machine persons' – but conceptually. If what is called Strong AI is true (computers can be conscious), then the mind may be theoretically reduced to a computer program – a set of algorithms and a certain quantity of data. But programs can be copied. In the sci-fi scenario where my consciousness is 'uploaded' to a computer, it might be possible to make copies of 'me'. I may not need to be 'embodied' (as it is traditionally thought of), and the question of my autonomy is also problematic, for if I am no more than a set of rules and algorithms, then in what sense do I have free will?

These problems seem to highlight the fact that personhood is not a simple matter of yes or no, but one of degree. Once we define personhood in terms of a list of features, then it seems inevitable that we will hit problems as new knowledge or circumstances provide unforseen ways of meeting those criteria (or some of them). It is only relatively recently that the linguistic capabilities of certain animals have been discovered, or that the computer model of the mind has evolved. Such developments have therefore upset our traditional notions of personhood – and will continue to do so. Faced with decisions as to whether or not someone is a person, we may therefore perhaps admit that we are faced with a value-based decision. If an Alzheimer's patient loses those memory connections that Locke thought essential, or a car accident victim the capacity for rational thought, then the decision to consider such individuals persons (or not) is a question of what we value. But this may differ from individual to individual, or culture to culture. Perhaps, then, personhood is simply a highly problematic concept.

A possible alternative to this, however, has been proposed by Peter Strawson. Perhaps, he argues, the notion of a person is 'logically primitive', and is therefore not a matter of degree: you either are or aren't. By this, he means that we do not decide whether someone is a person by looking at which characteristics they possess; rather, it is the other way around: we decide what characteristics a person should have by analysing what people generally think of as persons. So, for example, in considering what a person is, we look at a friend and ask the question, 'What characteristics does she (and all other similar people) possess?' One way of thinking about this is to say that a person is a 'natural kind' of thing. So, just like a tree, or a stone, or a mountain, we 'discover' persons in the world, and then we identify the characteristics they possess.

The problem with this is that it is difficult to justify the idea that persons 'just exist'. After all, people can disagree about what constitutes a mountain, or a tree, or any other natural kind, so why not persons? For instance, in 2006 Pluto 'lost' its planet status, and was reclassified as a 'dwarf planet'. Couldn't this happen with persons? Or, going the other way, might we decide that certain animals or machines are persons after all? Strawson's position therefore seems to beg the question, for, even if the concept is 'primitive' and not to be analysed into separate features, it may still be controversial as to whether something is or is not a person.

We've done no more than suggest some of the potential problems and issues surrounding the question of personhood, but as you can see it is a fascinating and complex debate. But it raises one very difficult question. If one of the things that defines us is our autonomy, our capacity to make rational choices, then what reasons do we have to think that we do in fact possess this capacity?

The problem of free will

Whilst some things are out of our control, or we occasionally seem to lack will power, we like to think that we mostly have choice. You may struggle to keep to your diet, but ultimately it is down to you whether you eat that piece of cake or not. This view is known as *libertarianism*, and we might consider it the default position. Mostly, we think of people as responsible for their actions and decisions, and only make exceptions for those occasions when our freedom is compromised – such as when someone blackmails or coerces us, when we are drunk or under the influence of drugs or even simply strong emotions, such as grief or anger. Such cases of diminished responsibility in fact only make sense if we generally have free will. The idea of freedom is therefore central to human life.

The problems start, however, when we try to analyse human action. You may choose to eat cake (or not), yet that choice does not simply spring out of the blue, but is caused by something else – your desire to lose weight, or on the other hand to savour the taste of the cake. But do you choose to desire those things? Arguably not. The libertarian will respond that, even so, you are free to choose whether or not to act on those desires. Our choice may be limited, but it is still a choice. Or is it? If we look at the natural world, then we may argue that everything that happens has a cause. An apple falls from a tree. It may seem arbitrary as to whether it falls now or later, but in fact if we had enough information – about the strength of the wind, the weight of the apple, the thickness of the stem holding it to the branch, and so on – then we could theoretically predict exactly when and how it would fall. This was the dream of the French physicist Pierre Simon Laplace (1749–1827), a contemporary of Isaac Newton, who hypothesised that some all-powerful intellect, given enough data, could predict the course of the universe. Laplace's 'daemon', as it has become known, therefore suggests that the world is simply one big mechanism, and given enough knowledge about the workings of that mechanism, we could show how every event is in fact not free, but *determined* by the laws of cause and effect. *Determinism* therefore rejects libertarianism, for humans are a part of the great mechanism of nature no less than any other object or being.

Determinism can take other forms. The ancient Stoics argued that our lives are determined by Fate (fatalism), religious determinism might see human action as preordained by God (predestination), or modern evolutionary biologists might argue that all our instincts and desires spring ultimately from our genes (genetic determinism). But whatever route the determinist takes, each will propose that things happen because *they cannot be any other way*. They are necessitated (by fate, God, physics or genes).

One libertarian response to this is to propose that, even though certain events are in fact necessarily linked in this way, the human will is not one of them. Such a position was held by Descartes, who argued that, whilst the laws of cause and effect determined the mechanical universe of physical matter, the mind (or soul) was *immaterial*, and therefore existed outside of this physical order. As we've seen, there is a well-known problem here: if the mind has no material parts, and the body no immaterial parts, how do they interact? We now know that damage to the brain affects the mind, and that even our thoughts and beliefs can have physiological effects. Descartes did not deny this, and considered mind and body to be intimately connected – but how? The problem seems a fatal one for dualism, and perhaps therefore for libertarianism. If the idea that some mind or will can exist outside of the physical order is confused, then the idea of free will would also seem to be so. But even if such a thing could exist, we would have to assume that certain thoughts or acts of intention were themselves uncaused, or more precisely *their own* cause – what is termed *causa sui*. But belief in this seems almost like an act of faith. Why did you choose one action over another? It seems sensible to say, 'because of X'. We might distinguish between 'reason' and 'cause' here – between understanding why something happened, and what brought it about. A libertarian might argue therefore that we are still free, even though there is a reason or explanation for our action. However, it still remains an open question as to what caused that action. If you chose X instead of Y, then your reason might also point to your motivation: you ate the cake because you were hungry (or greedy). But then, doesn't your greed *cause* your action? It may therefore not be so easy to distinguish between reason and motive, and therefore to escape determinism. However, even if it were possible, the idea of something being self-caused still seems like wishful thinking.

But, a libertarian might argue, even if we abandon the idea of *causa sui*, we may still point to the fact that not everything in nature is determined or fixed. We might cite quantum physics here. At the quantum level, certain outcomes do not obey fixed laws but – at most – statistical probability. Doesn't this suggest the possibility of freedom? Well, no. The fact that something has a random element or an unpredictable cause does not make it free. In fact, it might suggest the opposite. A thought which just pops into my head is not one that I would say I have freely chosen. Free choices are often not arbitrary, but suggest rational purpose. It is the fact that my choices *can* be explained, that they fit into the pattern of my life, that makes them *mine*, and not that they spring from some arbitrary whim. This point actually leads us on to an interesting alternative to both libertarianism and determinism.

Compatibilism, as the term suggests, argues that belief in free will and determinism are in fact compatible. This position can also come in different forms, but we're going to briefly outline that held by David Hume. Hume defines free actions as those which have been caused by an agent's will and desires. So, if you want to eat the cake, and you are under no compulsion to do or not do so, then your action is free. However, if some maniac forced you to eat the cake at gun point, then your actions would not be free but coerced. Both actions are caused, but only the former has the *right type* of cause. Simply put, those causes which come from inside us are what Hume calls 'spontaneous' and represent the basis of our free acts of will; those causes which come from outside us, even if they fall in line with what we would have chosen, are not the cause of free acts. Even if you would have chosen to eat the cake anyway, the fact someone has a gun to your head takes away your choice (or at least, your choice to not eat the cake *and live*).

On the plus side, compatibilism highlights the importance of causation in any account of free will. As already noted, the fact that our actions are linked to our desires and intentions is what makes us accountable for them (for good or bad). Hume therefore rejects certain aspects of libertarianism (that free actions are self caused or somehow indetermined), whilst retaining the possibility of moral accountability. However, the problem with this view is that – if you will forgive the pun – Hume wants to have his cake *and* eat it. If everything is caused, then the only difference between free and unfree actions would seem to be how we label them – as 'internal' or 'external' to the subject respectively. One problem, therefore, might concern whether it is in fact possible to maintain this distinction. If you want to eat cake, the cause is your internal desire (for sustenance or gustatory pleasure). But imagine that a vindictive neuroscientist were to play with your brain so that you no longer wanted cake, or even perhaps wanted it all the time. Is your resulting attitude to cake 'internal' or 'external'? It's 'inside' you, but it was put therefore by someone else (an external cause). We might make a similar point more simply. Many of our aspirations are culturally or genetically determined, or put there by upbringing or education. If you suffer a trauma, you might develop a compulsion to behave in a certain way (a phobia or a neurosis). And so on. The point is that, at least in some cases, Hume's labels do not always seem to serve the purpose that he wanted them to. And if so, then his compatibilism seems to breakdown also.

The problem of free will represents an ongoing debate. Some version of compatibilism would seem to give us the best of both worlds – a respect for scientific causation and moral meaning – but this is also difficult to defend.

Conclusion

Almost everyone now agrees that mind is somehow made possible in humans by the functioning of our brains. Yet the study of the brain is still in its infancy. There is still so much we have to learn about it. The philosophy of mind, however, has been carried out for centuries without even this basic knowledge about brains. Given that, one might think it remarkable that the subject has progressed at all. While it does seem true to say that the philosophy of mind has taught us a great deal, we should perhaps accept that the solutions to the big problems will only come when we understand better how the brain works. Philosophy has done its best to understand mind but some problems will take greater scientific knowledge to really solve.

Summary

The main question in the philosophy of mind concerns the mind's relation to matter and, in particular, to the body. Why is it that we do not seem able to understand mind in terms of the movement of physical matter when it seems everything else in the universe can be explained in this way?

Dualism's answer is that mind and body, since they have two very different sets of properties, are two different kinds of **substance**. The main problem with this theory is explaining how two so very different things could interact, especially since it seems true that mind and matter causally interact with each other.

Behaviourists argue that all **mental** concepts refer not to private, non-material things and events, but to publicly observable behaviours or dispositions to behave. The main problem with this view is that not all mental states have some kind of behavioural manifestation.

Physicalism is the view that any mental event is identical with some physical event, which in the case of humans will be a brain event. The reason that a brain event doesn't seem to be the same kind of thing as a mental event is simply that there are two ways of experiencing it – from the 'inside' and from the 'outside'. The major difficulty for physicalism is explaining how brain events and mental events can be the same when they seem to have such radically different properties. Double aspect theory and neutral monism suggest a response to this, arguing that the mental and physical are different aspects of the same underlying 'neutral' property, but this account leaves the relationship between physical and mental events and states problematic.

Functionalists argue something has a mind if it is capable of processing inputs and producing outputs in an intelligent way. It is neutral as to what kind of thing, organic or silicon, does this and what it feels like to be such a mind. The major objection to functionalism comes from Searle's Chinese Room argument, which attempts to show that a functionalist system could be just a rule-following device with none of the understanding required for true intelligence.

Non-reductive materialism argues that physical brains can have mental properties, but that these cannot be captured in a purely physical description. The mental 'supervenes' on the physical, meaning that consciousness is an emergent property of physical brains. But this approach does not seem to fully account for the **qualitative** nature of consciousness, and arguably leaves us with **epiphenomenalism**, which sees mental experience as an ineffectual by-product of the brain.

Eliminativism takes the drastic response of trying to 'eliminate' the traditional mental vocabulary and to replace it with a more respectable scientific one.

The problem of other minds is the problem of how we can know other people have minds when we cannot know they have an inner life – we can only observe their behaviour. One solution is the argument from analogy, which says that we attribute mental states to others because they resemble us in key respects. We ourselves have minds, so it seems reasonable to attribute mental states to others too. Putnam's solution is that the hypothesis that others do have minds is simply the best explanation for why they behave as they do.

The problem of personal **identity** concerns what it is that makes a person the same person over time, given all the changes a person may undergo. A traditional view is that personal identity is determined by the continued existence of a non-physical soul. **Psychological reductionists** claim personal identity is a matter of psychological connectedness and continuity. **Animalists** claim personal identity is simply the continued existence of a particular human animal.

The question of personhood looks at what list of features a person might be said to possess. Common candidates are consciousness, rationality, autonomy, physical embodiment, the ability to use language, a sense of self, the ability to set and revise goals and aspirations, and the capacity to fulfil a social role. Personhood may therefore be a matter of degree, and some argue that certain animals meet enough of these criteria to be considered persons, whilst certain humans – at certain times or in certain circumstances – do not. It may even one day be possible to consider machines as persons, or for human persons to exist in non-traditional forms. The idea that 'person' is a basic concept seems interesting, but problematic.

Libertarians argue that humans possess free will, based on the fact that we could have chosen to act differently to how we actually did. In line with scientific notions of causation and the materialist view of mind, **determinists** argue that such choice is illusory. **Compatibilism** attempts to establish a middle ground, acknowledging causal determinism whilst defining free actions as those which are not coerced.

Glossary

Animalism   The view that personal identity involves the continuation of the physical body, especially the brain.

Category mistake   To think of one kind of thing or phenomenon as though it were a different kind of thing or phenomenon. For example, to think of a university as a kind of building rather than an institution.

Causa sui   The idea that something can be the cause of itself.

Compatibilism   The view that, whilst our actions are physically determined, we must consider those actions free which are not compelled by some external source.

Determinism   The view that our actions are determined in advance, generally because we are physical beings, and so are bound by the laws of cause and effect.

Eliminativism   The view that traditional mental concepts are mistaken explanations of the mind, and should be 'eliminated', to be replaced with scientific explanations.

Epiphenomenalism   The view that mind is a non-reducible property of matter, but that it is ineffectual (it has no causal powers).

Identity   Strict identity means that if X is identical to Y, all and only the properties of X are properties of Y.

Libertarianism   The view that faced with options, we are not inevitably caused to choose the one we do, but we could choose otherwise.

Logical behaviourism   The view that all mental concepts refer to behaviours or dispositions to behave.

Mental   Everything that is characteristic of conscious beings, such as thoughts, sense perceptions and emotions.

Methodological behaviourism   The view that the best way to study the mind is to study behaviour.

Monism   The view that there is only one substance, rather than the two postulated by substance dualism.

Neutral Monism   The view that the mental and physical are different aspects of the same underlying substance, which is itself 'neutral' (neither mental nor physical).

Non-reductive Materialism   The view that the mental is a non-reducible aspect or property of the physical.

Physical   All that is the subject of the physical sciences.

Psychological reductionism   The view that personal identity consists in the continuation of mental properties, such as memory, personality traits or intentions.

Qualia   The way experiences feel to conscious beings. 'What it feels like' to have a thought, perception, emotion and so on.

Qualitative identity   The sense in which two objects, though distinct entities, can be called identical because they share all the same properties except their location in time and space.

Quantitative identity   The kind of identity where two apparently different things are in fact one and the same thing.

Semantics   Meaning in language.

Substance dualism   The view that there are two different kinds of substance, the mental and the physical.

Syntax   The formal rules which govern the construction of sentences.

Further reading

The classic exposition of dualism is René Descartes's *Meditations on First Philosophy*, which is one of the books covered in the companion volume to this one, *Philosophy: Key Texts*. A devastating critique of the Cartesian view and a major work for behaviourism is Gilbert Ryle's *The Concept of Mind* (Penguin), which is a lucid read.

A brilliant anthology of academic philosophy and weird sci-fi is *The Mind's I*, edited by Douglas R. Hofstadter and Daniel C. Dennett (Penguin). It contains many fascinating riffs on functionalist themes as well as covering a lot of other ground. John Searle's *Minds, Brains and Science* (Penguin) is a very readable précis of Searle's own work in the area. Tim Crane's *The Mechanical Mind* (Penguin) is a very clear and informative book which brings the debate right up to date.

Personal Identity, edited by John Perry (University of California Press), is an authoritative but select set of readings on the theme of the title. It includes Parfit's original paper on personal identity. For an original take on the problem of other minds, try Simon Glendinning's *Being with Others* (Routledge). Julian Baggini's *The Ego Trick* (Granta) is a wide-reaching and accessible treatment of the question of personhood and identity.

Peter Singer sets out his controversial views on personhood in *Practical Ethics* (Cambridge University Press).

David Hume's compatibilism can be found in his *Enquiry Concerning Human Understanding* (section 8).

4
Philosophy of Religion

What is the philosophy of religion?

The philosophy of religion is largely concerned with investigating the rational grounds for religious belief. It differs from theology in that theology starts from a particular religious belief or set of beliefs and seeks to understand and explore questions in religion from that starting point. The philosophy of religion, on the other hand, is not supposed to start with any assumptions or prior beliefs. Its goal is to examine the basis of religious belief and to do that it cannot assume that any religious beliefs are true or false.

In practice this distinction between the philosophy of religion and theology is not quite so sharp. Many of the arguments we will examine may look like attempts to establish religious belief on rational principles, but actually turn out to have their origin in attempts to provide rational explanations within religious belief systems. Nonetheless, our concern here will be with the philosophy of religion as contrasted with theology. It will start not from the assumption that any religious beliefs are true, but with an open-minded approach to arguments for and against religion.

Many of the arguments that will be considered appear in different forms in different classic texts. For example, the ontological argument for the existence of God has been put forward in different forms by both St Anselm and René Descartes. Because of the brevity of this book, we will not be presenting versions of such arguments specific to individual texts. Our aim is rather to examine the general forms of such arguments and the general objections which can be raised against them. That way we can identify the issues which cut across many different versions of the arguments without getting bogged down in details specific to one or two writers.

There is another issue which concerns the pronoun used for God. God is usually referred to as 'he' (or 'He'), in accordance with the very clearly male terms used to describe him, such as 'father'. However, the idea that God is male is somewhat baffling. After all, God is supposed to be neither human nor material. In any case, the whole category of maleness only has sense in the context of biological creatures which sexually reproduce, and whatever God is, it isn't such an animal. It would be equally absurd to rectify this by supposing God to be female and to use the pronoun 'she'. We could call God 'it', but since in English 'it' refers to objects rather than beings, this too is unsatisfactory. So in the absence of a perfect solution, we shall stick with calling God 'he', mindful of the fact that this does not assume his maleness.

A final point to bear in mind is that the agenda of the philosophy of religion as studied in the English-speaking world is largely set by issues arising out of the Judaeo-Christian tradition. This is, of course, a limitation, since if our starting point were some of the Eastern religions, for example, different philosophical questions would arise. In following this agenda, then, we are following what the syllabuses of many philosophy of religion courses dictate.

What is God?

Much of what we will be discussing in this chapter concerns the existence or non-existence of God. But what do we mean by God? In the Judaeo-Christian tradition, God is usually characterised by what we can call the three omnis, 'omni' being a prefix meaning 'all'.

First, God is taken to be omnipotent or all-powerful. That means that God can do anything. If God wants to destroy everything in an instant, or create infinite matter out of nothing, then he can do so. But could God create an open door that is shut, or a square circle? Could God make one and one equal 3? This seems absurd and many theologians have been happy to accept that God cannot do things which are logically impossible such as these. In this way, we can see that things like square circles are just nonsenses, and to say that God cannot create them is not to place limits on his power.

Second, God is taken to be omnibenevolent or all-loving. In the words of the famous hymn, 'God is love'. Therefore, there is no limit to God's caring. God would not allow anyone to suffer because he had run out of love. This is important for the question of why there is suffering in the world, as we shall see in the next section.

Third, God is taken to be omniscient or all-knowing. No-one can hide from God because God can see everything and knows everything, including your most intimate, private thoughts. God is the ultimate Big Brother.

In addition to these three characteristics, some add that God is omnipresent or everywhere. This is actually a matter of dispute. While some theologians understand God to be at all places at all times (or 'immanent' in creation), others see God as existing somehow 'outside' of his creation (or transcendent). Because of this disagreement, the idea that God is omnipresent is not part of the core of the Judaeo-Christian conception of God.

Some people are concerned by the fact that God is supposed to be omniscient because it seems to present a problem for human free will. For example, if God knows that I am about to choose coffee rather than tea, does that mean my choice was not really free, that it was somehow predetermined and beyond my control?

Some argue that this worry is based on a misunderstanding. The fact that God knows what will happen next does not necessarily mean that the future has been fixed by factors our choices cannot alter. If God is transcendent and exists outside of space and time, for example, then the fact that he can see the future does not mean the future is not the result of our free choices. God could know what we will do freely without that in any way compromising our freedom. Even if God is immanent in time and space, the mere ability to see the future does not mean the future is fixed.

A far more serious problem for the conception of God sketched out so far concerns the question of why there is evil and suffering in the world. This is the so-called 'problem of evil'.

The problem of evil

The problem of evil is misleadingly named because it is not just the problem of evil in the sense of the wicked things people do. It is really a problem of 'bad things'. These bad things can be classified into two types. First, there is moral evil, which are bad things that are the result of human action, such as torture and cruelty. The second type is natural evil, which are bad things that just happen, such as floods, disease, earthquakes and accidents.

The problem for the traditional conception of God is that there is a lot of both kinds of evil about. In fact, there is so much that it leads many to ask how the existence of such suffering is compatible with the existence of God as traditionally conceived.

The problem can be stated starkly. We know that there is evil in the world (in the senses defined). If God exists, then how can we explain this evil? There seem to be three possible explanations. It could be that God doesn't know about it, but that would mean God isn't omniscient. It could be that God doesn't care about it, but that would mean God isn't omnibenevolent. It could be that God can't stop it, but that would mean God isn't omnipotent. So it seems that the only way to reconcile the existence of evil with the existence of God is to radically change our idea of what God is: God cannot be omniscient, omnibenevolent and omnipotent.

Some people claim that this is enough to show that God doesn't exist, at least not the God many people worship and believe in. But is there a way out? Is there an explanation of how God could know about suffering, care about suffering, be able to do something about that suffering, yet still allow it to go on? Attempts to offer such explanations are known as theodicies and they come in many forms.

Some theodicies are extremely implausible. For instance, some deny the premise that there is actually any evil in the world at all. Things may look bad from where we're standing, but that's just because we can't see the whole picture. From where God's sitting, everything looks fine. It is hard to see how anyone could seriously believe this, at least while keeping their humanity intact. To look at the horrors of Auschwitz, for example, and say that it only looks bad because we can't see the whole picture seems to be callous at the very least.

More plausible theodicies do not deny the reality of evil, but attempt to show that, in the long run, it is better they exist than that they don't. Just as a dentist asks you to put up with some pain because you'll benefit in the end, so, on this view, God allows us to suffer because it is necessary for our eternal salvation. This doesn't deny the reality of suffering, but it explains why it is necessary.

But what could possibly make all the suffering in the world worthwhile? One surprisingly popular answer is the so-called free will defence. We may say surprisingly popular because it seems so obviously inadequate. The free will defence argues that God had two choices: he either created creatures with free will and the opportunity to freely choose good and thus enjoy eternal life; or he didn't create such creatures. The universe is a better place if such creatures exist. So God created them. But if such creatures exist, then they are bound to choose bad as well as good, causing suffering. So evil is bound to exist, but this is a price worth paying.

As it stands, this defence is hopeless because it only covers moral evil, not natural evil. It still doesn't explain disease, earthquakes and so on. So the free will defence has to be modified to say that such things are necessary in order that we can learn from them and grow spiritually. In other, words, it is only by confronting suffering that we come to be able to choose good.

Even in its modified form the defence is weak. The necessity of confronting suffering seems rather implausible. Some people suffer much more than others. Does that mean they are better people as a result? Do only they get to heaven? This leads into the general difficulty that the scale of the suffering seems disproportionate. Why do some people die slowly, in agonising pain, sometimes with no-one there to witness it and so learn from it?

It is also extremely dubious to suppose that this terrible suffering is really necessary. People can learn in different ways. For some people, it is enough to see that something is harmful for them to avoid it, whereas others have to actually experience the bad consequences before they shun it. This shows that there is nothing fixed and necessary about the way we learn. God could have made us better or worse learners by nature. God seems to be some kind of sadist if he has designed us in such a way that we can only learn through such terrible means.

In short, the free will defence fails to explain the variations in suffering we endure and the extremes which some people have to put up with. It also seems to be based on a cruel doctrine that we need to be made to suffer in order to learn. If the universe is this cruel, then surely that gives us more reason to doubt that it is under the control of a good God.

This leads to a different kind of way of putting the problem of evil. Let us accept that there is some rational way of reconciling God's existence with the existence of evil. If this could be done and God did exist, where would that leave us? For many, it seems we are left with the shocking truth that God is prepared to allow terrible suffering as a means to an end. We may feel that there are cruelties which God has allowed which could never be justified as a means to an end. If God allows these things, then that means God is not worthy of our worship. Put this way, the problem of evil shows that either God does not exist or that God is morally repugnant.

Faith and reason

Many believers find this style of arguing unsatisfactory. There seems to be something wrong about expecting God's ways to somehow be comprehensible to us. Shouldn't we just allow that God's purposes may be mysterious and that we cannot expect to fully understand them? We may not be able to see what could possibly make suffering worthwhile, but we can't see what choices God had, or how wonderful the rewards of life after death are. Can't we just trust that, after death, we will all come to see that God's purposes are indeed good?

This objection runs up against the problem of distinguishing the philosophy of religion from theology. In theology, it may be enough to say that we can understand so much but beyond that, all is mystery. If we are starting from a faith in God's goodness, then we can try and explain the existence of evil as best we can, but accept that our explanation may be incomplete. But the philosophy of religion does not start by presuming faith. If we cannot solve the problem of evil rationally, then our conclusion should be that it is not rational to believe in or worship God.

This, however, does invite a further, vital question. Though it may not be rational to worship or believe in God, doesn't faith go beyond what is rational? Must we be constrained by what is rational when it comes to religious belief?

There are many ways of considering this question, but if we are working within the philosophy of religion, the way to do this is to consider from a rational point of view what the limits of rationality might be and how faith can or can't go beyond reason. If we just say that faith has its reasons of which reason knows nothing, we have effectively given up on approaching issues of religion philosophically.

The idea that reason has its limits has a long pedigree in philosophy. Kant once said that his philosophy placed limits on reason so as to make room for faith. He attempted to show that there were some questions about which reason must remain silent, but which are still vital to human life. In these areas, it is legitimate to make one's decisions on the basis of faith.

A similar line of reasoning was followed by William James (1842–1910), who argued that there are many issues where it is acceptable to make decisions of belief on non-rational grounds, and God's existence is one of them.

James's argument rests on the idea that we sometimes have a choice between two or more competing hypotheses, but we lack evidential or rational grounds for making the choice. (For the sake of simplicity let us continue to talk of instances where there are just two options.) Of course, what we might do in such a situation is simply not make a choice. We can just suspend judgement and say we don't know which hypothesis is true. But in what James calls genuine options, we cannot do this. We have to make a choice and, in the absence of rational grounds for making that choice, we have to let our feelings – or our 'passional nature' – guide us.

These genuine options have three characteristics. First, the hypothesis in question must be a 'live' option. A live option is a hypothesis which is a serious possibility. If you were asked to consider the hypothesis that the moon is a lump of cheese, that would not be a live option. It is simply not a serious possibility. But the hypothesis that the mafia had JFK killed is a live hypothesis. You may not believe it, but it is a serious possibility. God's existence is, according to James, also a live hypothesis. Whether we believe in God or not, his existence is a serious possibility.

The second key feature of a genuine option is that it is forced. A forced option is one where you have two choices and there is no middle ground. For example, if asked whether you want tea with or without sugar, that is not a forced option because you could choose not to have tea at all. But if asked to accept that a particular statement is true, you either do or you do not. If you say, 'I'm not sure, I suspend judgement', then you have effectively refused to accept the statement. Belief in God is, for James, a forced option, because we either believe in God or we withhold our belief, by believing God doesn't exist or by suspending judgement. Either way, we have chosen not to believe.

The last feature of a genuine option is that it is in some way momentous. Watching a soap opera is both a live and forced option. It is a real possibility and you either watch it or you don't. But it is not momentous. Your life is not significantly changed depending on your decision. Belief in God, however, is momentous. It makes a great deal of difference to our lives (and possibly our afterlives) whether we believe in God or not. It affects the whole way in which we view the world.

So, for James, belief in God is a genuine option because it is live, forced and momentous. But neither reason nor evidence can decide whether we should believe in God or not. Therefore, we are entitled – or even obliged – to allow our feelings to guide us. If we decide to believe in God, therefore, we act on a faith which goes beyond reason, but only because our decision must be made beyond reason's domain.

James's argument is a very interesting and sophisticated one, but it does have many weaknesses. First, many atheists do not think that God's existence is a live option. Their reflections lead them to believe that the very idea of a God in the Judaeo-Christian mould is ridiculous. For such people, God's existence is as dead an option as the Moon being made of cheese.

Second, we might resist James's definition of a forced option. On James's account, it seems that suspending judgement is never permitted, because to suspend judgement is to withhold assent and this is classified as rejecting a belief. But surely there is a difference between rejecting a hypothesis and suspending judgement about it. This difference is deemed unimportant by James.

Third, although there may be people for whom reason and evidence leave the issue in the balance, we might well think they settle the question for us. It may well be the case that one cannot prove whether God does or doesn't exist. But the balance of evidence and arguments may tilt much more one way than the other. If this is so, then we don't need to rely purely on our passional nature. Our brains could still have the most important role to play.

James's argument aims to justify making a decision of faith without the support of reason by showing that by the standards of reason itself, such decisions are justified. It is certainly a clever argument, but whether it succeeds is a matter for debate.

Betting on God

Blaise Pascal offered a very different kind of argument which attempted to justify belief in God in the absence of proof or conclusive evidence. His argument is known as 'Pascal's Wager' because it attempts to show that belief in God is like a bet you would be foolish not to make.

The essence of the argument is that we have two possibilities: God does or doesn't exist. We don't have proof either way, so you've got to choose which one to believe. If you choose to believe in God and worship him, two things could happen. If God exists, you've chosen the right answer and heaven awaits (along with some rewards in this life to do with tranquillity of mind and so on). If God doesn't exist, you still get the rewards in this life. Your piety would have come at a small cost of course, but since death is the end, nothing much matters anyway.

If you choose not to believe in God, there are likewise two possibilities. If God doesn't exist, you were right, but death is the end and it's all meaningless anyway. You win, but your victory is hollow. If God does exist, your disbelief means you risk hellfire and damnation, or at the very least miss out on fast-track access through the pearly gates.

So which is the better bet? It would seem that belief in God is. Only this one gives you a chance of eternal life and it comes at little cost. The other choices have few potential rewards and carry great risks. So belief in God is the best bet.

The argument is clever, but it is sometimes hard to see why it has commanded so much attention. The first problem is, if we believe in God, which God do we believe in? If we choose the wrong religion or sect, we also risk hellfire and damnation. More serious still is the question of why God would accept into heaven people who choose to believe in him on the basis that it's a good bet instead of others who don't, but who live good lives. Pascal acknowledges that belief must be sincere but he argues that, once you accept the bet, if you just practice living a religious life you will come to believe sincerely. But this seems to be a double-bluff: you first trick yourself into believing sincerely, and then God will accept this sincerity and let you into heaven.

Both these problems touch on the wider issue that, for the non-believer, the whole idea that God decides how to reward people on the basis of what they believe about him is crazy. Is God some kind of insecure egomaniac who treats people better or worse depending on how much they worship him? The atheist finds something strange in the mindset of religious believers who think that decisions about eternal life and damnation are made on this basis. To put it in terms of another bet, the atheist might think that if there is a God, it is much more likely that he decides what happens after life on the basis of how a person has lived than on whether they join the right religion.

The status of religious language

Just as many religious believers think there is something inappropriate about trying to understand religion in purely rational terms, many others think that it is inappropriate to try to understand religious language in ordinary terms. When, for example, a Christian priest takes the bread and wine in a communion service and says, 'This is the body and blood of Jesus Christ', it would be crass to take these words in their everyday senses. Normally, if we say something is the body and blood of someone, that means, if we were to analyse it, we would find it was composed of flesh and blood. Hardly anyone thinks this is what would happen were you to analyse the communion bread and wine. Whatever it means to say the bread and wine is flesh and blood, it isn't that.

However, it is difficult to move on from this to find a way of understanding religious language that is satisfactory. For a start, most religious believers would not want to say that the language they use is simply metaphorical or figurative. To understand how Jesus is the son of God, for instance, we may have to understand 'son' differently from normal, but Christians surely don't mean that Jesus isn't really God's son and that the phrase 'son of God' is just a metaphor. Of course, religious texts may include metaphors, but if all religious language were understood this way, believing in a religion would not require belief in anything literally true, but merely the admiration of a kind of body of poetry. Some religious people are prepared to accept this, but it seems most do not.

So the dilemma facing religious believers is this. If religious language is interpreted as normal language, much in religious creeds just seems to be absurd or demonstrably false. Jesus can't literally be all God and all man. He can't literally be the son of God. The communion bread and wine can't literally be the body and blood of Christ. But if religious language is taken to be figurative or metaphorical, religious beliefs lose their substance. For instance, belief in life after death does not add up to much if this is just a belief in a metaphorical life after death. An atheist can believe in that kind of immortality. And if 'son of God' is a metaphor, what makes Jesus so special? Aren't we all, metaphorically speaking, sons and daughters of God? But if religious language is neither literally nor metaphorically true, what kind of status does it have? And doesn't the whole attempt to make an exception for religious language look like a desperate measure to preserve truth and meaning in a body of belief that is just out of kilter with the rest of our knowledge and beliefs?

In the twentieth century, some have seen a solution to this problem in the later philosophy of Ludwig Wittgenstein (1889–1951). The way in which Wittgenstein understood language seems to make room for different types of language to have different rules, without needing to make a special case for religion. Wittgenstein rejected the model of language which saw words and sentences as mapping directly on to the world, rather like the way captions map on to the pictures they are placed under. For example, it is common to think that a sentence like 'the cat sat on the mat' means what it does, and is true or false, because of the relations the words in the sentence have to objects in the real world – the cat and the mat. On this model, meaning and truth in language is just a matter of words and sentences corresponding to things in the world.

The problem is that if you look at what rules govern this correspondence, things begin to look much more difficult. For instance, what if we say, 'Jenny is playing a game'? What rule determines whether these words correspond to reality? You might think the answer is simple: the words correspond if there is a person called Jenny and she is playing a game. But the hard question is this: what rule tells us if Jenny is playing a game? What are the rules that tell us when a word like 'game' is being applied correctly? Attempting to answer this question can be frustrating, because in one sense we all know full well what playing a game involves. But if you try to articulate that in a clear set of rules, you will almost certainly fail. There are just too many ways in which one can play a game. Further, the same activity, such as a fight, can start as not a game and become a game, or the other way around. The word has too fluid and flexible a meaning to be captured in a finite set of rules.

Wittgenstein's point here is that using a word correctly is not about learning a set of rules so that we can label items in the world correctly. It is much more like learning a skill. We understand what a word means when we can use it correctly. Compare this to learning how to use something like a baseball bat. We know someone has learned how to use a baseball bat, not when they can tell us all about bats, but when they can go out into the field and whack the ball well. In the same way, learning to use language is about using words appropriately and in the right context. This is captured in Wittgenstein's advice that to understand a word, you shouldn't ask for the meaning, you should ask for the use.

How does this relate to religious language? Wittgenstein's theory is seen by some as a rebuttal of those who demand of religious language that it operates in ordinary or scientifically explicable terms. If you ask to examine the communion wine to see if it is blood, for instance, you are making the mistake of assuming that there is a clear rule which governs the use of the word 'blood' and that this rule is basically a scientific one. However, for the religious believer, there are other uses of this word. 'Blood' has a sacred significance and a use in the communion service which can't be simply explained in terms of mere metaphor or science. The only way to really understand this use is to live within the religious community and use the word for yourself. Just as you can only learn how to use the baseball bat by practising in the park, so you can only learn how to use language by practising it in the community in which it is used. So to understand religious language, you need to see how it is used in the religious community.

Wittgenstein's theory is extremely subtle and rich and merits a close reading. Its main danger is that it can be used as a justification for obscurantism – the covering up of vague or confused ideas in a veil of impenetrable language. After all, couldn't anyone, if their beliefs are under attack, turn around and say, 'You just don't understand how these words are used in our language community'?

In addition to this, Wittgenstein's views may also lead to relativism, where there are no common standards to decide between competing claims to truth and where every community has its own truths. This is a consequence many Wittgensteinians are prepared to accept, but it troubles many others who believe truth and falsehood depend not on what we say and think, but on how things are.

The ontological argument

The issues we have looked at so far, surrounding the concept of God, the nature of evil, religious language and the relation between faith and reason, are perhaps the most interesting in the philosophy of religion. But when the subject is taught, these issues are often considered second, not first. Priority in the syllabuses tends to go to a series of largely medieval arguments for the existence of God. These arguments are certainly of interest, as we shall see. And of course, it is natural that the question of the existence of God would be among the first those new to the subject would seek to investigate. However, since these arguments are at best inconclusive, and at worst weak and unconvincing, they have perhaps commanded more attention than they deserve.

One of the most interesting and difficult of these is the ontological argument for the existence of God, which appears in its most famous guises in the writings of St Anselm and Descartes. As with many of these arguments, there is no one single 'Ontological Argument'. Rather, there are a number of different arguments, all of which share a basic common form. Ontological arguments attempt to show that God must exist as a matter of necessity and that we can know this simply by considering what the concept of God means.

In its simplest form, the argument attempts to show that it is a contradiction to say that God does not exist. Consider as an example what we can and cannot say about triangles. Without making any presumptions about whether triangles actually exist or not, we know by considering what it means for something to be a triangle that triangles must have three sides and that a four-sided triangle is a contradiction in terms. Now consider the concept of God. God is, as we have seen, all the omnis – omnipotent, omniscient and omnibenevolent. But surely something which has all these features must also exist. You can't be all-powerful if you don't actually exist. So it seems existence is built into the concept of God. So just as a four-sided triangle is a contradiction in terms, so is a non-existent God. Therefore, God must exist.

Although this is a simplified version of the argument, it does contain the essence of all ontological arguments, as can be seen by looking at a more sophisticated formulation. One seemingly unobjectionable definition of God is 'the greatest being imaginable'. Let us now suppose that such a being does not exist. Now, though, it seems that we can imagine a being greater than this, namely, the greatest being imaginable which actually exists. But, of course, if such a being can be imagined, then our original, non-existent God is not the greatest being imaginable after all. The only way to get out of this contradiction is to suppose that such a being does exist. That is the only way the concept of the greatest being imaginable makes sense and doesn't contradict itself.

As is clear, although the formulation of this argument is a little more sophisticated, in essence the same point is being made. God's existence is deemed to be necessary because the concept of a non-existent God is taken to be in some way incoherent or self-contradictory.

The problem with this argument is evident as soon as we apply the same logic to something else, like the greatest athlete imaginable. If the greatest athlete imaginable doesn't exist, then it seems we could imagine an athlete greater than this, namely the greatest athlete imaginable who does actually exist. This would make the non-existent greatest athlete imaginable not the greatest athlete imaginable after all. So it seems the greatest athlete imaginable must exist.

As should be clear, the same argument could apply to the greatest pizza imaginable, or the greatest symphony imaginable. Worse, it could also apply to non-existent entities. What about the greatest dragon or phoenix imaginable? Or the greatest half-man, half-cheeseburger imaginable? All these things must exist if the logic of the ontological argument is right.

Of course, there have been attempts to show that God is a special case, and that the logic of the ontological argument can't be extended to just anything. But most philosophers do accept that the logic of the argument is flawed. So where does the mistake lie exactly? The problem seems to be that the argument makes a leap between concepts and actual existence. But there is no direct link between the two. For example, in the case of triangles, the fact that a triangle must have three sides does not mean that any actual triangles exist. It does mean that if a triangle exists, then it must have three sides, but this is still an 'if'. From what must be true about the concept of a triangle, therefore, nothing about the actual existence or not of triangles can be inferred.

Similarly, if we consider the concept of God, we might conclude that if God exists, God is the most perfect being imaginable. But this is still an if. We cannot conclude that God must exist because the concept of God is the concept of a supremely perfect being. Considerations of the concept of God can never tell us whether there is an actual being in the universe to which the concept applies.

The ontological argument is therefore considered by most philosophers to have failed. But there are other arguments for God's existence which we also have to consider.

The cosmological argument

The ontological argument has a fishy smell about it and is intuitively unpersuasive, but it is difficult to pinpoint exactly what is wrong with it. The cosmological argument, on the other hand, is one of the most intuitively plausible arguments for the existence of God, but its faults are all too glaring.

The cosmological argument is really little more than the argument that everything must have a cause and therefore the universe itself must have a cause. Since that cause cannot be the universe itself, it must be something else, something powerful enough to bring everything into existence. God is the best candidate for this, since only God seems powerful enough to be this cause.

One important feature to note about this argument is that, unlike the ontological argument, it is based on the evidence of experience rather than watertight logic. In philosophical terms, it is an *a posteriori* argument, not an *a priori* one. This means that we should not expect the conclusion to follow as a matter of necessity from the premises. It is enough that the conclusion is the best way of explaining the evidence.

The problem with the argument is that there is no justification for virtually every part of it. Even the basic premise that everything has a cause is debatable. It is not out of logical necessity that we say everything must have a cause. The idea of an uncaused event is not a logical contradiction in the way that a square circle is. Rather, we say everything must have a cause because this is what experience teaches us. But experience only teaches us about events in the universe as it actually exists. Experience is silent about what happened before the universe existed, or at the point where it came into existence. So although experience does teach us that every event *in* the universe has a cause, it does not and cannot tell us that the universe as a whole must have a cause.

Nevertheless, some might say that if there are two hypotheses – that the universe has a cause or it doesn't – the hypothesis that it does is more plausible. This response faces two problems. First, this plausibility seems to be based on the assumption that everything has a cause, which, as we have seen, has no foundation in logic or experience. Second, if we say that God is the cause, we are saying that there is at least one thing in the universe which does not have a cause – God. So we are contradicting our major premise that everything must have a cause. Third, even if we accept that the universe has an uncaused cause, the jump from this to God is extremely large. All we need to end the causal chain is the idea of an uncaused first cause. Why should we attribute to this all the characteristics of God?

The cosmological argument seems, then, to boil down to this: there must be at least one uncaused cause in the universe and that God is the best candidate for this. Although the first part of this proposition seems reasonable (though not beyond dispute), it is the second part which is really speculative. In essence, the argument seems to be that we have no idea what kind of thing this uncaused cause could be so we'll say it's God. This is a very weak form of argument. Historically, God has always been invoked to explain the mysterious or unexplained. When people didn't know where thunder came from, they attributed it to God. When they didn't understand meteorology, they thought God was pulling the weather levers. Such a 'God of the gaps' is very vulnerable to advances in knowledge. As soon as we understand how a part of nature works, another role for God goes. Now God has been demoted to the first cause, the last part of nature where it is felt we need to invoke God to explain things. But this is a dangerous place for God to be, for modern physics is even grappling with the question of how the universe began and is coming up with explanations which do not need God. An argument for the existence of God which is based on needing God to explain the unexplained would therefore seem to be a very weak, vulnerable and discredited form of argument.

The teleological argument

The teleological argument starts with the observation that the universe is intricate and orderly. As one of the original proponents of the argument, William Paley, noted, when we find something like a watch, inspect it and find all its parts are working harmoniously and in an orderly fashion, we reason that someone must have designed and made the watch. We do not think that such objects just spring into existence or grow on trees. But if we reason thus when we look at something so simple as a pocket watch, surely when we see something so vast and intricate as the universe, it is reasonable to suppose that an intelligent designer and maker created it. The only thing we can conceive of which comes close to the description of such a creator is God, for only something all-powerful and all-knowing would have the intellect and resources to design such a universe.

The argument has two main weaknesses. First, the analogy between the watch and the universe is very weak. We know that artefacts such as watches have makers because we have experience of watches and watch-makers and we know that you can't have the former without the latter. But this is not the case with nature. We do not find a beautiful wilderness and assume it must be the work of a landscape gardener. It is only when a landscape has been clearly ordered in a particular way, typical of the work of humans, that we believe a gardener is responsible. What this example shows is that the hallmarks of intelligent design are only found in certain kinds of things. Wildernesses, animals and natural phenomena do not bear the hallmarks of intelligent design in the same way as watches, cars and buildings do.

Further, we have no experience at all as to what the ultimate causes of things in nature are. As far as we do have experience of the causes of natural phenomena, these are definitely not intelligent designers. Mountain ranges are caused by shifts in the Earth's plates, storms by falling air pressure, cliffs by gradual erosion of the coastline. In so far as experience tells us anything at all about the causes of things in nature, it tells us they are not the product of intelligent design.

But surely, it might be argued, the best explanation for the overall order of the universe is that there is an intelligent designer? The analogy with artefacts may not work, but none the less, we know that had just a few things been slightly different at the start of the universe with the Big Bang, none of this would be here at all. Surely something intelligent must be behind it?

The idea that God is the best explanation for the order we find in the universe leads to the second main objection to the teleological argument. The problem is simply that God is not the best explanation at all. To say God created the order of the universe is to say we don't know how the order in the universe came about, we just think God is responsible for it. This isn't an explanation. It would be like saying that you can explain how a murder was carried out simply by identifying someone as the murderer. But what is worse, science can explain a lot of the order in the universe without the need to invoke God. Most powerfully, evolutionary theory turns the idea of intelligent design on its head.

It is worth spending a little time looking at evolution because it is often misunderstood. Consider something like the human ear. Pre-Darwin, it would seem natural to think that something as useful as the ear must have been the product of some kind of design. God gave us ears to hear – how else could we have got them? Evolutionary theory explains how we got ears without the need for the intervention of a benign, intelligent designer. This is, crudely, how it works.

When an animal or plant reproduces, it never reproduces itself exactly. Rather like a photocopier, or a game of Chinese whispers, small changes or 'mutations' occur from generation to generation. Some of these random mutations will benefit the offspring and some will not. So, for example, an early ancestor of *homo sapiens* reproduces and one of its children has a minute sensitivity to sound whereas another does not. This sensitivity gives that animal an advantage over its peers, since it provides an early warning system for approaching danger, for example. So that particular animal is more likely to survive, reproduce and pass on this sensitivity to its own offspring. These will, in turn, have an advantage over their peers. So, over time, the proportion of these animals which have this sensitivity to sound increases. Further, those which have a greater sensitivity to sound will stand more chance of survival than those who have a lesser sensitivity. So a process begins by which, generation to generation, without intelligent design or purpose, those with a greater sensitivity to sound tend to survive more than those with a lesser sensitivity. And so, over time, this sensitivity develops until many millions of years later, we have the human ear.

Many creationists will say that evolutionary theory is incomplete and contested. In fact, it is one of the most tested and proven theories in science. It can be hard to fully conceive because it works over vast time-scales. It is virtually impossible to really imagine an ear developing over millions of years from a small mutation which first gave an animal a minute sensitivity to sound. But the failure here is purely one of imagination. One can understand how the process works and even observe the process at work in experiments on fruit flies, for example, which breed quickly enough for scientists to actually witness evolution at work.

Evolution shows how you can end up with order in the universe, even organs which appear to be designed to fulfil a function, such as hearing, without the need for an intelligent designer. Other branches of science, such as physics, explain the order in parts of the universe other than human life. In the light of this, it is hard to see how the hypothesis of an intelligent designer is the best explanation for the order of the universe.

However, there are those religious believers who accept the basics of evolutionary theory, but who argue that it does not fully account for natural complexity, and that in order to achieve a successful explanation we must combine scientific findings with the notion that a divine designer had some hand in evolution. For instance, *theistic evolution* holds that natural selection is a process created by God to achieve his ends. As such, this may be distinguished from full-blown literalist creationism, which must somehow account for the fact that life and the Earth itself does not appear to have been created in seven days (as Genesis – interpreted literally – teaches). Nonetheless, theistic evolution claims there are features in the natural order which natural selection or some other blind process cannot account for. Theistic evolution is very much a minority view among the scientific community, although it is held by some prominent scientists.

Religious experience

The apparent failure of the traditional arguments for the existence of God doesn't bother most religious believers. One reason for this is that belief in God is very rarely founded on such arguments. People do not read about the cosmological argument and go off and get baptised the next day. What does tend to ground religious belief is personal experience. The physicist Russell Stannard, echoing Jung, captured this when he said in an interview: 'I don't have to believe in God, I know that God exists – that is how I feel.' At the end of the day, all we have considered so far in this chapter is irrelevant to many with faith. What counts for them is the inner conviction that God exists, often based on a feeling that they have had some direct experience of God's existence.

These experiences may take many forms. They may be visions of saints or prophets. They may be no more than inner convictions. They may be a sense of God in nature. Rather than look at each type of experience individually, we will just talk about religious experience as one kind of thing which is characterised by any kind of personal conviction that God exists based on one's own private experience. (Public experience of miracles is discussed in the next section.)

The philosopher Alvin Plantinga has argued that it is quite right to take the evidence of such experiences as basic beliefs, beliefs which form the foundations for our other beliefs, but which themselves do not need to be justified by other beliefs. Just as we do not need to justify the belief that we exist and have experiences of objects and other people, so our experience of God's presence (if we have it) stands as basic and without need of justification.

It is easy to see why, for those who have such convictions, no further justification seems required. But there are several reasons for not just accepting the evidence of personal experience in this case.

First, many of the religious beliefs that are typically grounded in religious experience are very different from beliefs in things such as our own existence and objects that are grounded in ordinary experience. It is true that in both cases we cannot easily doubt that the experience is real. We cannot doubt that we seem to exist, we cannot doubt that objects seem to exist and the religious believer may not be able to doubt that God seems to exist. In each case, what is undoubtedly real is the experience. What can be doubted in each case, intellectually at least, is whether the experience corresponds to an independent reality. The arguments concerning the real existence of the self and the material world are many and complicated. But virtually everyone would agree that, even if we cannot adequately justify our conviction that we and the external world exist, we cannot dispense with the conviction that they do. People can, however, dispense with the conviction that God exists. In a recent survey, more than half the British population said that they didn't believe in God. The question wasn't asked, but it is clear that very few, if any, would have said they didn't believe in themselves or the external world. What this illustrates is that religious beliefs are dispensable in a way in which basic beliefs about self and world are not, so they are not basic in quite the same way. Therefore it is possible to argue that, because first-person experience is in general an unreliable basis for knowledge of the external word, it should not be used to justify beliefs which are not *indispensably basic*, even if people are absolutely convinced as to the veracity of their experiences.

Further, the beliefs which religious experiences claim to justify are disputable in a way in which other basic beliefs are not. For example, if you're sitting next to someone and they point and say 'there's a pink elephant' and you see it too, that is a reason to think the pink elephant is there. But if you can't see the elephant, the suspicion is that the other person is hallucinating or is making it up. Religious experiences are more like the latter experiences than the former. Someone can claim to be in the presence of God while the person next to them feels no such thing. That is to say, the belief created by the experience is not subject to independent confirmation in the way in which other basic experiences are. This is usually the hallmark of an experience which is not of something real.

The important thing to note here is that such experiences may be utterly convincing to the person having them. But we do not take the vividness of the experience to be evidence that the thing the experience is of really exists. We just accept that people's experiences can mislead them. In the same way, the non-believer will say that the conviction the believer has is no evidence that God actually exists and that they too should accept this.

But why should the religious believer doubt their own experiences? After all, it is not quite like the pink elephant. What they claim to experience isn't visible, for instance, so one might expect others not to be aware of it. And many religious believers share the same convictions. So there is some support from the experience of others.

The response to this is that religious experiences contradict one another. If religious experience were a reliable source of belief, then we would not find these contradictions. For instance, people use religious experiences to justify their beliefs in a variety of different Gods. People use it to justify a variety of different, conflicting actions. Some will say they felt God telling them not to work on the Sabbath, whereas others will say they felt God telling them to do the opposite. We should also remember that many criminals have reported that they were told what to do by God. The notorious 'Yorkshire Ripper', Peter Sutcliffe, sexually assaulted and killed several women because he heard God telling him to do so.

The point is that if religious experience were a reliable basis for belief, we would find that religious experiences produced the same beliefs time and time again. But what in fact seems to happen is that people have religious experiences and they interpret them or take them to justify whatever religious beliefs they already have or are dominant in their cultures. In this way, it seems that religious experiences are not a reliable foundation for religious belief.

To someone who has a religious belief, their own experience of what they take to be God often does seem to be enough to convince them of the veracity of their beliefs. The problem is that the question of whether something is true or false is separate from the question of how firmly one is convinced that it is true or false. One cannot use the firmness of one's convictions as evidence for the truth of that of which one is convinced.

In response to these points a religious believer might point out that the fact that religious experiences apparently conflict with one another is not in itself conclusive: false currency does not invalidate the genuine, even if it makes it more difficult to tell which is which. Also, believers will argue that there is in fact a common form and content to genuine religious experiences. As for the role of personal conviction, we might admit this to be a general problem, and not one specific to religious experience. My beliefs about everyday affairs may be equally without absolute justification – religious experience may therefore simply represent an extreme case of a general problem.

Miracles

There is one kind of religious experience which is not private but, at least in theory, public. Miracles have been reported in the literatures of all the great religions of the world. Do these miracles provide any evidence that God does indeed exist?

The general problem with miracles is our capacity to verify their occurrence. After all, we often seem to get reports of supposed miracles at second- or third-hand, appearing in ancient texts (the historical accuracy of which may be questioned), or in remote or inaccessible regions. Can it be a coincidence, the sceptic will ague, that miracles don't happen in Times Square or Piccadilly Circus, but only places where their veracity cannot be checked?

Such is the rarity of anything that even looks like being a genuine miracle that it became headline news for several days when a statue of an elephant in a Hindu temple in North London seemed to start absorbing milk offered up to it from spoons. Yet, the sceptic will again observe, it is the human desire to believe that is the key factor here. The fact that it was made of a porous stone and that much of the milk ended up on the floor below it did not stop people being amazed by the statue's 'drinking'.

The Roman Catholic Church also continues to record miracle healings at Lourdes. However, it is a fact that some people do get better for no apparent reason, especially if their mental attitude is positive. This suggests that if thousands of sick people passed through any spot in the world, believing it would help them, some would get better without any obvious reason. But at Lourdes, such a recovery is called a miracle.

The point is that, by scientific standards, there appears to be a lack of reliable evidence that miracles take or have taken place. What, then, is the philosopher to do? Dismiss the whole issue as superstitious nonsense? Against the sceptic we might argue that miracles are, by definition, rare occurrences. Let us therefore, for arguments sake, set our scepticism aside, and focus on the question of whether a miracle may count as evidence for the existence of God.

To answer this we need to consider what a miracle is. Many follow Hume in defining a miracle as a violation of the laws of nature. Some disagree with this and say that a miracle can be merely an extraordinary event or even an ordinary event with religious significance. A bus normally turns left on its route, but instead turns right, and thereby affects events that would otherwise have turned out differently (perhaps it allows someone to get to an important appointment, or causes a violent mugger to run off). There is no breach of natural law here, but if such an unusual occurrence proves significant then we might consider it miraculous. However, even if we accept that 'miracle' can be defined in this way, since such events can be dismissed as mere coincidence or luck, they can't really provide conclusive evidence for God. Therefore, let's follow Hume's definition, and consider a miracle to be an occurrence where a law of nature has to be breached.

Hume went on to argue that we can never have any good reason to suppose such miracles can occur. This is because all of experience confirms to us that natural laws are never breached. Therefore, whenever one seems to be breached, it is always more reasonable to assume that we have been tricked, or that there is another kind of unseen, natural cause in operation, or that what we thought was a law of nature is not, in fact, so.

For example, let's say you see a good illusionist, such as David Copperfield, make a huge truck seemingly disappear. That would seem to be a miracle. But you would be very gullible if you thought that Copperfield had actually broken the laws of nature. You would assume one of the three things set out above. One possibility is that this is a trick and he hasn't made the truck disappear at all. Another possibility is that he has made it disappear, but by some unseen cause, such as a hidden trap door. The third, most outlandish, possibility is that Copperfield has discovered a new law of nature which explains how objects can be made to disappear into thin air. The one thing you wouldn't think was that he had performed a miracle.

If this is what you would think when you saw someone make a truck vanish in front of your very eyes, why should you think anything different for other alleged miracles? It seems bizarre that we can see someone perform a very impressive trick, such as seeming to cut a person into two, and accept that it is just an illusion, but we can also see something relatively unimpressive, like a statue absorbing milk, and think this is a miracle. Hume's argument is that experience teaches us that we always have more reason to suppose that natural laws have not been breached than that they have. It is just gullible to think anything else.

A critic would point out that Hume seems to rule out miracles almost by definition: if they are supported by general and repeated experience, then they are simply evidence of unknown natural laws; rare, non-repeating occurrences seem to rule themselves out. But miracles are not law-like things – as Hume himself argues, they are tradition-ally the suspension or contravention of known laws. However, Hume's more general point – concerning the role of such reported occurrences in proof for the existence of God – seems correct. There is almost always a more likely explanation for such things. It is our potential knowledge of miracles which therefore seems problematic: even if they do occur, it would be almost impossible to prove them. Does this leave it as a matter of faith? With faith comes once again the possibility of self-delusion – and such a possibility will not appeal to the non-believer or even agnos-tic. It seems then that miracles, traditionally defined, can play no part in the objective proof for the existence of God, though – if they exist – they might play some role in the establishment of personal conviction.

God and morality

One reason why people think it is important that God exists is that without God, it might seem that morality is impossible. The existence of moral law implies the existence of a moral lawgiver. The only being in a position to issue such laws is God, so if God doesn't exist, then morality is not possible.

Some have even used this as an argument for God's existence. Given that there is such a thing as morality, and given that only God can be the source of it, God must exist. This argument's first premise is ques-tionable, since the fact that we do follow moral rules and believe there is a morality is no guarantee that morality exists independently of us. It could just be that when we think we are following real moral laws, we are merely following human conventions or laws established by us rather than God. So although it is unquestionably true that morality exists in some form, it is not obvious that this is morality in the sense of a set of laws laid down by divine authority.

The second premise of the argument is more interesting, for whether or not the argument from morality's existence to God's existence works, there is still an issue of whether or not the very possibility of morality somehow depends on God.

In fact, a very persuasive argument that morality does not depend on God was put forward over 2000 years ago by Plato, in a dialogue called *Euthyphro*. The argument is very simple and is based on the possible answers to a simple question: Does God choose what is good because it is good, or is what is good good because God chooses it? (Plato's question talked about gods rather than God, and holy rather than good, but the basic point is the same.)

Consider the second possibility. If the good is simply what God chooses, then it seems the distinction between good and bad is arbitrary. What would stop God deciding that murder is good and kindness is wrong, for example? If good and bad are arbitrary in this way, then they lose their moral force.

Surely, then, the first option must be correct. God's choice of good and bad is not arbitrary. It is not the fact that he chooses the good that makes it good, he chooses the good because it is good. But that means that good things are good independently of God. God's choosing does not make them good – they are good already. That means their goodness does not depend upon God.

But if good and bad do not depend on God, that means we do not need God for there to be good and bad. If God doesn't exist, therefore, good and bad still can. So there is no dependency between God and goodness. So the existence of morality does not prove the existence of God and the non-existence of God would not threaten morality.

This argument is considered by many to be decisive. Some have tried to reply to it. For example, it is argued that God *is* goodness, so the question set out in the *Euthyphro* Dilemma is misleading. God doesn't choose what is good, God just is good. But then we could still pose the same basic dilemma in a different form: is God good because goodness is just whatever God is, or is God good because goodness is embodied in God? In other words, would God be good whatever his nature – all-loving or all-hating – or is God good because what it means to be good is fully manifest in God? The answers lead to the same conclusion: if goodness is not arbitrary, God's goodness must reflect the nature of goodness itself, which means that the concept of goodness is divorceable from that of God.

Conclusion

The philosophy of religion is in some ways one of the most interesting areas in philosophy because it deals with big questions that trouble most of us at some time in our lives. However, as you will have seen, many of the attempted proofs of God are at best inconclusive. This is not a particularly controversial conclusion, for most philosophers would agree. Where then does this leave us? Must faith remain a purely private concern? This throws up interesting questions, which are arguably more interesting: What is the relationship between reason and faith? Can believers utilise a conception of God which is internally coherent, or fits with the scientific worldview? Arguably, philosophy syllabuses have given too much space to the problematic attempted proofs of God's existence and not enough to more interesting questions.

Summary

The philosophy of religion explores the rational justifications for religious **belief**. In Western philosophy, these debates centre on the existence or non-existence of a God who is **omnipotent, omnibenevolent** and **omniscient**. One problem with this conception of God is that it seems it cannot be all these things given that there is **evil** in the world. Attempts to explain how the traditional conception of God can be reconciled with the existence of this evil are known as **theodicies**. The most well known theodicy is the free will defence, which says we need evil in order to truly exercise our free will.

Many believe that **faith** can step in to provide justifications for religious belief when reason cannot. James, for example, thought we were entitled to allow our passional natures to determine whether we believe in God, because God's existence cannot be proved or disproved yet it is a real possibility, its significance is enormous and we have to choose to believe or not. **Pascal** argued that we should believe in God because we cannot know if God exists, but it is a safer bet to suppose that it does.

Some people believe that religious language is different to normal language. It should not always be understood literally, but nor is it merely metaphorical or poetic. On a Wittgensteinian view, you only really understand religious language if you live within a community of believers and learn how to use it.

The ontological argument for the existence of God attempts to show that God must exist because the concept of a non-existent God is self-contradictory. The main objection to this argument is that it jumps from truths about concepts to truths about real existence.

The cosmological argument attempts to show God must exist because the universe requires an uncaused first cause. Critics claim that we have no reason to suppose such a cause is necessary and even if it is, it is not clear why we should suppose this cause to be God.

The teleological argument states that God's existence is the best explanation for the high degree of order we see in the universe. Critics say that there is no evidence that this order is the product of rational design and that it can be explained though physics and **evolutionary theory**.

Some believe that religious experience is the main basis for religious belief. The problem with this as a justification for God's existence is that the fact that we feel something must be true is not usually considered a good reason for accepting that it is actually true. The public experience of **miracles** is not sufficient to justify belief in God because there is a lack of scientifically reliable evidence to suppose such miracles have occurred.

It has been argued that God is required for morality to exist, but because the concepts of God and goodness can be separated, this claim seems to be untenable.

Glossary

Basic belief   The idea, utilised by Alvin Plantinga in philosophy of religion, that certain beliefs, including belief in God, may be taken as foundational and self-justified if they form the basis of a coherent worldview.

Creationism   The view that the universe and all life in it was created by God; in its fundamentalist guise, the doctrine that the Earth and all life was created in its final form in seven days, as told in the book of Genesis.

Euthyphro Dilemma   Does God choose the good because it is good, or is the good good because God chooses it?

Faith   Belief or trust which is not justified by reason.

Genuine option   A potential belief which is a real possibility (live), which we must decide on (forced), and which is of great significance (momentous).

Immanent   With regard to God, existing within creation.

Miracle   Usually defined as something of religious significance which breaks the laws of nature, but sometimes as any event of religious significance.

Omnibenevolent   All-loving or all-good.

Omnipotent   All-powerful.

Omnipresent   Existing everywhere at all times.

Omniscient   All-knowing.

Pascal's Wager   That given God's existence cannot be proved or disproved, it is a safer bet to believe in God than it is not to.

Problem of evil   The problem of reconciling the existence of God as tradition-ally conceived with the existence of evil and suffering.

Theistic evolution   A position which attempts to combine a certain religious perspective with an interpretation of evolutionary theory.

Theodicy   An attempted solution to the problem of evil.

Transcendent   With regard to God, existing outside of creation.

Further reading

There are many introductions to the philosophy of religion. *The God of Philosophy* by Roy Jackson (Acumen) and *The Puzzle of God* by Peter Vardy (Fount) are two of the best for a straight, syllabus-based approach. Coming from a different angle, *Arguing for Atheism* by Robin Le Poidevin (Routledge) is also an introduction but one with a rare, explicit non-believer's stance.

One of the most interesting modern writers on religion is Don Cupitt and his *The Sea of Faith* (SCM Press) is a brave attempt to construct a non-superstitious conception of religion which does not see God as having a real existence. Alvin

Plantinga is also an interesting contemporary religious philosopher and *The Analytic Theist: An Alvin Plantinga Reader*, edited by James F. Sennett (Eerdmans William B. Publishing) is a good place to start.

A classic, fascinating and very readable text which attempts to defend religious belief against scientific reductionism is William James's *The Varieties of Religious Experience* (Penguin Classics).

5
Political Philosophy

What is political philosophy?

Politics is a subject which divides people in many ways. It divides people according to their convictions, with people on the right, for example, often suspicious, disdainful or even loathing of people on the left, and vice-versa. It also divides people according to their interest, with some people seeing politics as by far and away the most important part of life, while others can't even see the point of walking down the road to vote once every five years.

These different reactions can perhaps be understood. Politics is about the way in which our society is ordered by its institutions, its rulers and its laws. In this sense politics surrounds us and determines how we can live on a day-to-day basis. People disagree in their convictions because people can have very different ideas about what the best way to live is. But people can also disagree about the importance of politics, because some see the political background to our lives as something we can ignore while we get on with living, whereas others are highly aware of the impact the political system has on many areas of our lives.

Political philosophy is about how we justify the various forms of government, political ideologies, laws and other features of the state. It is not the study of how different regimes and systems actually work, but an investigation into what principles and arguments can be used to support or criticise general forms of political institution and belief. Political philosophy thus delves beneath the hurly-burly of much political debate and examines more enduring questions.

Political philosophy is of interest not only to philosophers, but to students of politics and citizens interested in civic life. To address all these potential readers will require us to look at a selection of topics which,

147

though perhaps not typical of many undergraduate syllabuses, nevertheless touch on the major issues of rights, freedom and the legitimacy of the law. But to start with, we will look at some of the most important political ideologies.

Liberalism

Liberalism may seem an odd place to start, especially for British readers, since in many Western countries the most powerful political parties describe themselves as socialist or conservative. In Britain, the Liberal Democrat Party and its successors have been in a distant third place for most of the last century, finally forming part of a coalition government in 2010 with 23 per cent of the vote.

But liberalism (with a small l) has been as successful in the West as the Liberal Democrat Party has been unsuccessful. The fact is that liberalism is the dominant political ideology of modern times and the socialist and conservative parties have accepted and worked within a broadly liberal framework. 'Liberal' may have become a term of abuse in some North American circles, but North America is still the liberal nation *par excellence*.

So what defines liberalism? Liberalism is based on the belief that individuals should have the freedom to live their lives as they see fit and that this freedom should be enjoyed by all members of society equally. In this way, the individual is of paramount importance. The interests of the state or the interests of a particular social class should never be used as a reason to restrict the freedom of individuals. In fact, the only justification for limiting the freedom of individuals is to safeguard the freedom of other individuals. As John Stuart Mill wrote in *On Liberty*: 'The only purpose for which power can be rightly exercised over any member of a civilised community, against his will, is to prevent harm to others.' People should not be forced to do things against their will for the common good. Nor should they be forced to do things for their own good if they don't want to. Nor should someone be forced to do something just because it is in the interests of a ruling class that they do it.

Understood in this way, we can see how Western democracy is essentially liberal in nature. The rights of the individual are often enshrined in constitutions and laws. Indeed, the idea of a liberal society is closely tied in people's minds to the idea of a democratic society. Countries where people are forced to work to further the state's interest or where slavery – official or unofficial – still exists are usually characterised as undemocratic or totalitarian. In fact, both these possibilities are compatible with democratically elected governments and a non-democratic government can institute a liberal regime. The trend, however, has been for more democratic societies to be more liberal also.

Liberalism is therefore a deeply entrenched feature of Western politics. But what is its justification? Several could be offered. One is that it is the ability to make autonomous, free choices for ourselves that is the most valuable characteristic humans have. It is what distinguishes us from other animals and gives our lives special value. Therefore, our political systems have to respect this faculty by allowing us to use it to the greatest degree possible. In this way, liberalism allows humans to flourish to their full potential, by maximising our capacity to enjoy freedom of choice.

A second cluster of arguments are based around the fallibility of human judgement and the plurality of human values. Arguments of this sort stress that no-one is able to say with any certainty that they know what the right way to live is. Further, it could be the case that human values are plural, which is to say that there is more than one way to live a good life. These two points, separately or combined, make a good case for saying that it is better to allow people, as far as is possible, to choose how to live their own lives than to impose a way of life on them. No-one else is in a position to decide what is best for other people, either because no-one has enough authority or because there is no one thing which is best for everyone anyway.

A third, more pragmatic, argument is just that society and individuals do much better if they live in a basically liberal society. It is no coincidence, it is argued, that liberal countries tend to be wealthier and more stable than their authoritarian counterparts.

Critics of liberalism often argue that it places too much stress on individual liberty. First, individuals may not be quite as free as we take them to be. Their so-called free choices are largely determined by their environments. For instance, the kind of free-market capitalism that tends to operate in liberal countries manipulates citizens to become voracious consumers, persuading them that they need to spend more and more to be happy. People are very much constrained by society and the liberal myth of the free, autonomous individual allows us to turn a blind eye to the many ways in which people are manipulated by corporate and government interests.

Second, individual liberty may well be a good, but liberals tend to overstate the importance of this good. We also need to be happy, to be able to live together in communities and to all enjoy a decent standard of living. Arguably, liberal societies sacrifice these goods for individual liberty. The stress on the individual erodes community life, weakening the bonds that tie society together. Inequality is tolerated as the price of freedom, which means millions live in poverty. Some would also argue that all this freedom is not making us happier. In fact, caught up in a consumerist free for all, we are often left unhappy because we cannot live up to the ideal of the perfect lifestyle sold to us by advertisers and the media.

These critiques of liberalism really call for a scaling down of the importance placed on individual liberty, not the end of liberalism altogether. Some critiques go even further. Religious fundamentalists sometimes argue that liberal societies are sinful, because they place more importance on individual liberty than God's law. In this way, liberal societies replace God with individual people, which is the height of human arrogance. Of course, one can only buy into this critique if one shares the fundamentalist convictions of those offering it, but it is worth at least being aware of this point of view, if only to understand the hostility Western liberalism faces in parts of the Islamic world in particular.

Socialism

Although liberalism is the dominant political ideology of the West, others have also made their mark. Socialism is one of the most important. Like liberalism, socialism is really a broad family of political ideologies rather than a single one. It has been advocated by many democratic parties in the West and is also an important part of the communism of Marx, Lenin and Mao.

Socialism is best understood as a critical response to capitalism. In a capitalist society, individuals or corporations own and control the various forms of production, such as industry, transport and services. These corporations compete with each other to create the most profit for themselves. But the actual work that is needed in these industries is done by paid employees. So the people who do the work are not the people who own the capital – the assets and the profits of the companies.

What is more, in order to make more money, corporations have to become more and more cost effective. If one company is making a product which sells for five dollars, for example, a company in competition has to produce a better or a cheaper product. If it doesn't, it will lose out to the other company and eventually go bust. One of the easiest ways to cut costs and hence make more profit is to pay its workers less. Obviously, companies are not always cutting the wages of their employees.

But it is the case that there is a constant pressure to keep wages as low as possible in order to maximise profit.

Socialism takes a look at this situation and declares it obviously unfair. Why should workers be paid as little as possible so that owners can earn as much as possible? Why should wealth be concentrated in the hands of the few owners and not spread to the hands of the masses who actually do the work? Surely, this is unjust?

The socialist answer is to ensure that the workers themselves control the means of production and that there is a fair distribution of profits among the whole workforce. If this happened on a company-by-company basis, there would still be a situation where some groups of workers would effectively have control over others, since the most successful companies would put a squeeze on the less successful ones. Perhaps for this reason, most socialists have argued that the state should take control of industry on behalf of all workers, thus ensuring a genuinely fair distribution of profits throughout the economy. A socialist society would thus ensure a fair society. As Marx put it, each would give according to their abilities and receive according to their needs.

It should also be noted that some associate radical socialism with dictatorships, largely because the Communist world was not (and is not where it still survives) democratic. But there is a long tradition of democratic socialism which utterly rejects this communist model.

The case for socialism is therefore largely a moral one. Socialism is fair, whereas its alternative is not. Does this mean we should all be socialists?

Arguments against socialism can be pragmatic or principled. Pragmatic arguments state that socialism may well be the ideal, but that in practice it just doesn't work. Any credible political philosophy has to start with the reality of human nature and the fact is that socialism runs counter to this. People do better whenever they strive as individuals for their own good. As a result, society does better when people are allowed to get on with it rather than have their affairs ordered by the state. This idea is put most forcibly by Adam Smith, who argued that when individuals each pursue their own interests, the interests of the whole are also served by what he called the 'invisible hand'. On this view, if we try and pursue the common good directly, we often fail. But if we pursue it indirectly, by each pursuing our own good, we find the goal is achieved.

Further, as Lord Acton said, power corrupts, and absolute power corrupts absolutely. Socialism requires a great deal of power to be placed in the hands of a few. Experience should have taught us that when this happens, people do not pursue the common good but look after themselves. Socialism thus faces a double disaster: those who have power have all the power and look after themselves. Meanwhile, the workers, who no longer see a link between the effort they put in and the wages they receive, lose the incentive to work hard.

These arguments are all pragmatic in that they are based on the idea that socialism, though a noble ideal, cannot succeed. There are also principled objections. These tend to be rooted in a vigorous defence of liberal individualism. It is of uttermost importance, it is argued, that people choose how to live their own lives. In a genuinely free society, if anyone wants to start a business and become a member of the owning classes, they can. If they would rather lead a quite life, work for an employer and draw a wage, they can. The socialist presents a caricature of society when she argues that people are divided up into owners (the bourgeoisie) and employees (the proletariat). In modern Western states, people can move between both classes, or even be a bit of both. For example, one can be an employee and yet own property. Further, many employees have more wealth than many owners. What's important is that people decide for themselves how to live rather than have their lives ordered by a too-powerful state that decides what is best for them.

Conservatism

Intellectual debates about political theory have tended to focus mainly around liberalism and socialism. Yet one of the most powerful political forces is conservatism. Conservatism is essentially about preserving the institutions and social structures each generation inherits. It is not against change completely, but it argues against wholesale change, preferring instead a gradual evolution of social and political structures. Its enemy is therefore radicalism of any sort, which attempts to bring about a root and branch reform of society in order to achieve a brighter tomorrow.

Conservatism has been justified in a variety of ways. For Edmund Burke (1729–1797), the basis of conservatism is that each generation is only a temporary custodian of society. Their duties lie not only to themselves, therefore, but also to other generations past and present. They should thus exercise caution before overturning their inheritance, which is the product of the cumulative wisdom of successive generations. There is something arrogant about any generation which thinks it alone has found the answers to society's ills and rejects all that has come before as outdated. They also have a duty to the next generations not to squander their inheritance, but to build upon it.

Apart from these arguments about responsibility, Burke also thought that continuity was essential for the smooth operation of society. If society changes too quickly, then by the time someone has been educated to be a good citizen, society has changed and they no longer know how to function in it. Hence, the preservation of existing structures, morals and institutions is a prerequisite for a harmonious society where everyone knows their place.

Conservatism can also be justified by a pessimistic view of human nature. Many conservatives think that human beings are essentially greedy, egotistic, self-serving and prone to error. Humans therefore need to be constrained by firm institutions and practices that keep their baser instincts in check. Traditional institutions are the best way of achieving this, since they provide order, certainty and continuity. It is foolish to think that we can do better by destroying the past and starting again because humans are neither wise nor benign enough to create moral and effective societies from scratch. Experiments in the Communist world provide evidence for this pessimistic credo.

The conservative philosophy is sometimes summed up in the principle that it is easier to destroy than to build. The present is the result of centuries of gradual evolution and we bring it down at our peril.

Critics of conservatism often point out that the institutions and practices that it aims to preserve often serve the interests of a narrow section of society. In Britain, for example, the second chamber of parliament still contains many people who are there simply because they inherited a title. Being born into the aristocracy gave these people an important role in the governance of the country. Conservatives who argue that we should not change the system are therefore supporting the interests of the aristocracy over those of wider society. Of course, the conservative will respond that the two are connected – preserving an institution like the House of Lords is not just for the benefit of the lords themselves, but for society as a whole. However, when in this, as in other cases, what is being directly preserved is the status of an elite, this defence can seem a little thin.

It can also be argued that conservatism can be used as a justification to preserve all sorts of terrible things. Slavery, for example, was defended on conservative grounds, as was the lack of votes for women. So it is evident that only the most hard-nosed of conservatives will refuse to admit society does need to change from time to time and sometimes such changes need to be quite radical. This means a credible conservatism might end up looking like little more than an urge to caution. Anything more may seem dangerously reactionary, resistant to any change in society, for good or for bad.

A final criticism is that conservatism fails to take account of the way in which the world as a whole is changing. Change for change's sake may be foolish, but the world is now so different to how it was even 20 years ago that to argue political institutions need not change very much could look like wishful thinking. Change is happening whether we like it or not and any political ideology which refuses to accommodate this is doomed to failure.

Anarchism

Liberalism, socialism and conservatism are the three main political ideologies of recent history. A radical alternative, which has never been put into practice for more than short periods, is anarchism – the absence of government.

Anarchists have an image of being violent rioters, punks or both. Anarchy is often used as a synonym for a lack of order or for chaos. The image is unfortunate because the most eloquent of anarchist writers have demonstrated an optimistic idealism rather than a dark nihilism. Anarchism means the end of government, but for many anarchist thinkers, this would not mark a descent into chaos but a new dawn where people would live in harmony together, governed not by rules but self-restraint.

The anarchist position is based upon a rejection of the legitimacy of any kind of government. This can come from a perspective close to that of liberalism. Each person should be considered an independent, autonomous agent, capable of making their own choices. Anything which diminishes that autonomy needs to be justified. But whereas the liberal believes that some government is required in order to protect individual freedoms, the anarchist thesis is that any power the state takes on diminishes the freedom of individuals. Why is this so? According to Mikhail Bakunin (1814–1876), the reason is that government, by its nature, is the seizure of power by a minority to govern over the majority. Government is only government if it has power over those it governs. And if it has that power, it sets itself up as superior to the governed. Therefore, government by its very nature involves a dynamic of oppression.

Interestingly, anarchism had one of its periodic flourishes during the Russian Revolution. The anarchist Makhnovists disagreed with the communist Bolsheviks about the necessity to set up a form of central state socialism. It was always the dream of communism that the strong state would be a temporary measure and that after a while, once the new order had been established the state would just wither away. The Makhnovists argued that this was pure fantasy, and that power, once granted, tends to be retained. The Makhnovists lost out, but as history showed, they were at least partly right in that the Communist Party maintained a strong grip on power in the USSR until its downfall in 1989.

The central plank of anarchist philosophy is therefore that one cannot cede power to any government without that power being misused. The only alternative is to work without government. This does not mean the collapse of society. On the contrary, society will be stronger because people will enter into entirely voluntary partnerships with each other. In the fashionable terminology of management consultants, social organisation will emerge from the bottom up, rather than being imposed from the top down. And, again in an echo of management consultancy, it is thought that such bottom-up arrangements will be more effective and durable.

A vital corollary of this is that anarchism would see private property abolished. The whole idea of private property only makes sense within a legal framework where property rights are guaranteed by the state. So if there is no state, there is no private property.

Anarchism can therefore be an extremely attractive prospect. But it faces difficulties, both practical and philosophical. Philosophically, the weakness of anarchism is that it is based on an extreme form of liberalism, where the freedom of the individual is more important than anything else. If we don't accept this basic premise, the intellectual case for anarchism weakens. If we accept, for example, that some things are more important than people not having their freedoms in anyway limited by state power, the strong anarchist objection to the state seems misguided. For instance, having to pay taxes may be a small price to pay for having good healthcare for all.

So it seems the case for anarchism must rest on its empirical claims about what actually is the most effective form of society. What we then need to judge is whether the anarchist is right in saying that the existence of the state will always lead to a situation where power is exercised by the few over the many and that this will be worse on balance than what would happen without the state. Most people think that this anarchist claim is highly implausible. Rather than co-operating happily together, most think that without the state, worse forms of oppression will arise. When the state goes, it is replaced with gangs and warlords.

Lawlessness will not reduce oppression, it will merely allow new forms of oppression to thrive, without any external checks.

Anarchists reply that we only think this because we have been conditioned to think that the state is necessary. What we need to do is to relearn how to live without it. This claim is hard to test but even if we try to be as optimistic as possible, the anarchist vision does seem utopian.

However, some political theorists have taken a leaf from the anarchists' book. Libertarian philosophers such as Robert Nozick (1938–2002) have agreed with the anarchists that any transfer of power from the individual to the state has to be justified and that the state has too much power at present. But they disagree that the state can be dispensed with altogether. More fundamentally, they see the right to retain the fruits of one's labour as central to human freedom and therefore at the very least property rights have to be protected by the state. Libertarians, therefore, argue not for an abolition of the state, but for a minimal state which does only what is strictly necessary to guarantee individual freedom. Libertarian arguments have been very important in academic political philosophy in the last quarter of the twentieth century and have also influenced the neo-liberal policies of conservative governments such as those of Ronald Reagan in the United States and Margaret Thatcher in the United Kingdom.

Freedom

We have talked so far about freedom in several contexts. Freedom is rather like mother and apple pie. Everyone's for it and no-one is against it. But people disagree about just what freedom is. Socialists argue that their ideal society has more freedom than a capitalist one, whereas capitalists look on the large role of the state in socialist countries as an affront to freedom. How can everyone seem to both agree and disagree about the same thing at the same time?

The seeming paradox is largely a result of an ambiguity in the meaning of 'freedom'. Isaiah Berlin (1909–1997) distinguished between negative and positive freedom. Negative freedom is freedom from outside interference. It is the freedom to go about one's business without any external forces limiting what one does. It is called negative freedom because it is essentially an absence of coercion.

Positive freedom, on the other hand, is the freedom to do things, to live the best kind of life one can and to fulfil one's potential. It is called positive freedom because it is about what one can do as a result of having that kind of freedom. It is about being empowered to achieve something, or to be given the means to do so.

Although both forms of freedom merit the name, they are very different kinds of things and are often in conflict. For example, consider a pure capitalist society, without government support to the worst off in society. Such a society could have plenty of negative freedom. You could do what you want and no-one will stop you going about your business, as long as you don't interfere with the freedoms of others. If you want to live by the riverbank fishing all your life, you can (as long as someone else doesn't own it). If you want to try and run a big business and get rich, you can. Such a society could have very few external constraints and so could be negative-freedom rich.

But what if you come from a poor family, or got ill and were unable to work as hard as other people? In such a situation, without any state to help you, you might find that you were unable to fulfil your potential. There would be many things you could, in other circumstances, do and achieve, but in a dog-eat-dog world, you just can't do them. Here, you are poor in positive freedom. There are no external constraints, but there is nothing to help you fulfil your potential and in the kind of society you're living in, without such help you are lost.

That's why in most Western societies we think the state should do more than just prevent people from interfering with each other. We should also help people to achieve their potential, by providing decent education, healthcare and housing, for instance. By doing this we can increase people's freedom to live the kind of life they choose without seriously diminishing their negative freedom. But there is some loss of negative freedom. At the very least, we need to tax income and profits to pay for the provision of these enabling services. This means interfering with the finances of individuals.

Isaiah Berlin cautioned, however, that positive freedom in particular was a concept that could be misused. In countries such as the old Soviet Union, governments interfered with people's negative freedom to an excessive degree in the name of positive freedom. Their claim was that in order for everyone to be free to fulfil their potential, strong state control of all areas of life was necessary. This was to misuse the word, for not only was it doubtful that the extreme form of government control exerted did significantly increase positive freedom, the price was too great a loss of negative freedom anyway.

Some libertarian philosophers would go further and say that it is a myth that positive and negative freedom have to be balanced. Rather, the best way to increase positive freedom is to increase negative freedom. In a society where the state intervenes very little, people are liberated to pursue their own interests in the knowledge that they will enjoy the full rewards. People who seem to need welfare and state benefits will actually find that their dependency is entirely learned and, freed from this unhealthy relationship with the state, they too will learn to stand on their own two feet with increased dignity. The very weakest in society will also be protected because humans are not nasty brutes and voluntary aid will ensure that no-one who needs help will lack it. In short, if the state steps back, people will be allowed to flourish and as a result, positive freedom will increase alongside negative freedom.

The libertarian position gained a lot of support in the wake of Nozick's powerful book, *Anarchy, State and Utopia* (1974). But many see the position as being unrealistic. Libertarians think life under the minimal state will be free and open, whereas critics think that life in such a world would be highly competitive, creating great differences between winners and losers. Those without capital, for example, will be unable to compete with the wealthy, who will inevitably own the majority of businesses and have access to the best education and healthcare, while the poor make do with the scraps that are made available by voluntary effort. In this way, libertarianism faces similar criticisms to those directed at anarchism. The ideal may sound fine, but critics doubt that things would actually turn out as the libertarian predicts.

Because the idea of freedom is so deeply entrenched in Western liberal politics, it is easy to forget that not everyone agrees that freedom is so important. In the United States, for example, the value of freedom is asserted as though it were the absolute good. When the United States goes to war, it is usual to hear that what is being defended is freedom.

But are we right to see freedom as of supreme importance? Many ethical theories place much value on other aspects of human life. Utilitarianism, for example, views the increasing of happiness and the diminishing of pain as being the main goals of ethics. If that is right, then we should not assume that maximising freedom is always the best way of achieving this. Certainly, many would agree that societies with a large degree of liberty for their citizens tend to flourish more than those where there is oppression. But this positive correlation may not hold under all circumstances. Increasing freedom may not always result in increases in other goods we value. It may even be the case that too much freedom has a bad effect. Implicit in the conservative philosophy, for instance, is the view that we need to have our behaviour checked by conventions and social rules to stop us descending into brutality. Many communitarian thinkers have also argued that we need the bonds, and with them the constraints, of community life in order to really flourish as individuals. Many of those who do not agree with the conservatives or the communitarians would nonetheless accept that it is too simplistic to say that freedom is the supreme good and it should be maximised at all cost.

Justice

Another word which, like freedom, everyone lays claim to is justice. No-one ever rallied popular support by claiming they wanted to promote injustice. But as with freedom, justice means different things to different people and in different contexts.

Justice appears as a concept in different spheres of political debate. As its name suggests, distributive justice is concerned with how society ensures a just distribution of goods and benefits. These goods not only include wealth, but access to services and benefits as well as political and legal institutions.

Retributive justice, on the other hand, is concerned with punishment. It is sometimes called legal justice, since it is the kind of justice meted out by the law courts. We will look at this form of justice in the section on punishment (below). Here, we will look only at distributive justice, bearing in mind that this term covers a wide range of goods, not just money.

Since at least Plato, many have agreed that justice is something like everyone receiving their due. A society is just if everyone gets what they deserve, unjust if they do not. The problem with this definition, however, is that it is extremely 'thin'. That is to say, it tells us what the broad nature of justice is, but it leaves wide open exactly what 'receiving one's due' adds up to. For instance, does everyone get what they deserve if we allow people to go out and create as much wealth for themselves as possible, or for everyone to get their fair share do we need to redistribute wealth in some way, taking taxes from the rich to help the poor?

One person who thought justice required the second of these options was Karl Marx (1818–1883). Marx argued that the only just way to distribute wealth was to take 'from each according to his abilities' and to give 'to each according to his needs'. To see why he thought this, we need to first look at how wealth is distributed in a capitalist society. Here, the amount of money one receives bears no relation to the amount of work one needs to put in. Someone can go and work in an office for 40 hours a week and receive, say, 200 dollars. But their work could create a thousand dollars for the owner of the company, who works no harder, and perhaps works even less than the office worker. The rewards of labour can thus be vastly disproportionate. To Marx, this is obviously unfair, since in effect this means that one person (the owner) is allowed to keep the wealth generated by another (the worker).

An improvement on this system would be if each person were to be paid the fair value of their labour. On this model, society is like a huge co-operative. Each person pays into society a certain amount of their labour and is allowed to withdraw from it the equivalent cash value. But even this system is not entirely fair. Some people are born stronger or cleverer than others. These people may be able to work more or better, not because they make more effort, but just because they have more natural ability. These people would receive higher rewards than others, but only because of their unearned natural abilities. Further, some people need more than others. Someone with a disability, for instance, often requires some extra assistance just so that they can enjoy a normal amount of mobility. But if everyone is paid according to how much they work, these people will not receive the extra they need.

So we end up with Marx's principle that the only fair way to distribute wealth is to give everyone what they need and ask of everyone only what they can do. This is fair, because everyone does what they can, so no-one is having an easier time of it than anyone else. Also, everyone gets what they need, so no-one suffers just because their needs are greater.

Some of the problems with this view have already been dealt with in the section on socialism: the alleged impracticality of the socialist programme and the way in which it requires an unacceptable denial of individual liberty are the two main recurring themes here. In addition to these criticisms, others focus more directly on the ideal of justice in Marx, which is linked very closely to that of economic equality. Implicit in the argument is the idea that justice will involve an equal distribution of wealth, weighted slightly to take account of differing needs. But must justice be so solely tied to equality of economic outcome in this way? Isn't it at least plausible to argue that justice requires allowing people to keep the extra wealth they create for themselves if they choose to work for it? Shouldn't we allow people to benefit from their natural abilities, even if that creates inequality? At the very least, this might have practical benefits, since people are more likely to use their natural abilities to their greatest extent if they will be able to receive rewards for doing so.

The relationship between justice and economic equality is a major issue in political philosophy. Many have followed Marx in arguing the strong equality of outcome view: that justice requires everyone getting the equivalent quantity of benefits. Others stress equality of opportunity: that everyone should be given the same access to wealth and other social benefits, but how much they actually end up getting should be down to a combination of work, talent and maybe even luck.

One of the most important developments in this debate in the last few decades came with the publication of John Rawls's *A Theory of Justice* in 1971. Rawls's difference principle confronts one of the major difficulties with Marxist and socialist conceptions of justice. This problem is that, while equality of outcome does seem to be desirable, pursuing equality of outcome at all costs seems to be disastrous. For reasons already explained, it seems that we need to allow individuals the freedom to create wealth for themselves – and with it inequality – in order to fully harness the range of abilities in the workforce. Limiting personal reward seems to be a recipe for economic stagnation which harms the interests of everyone.

Rawls's difference principle attempts to accommodate what is true in both the socialist goal of equality of outcome and its critique. The difference principle states:

> All social values – liberty and opportunity, income and wealth, and the bases of self-respect – are to be distributed equally unless an unequal distribution of any, or all, of these values is to everyone's advantage.
>
> (John Rawls, *A Theory Of Justice*)

The principle is simple. Equality is to be preferred, but not if the price of equality is that everyone is worse off. It is better to have some inequality and have everyone better off than total equality where everyone is worse off. Crucially, we should only tolerate as much inequality as is strictly necessary to improve conditions for all. The difference principle is not a green light to allow any amount of inequality.

The major problem with Rawls's principle is that in order to apply it, one needs to know exactly what the effects of different policies will be on general well-being and equality. In theory, this should be an empirical matter – something which should be worked out by economists, perhaps. But in practice it is very difficult to say exactly what the effects on equality and well-being different polices have, especially since the principle does not just apply to crude wealth, but all social values. Hence, we find people adopting the difference principle to justify a wide range of wildly different political ideologies. Socialists, conservatives and libertarians can all claim that their approach results in the minimum amount of inequality required to improve the lot of everyone. Deciding who is right, then, becomes a very difficult matter.

Rights

Along with freedom and justice, rights are something else which politicians of all stripes are keen to be seen to be defending. As with freedom, there are negative and positive rights. Negative rights are rights to non-interference. For example, the rights to free speech, freedom of association and free thought are all negative rights because in order to exercise them it is enough that no-one interfere with one's business. Positive rights, on the other hand, are rights to certain things, and for these rights to be maintained, it may be required that something be given or granted to someone. Rights to food, shelter and work are such positive rights.

Rights play an important part in contemporary political debate. Countries are sometimes refused recognition or access to trade if they do not guarantee basic human rights to their citizens. The United Nations Declaration of Human Rights is a document of paramount international importance, providing a benchmark against which regimes around the world are judged. There are also fierce debates about the number and scope of rights, with for example, 'pro-life' campaigners asserting the rights of the unborn child to life and the 'pro-choice' campaigners asserting the rights of the mother to choose what to do with her own body.

Rights are clearly important. But where do they come from? They are usually discussed as though they are somehow granted at birth to all human beings. On this conception, rights are 'natural'. We are born with them and to infringe them is to somehow breach a moral law of nature.

Many philosophers have found this conception of rights to be flawed. Rights just don't seem to be embedded in nature. Is a lion born with a right to hunt antelope? Does the antelope have any right not to be eaten by lions? These questions strike one as absurd, and considerations of this sort led Jeremy Bentham to declare that talk of natural rights is 'nonsense upon stilts'.

If rights aren't part of the fabric of nature, then they must therefore be a human construction. We are not born with rights. Rather, humans grant rights to other humans and sometimes also to other animals. Rights therefore need to be understood as legal rather than natural. They are legal in the sense that if they are not recognised by law, national or international, formal or common, they simply do not exist. We may well think something should be a right, but until it is legally recognised as such, it is not one. So, for instance, the right to join a trade union is a right which exists in some countries and doesn't exist in others. It is not that such a right exists everywhere, but just is not recognised; it simply does not exist *until* recognised.

This conception of rights as non-natural fails to satisfy some because it is thought that if rights are a human construction, they do not have the strong force we usually attribute to them. For example, the right to life is considered absolutely fundamental. But if rights are granted by humans, then it seems we have the power to decide this isn't a fundamental right after all. This seems to conflict with the very nature of rights as basic and inviolable.

In response, it can be argued that it is just wrong to think that moral concepts, such as the concept of rights, have to be non-human in origin to have any force. The force rights have depends not on their origin, but on our determination to uphold or trample over them. Take the right to free speech as an example. Whether this right is respected or not ultimately depends on the decisions human beings make. These decisions have to be made whether the right is natural or non-natural. If rights were natural, that would give them no special protection.

However, what we think rights are based on might make a difference. Some would argue that rights are based on considerations of what is inviolable about persons. For instance, we may think that fundamental to our morality is the idea of the individual as a free, rational agent able to make decisions for herself and live her life as she wishes. We use the language of rights to make plain what this conception of a person entails. Because we value human life in this way, we say humans have a right to life, free thought, free movement, free speech and so on. In this way, rights embody what is non-negotiable and they would seem to have a strong, perhaps inviolable nature.

However, others, such as Bentham, think that rights are only granted because there are benefits in doing so. For example, a utilitarian such as Bentham would argue that the highest good is to increase happiness and decrease misery. As a means of achieving this, it may be useful to grant people certain rights. These rights offer basic guarantees, in law, which provide the secure and stable environment for people to go about their business in a way conducive to increasing the general happiness. However, it should be clear that on this conception of rights, it is always conceivable that the rights might be revoked. Rights serve a secondary role here, acting in the service of the primary goal of increasing happiness. If, therefore, circumstances arose where it would serve the general happiness if rights were removed, there would be no reason for the utilitarian to hold on to them. Rights on this conception do not represent anything fundamental or inviolable. They are merely a mechanism used to achieve a higher goal.

Many would argue that this utilitarian conception does violence to the very concept of a right. Surely the whole point about a right is that it is something that cannot be taken away. But if rights are only justified by their usefulness, and this usefulness is not guaranteed to be permanent, rights become removable and, arguably, therefore not rights at all.

In defence of the utilitarian conception of rights, it is hard to see how many of the rights people now try and claim can be genuine if rights have to be inviolable in some way. For example, many would argue that in a rich, developed nation people have a right to decent housing. It is virtually impossible to make sense of this right if rights are inviolable. Surely one can only have a right to what is possible and whether it is possible to have a decent home depends on when and where you are living, not on whether you are a human being or not. If a nation goes bankrupt, how can it maintain the right to provide decent housing for all? Yet if rights are inviolable and the right to decent housing is a genuine right, then it seems we have to accept that such a country would be breaching the rights of its citizens if it failed to uphold their right to decent housing.

There are two ways out of this dilemma. One is to say that many of these rights people claim are not genuine rights at all. Many, if not all, positive rights would, on this conception, be seen as bogus rights. The other way out is to say that rights are non-natural and violable. There is nothing wrong with saying that everyone has a right to decent housing, as long as we accept that this right is something granted by society on the basis of what it is currently possible for that society to do.

In conclusion, conceptions of rights can be weak or strong, broad or narrow. Weak conceptions of rights see them as secondary, serving a greater good and not of independent value in themselves. Such conceptions of rights allow in a broad range of rights. Strong conceptions see rights as inviolable, perhaps even natural. Such conceptions of rights tend to allow a narrower range of rights as genuine.

Tolerance

Linked to the question of rights is the notion of tolerance. If we have the right to freedom of speech, for example, then others should be tolerant of what we say so that we do not live in fear of reprisal or discrimination. We might say then that the rights and freedoms embodied in a democratic society *imply* tolerance.

But why be tolerant in the first place? As mentioned earlier in our discussion of non-cognitivism in moral philosophy, to point out that people hold different values and opinions does not itself force us to be tolerant. Even if there is no objective means of deciding between such different values, the adoption of tolerance is itself an expression of value. So, tolerance is not forced upon us, but we may argue for it on the basis that it is a good thing or serves useful purposes. But is this true? Surely there must be things that we cannot tolerate – even if that is only *intolerance*. Perhaps also there are times and places where tolerance is unwise. Must we be always tolerant, or may we be selectively so?

Before we answer these questions, we need to get a clearer idea as to what tolerance involves. This in itself is a controversial question, but there are some common features on which philosophers mostly agree. Firstly, tolerance implies an attitude of active disapproval. We cannot be said to be tolerant of things that we actually like, or those things which we are indifferent to. Secondly, we cannot be tolerant of things that we are powerless to change. For instance, I might withstand torture, but I do not tolerate it. Tolerance therefore fundamentally must involve a different attitude or practice that we disapprove of, and that we are in a position to change, but choose not to. Tolerance is a choice.

But what would lead us to make this choice? What motivates our tolerance? We have already seen the link between rights and toleration. For everyone to possess rights and freedoms, the liberty to perform certain actions and hold certain beliefs should be mutually respected. A Christian might inwardly object to her neighbour mowing his lawn on a Sunday (thus breaking the commandment to respect the Sabbath). But the neighbour is not a Christian, and it is his free choice to mow his lawn instead of going to church. So, the Christian doesn't interfere in her neighbour's lawn mowing and he doesn't interfere in her religious observances. One central motive for tolerance is therefore that it leads to social harmony. Most modern societies are increasingly multicultural, containing many belief and value systems, and somehow we must all get along. Tolerance, then, is an essential attitude that enables this to happen.

This approach is, of course, essentially a *liberal* one. The earlier discussion of John Stuart Mill's liberalism is therefore relevant here. You may recall that Mill's primary arguments for freedom were that human beings are fundamentally autonomous (it is in our nature to make our own choices), we are fallible (our views may be mistaken) and that personal freedom is a vital ingredient in the flourishing of society. All these are good reasons to respect individual freedom and to impose the absolute minimum of external restraint. Of course, these are also good arguments for toleration. But there are other reasons to be tolerant.

In his essay on religious tolerance, John Locke largely prefigures Mill's position. For instance, he argues that, as earthly mortals, we are fallible judges of divine truth. However, he also points out that we cannot enforce religious conformity, and the attempt to do so would lead to greater social upheaval. Locke's position may be seen as being in line with certain traditional Christian attitudes. Christian pacifism, for instance, is usually taken to spring from the attitude that the means defeat the ends: to win by violence is to lose, because the aim is to spread peace and love. Similarly, then, you cannot force a change of heart upon someone, and coercion can play no part in religious conversion. Another motive for tolerance can therefore be that people must be allowed to make their own mistakes (something Mill also argues for), and like Mill, Locke takes the liberal view that government should have minimal involvement in the private affairs of its subjects – including their religious views.

But some would object here that such an attitude cannot be true tolerance. If you say to yourself, 'I disagree with his opinion, but he must find out for himself that he is wrong', then you are not according his different opinion any genuine value, for you still think that it's wrong and want it changed. Some will therefore argue that there is a paradox here: we are tolerant of beliefs in that we do not seek to change them; but we are *intolerant* of them in the sense that we reject them. Full tolerance, the objection implies, requires me to accept the validity of your differences with me. However, it is not clear why tolerance requires us to embrace beliefs we disagree with in this way. Indeed, it has been argued that this is a fundamental mistake which has led to excessively permissive attitudes. Because people believe that tolerance requires us not to judge others, we are obliged to embrace a relativism by which all values are considered equal.

There is perhaps another way in which we might not *disapprove* of others' choices, but merely admit that they would not be ours. This would be a form of *pluralism*, that is, the view that there are multiple possible forms of belief or action that are acceptable. This is different from arguing that we *don't know* what the correct choice is (so we must be tolerant), *for it assumes an equality between choices because there is no single correct choice*. However, a pluralist need not be a relativist (someone who rejects the idea that there are any universal truths). We might simply be pluralist in certain regards, or certain areas of life. You like jam, I like marmalade, but neither choice is 'correct'; they're both good. Pluralism simply extends this approach to certain areas of lifestyle choice and belief.

However, pluralism and religious tolerance are largely at odds. Occasionally, certain religious traditions will propose that other paths to truth are possible (for instance, Sufism or Quakerism), but that there is still a kernel of religious truth that is taken to hold all these divergent beliefs together. However, religion is rarely this flexible, and is often itself representative of intolerance, especially where religious teachings are taken as unquestionable, fundamental truths (fundamentalism). Believers of this type will therefore argue that tolerance is an overrated virtue, and that there should be strict limits as to what are acceptable forms of thought and behaviour. Without such limits, it is argued, we open society to moral and spiritual decline, for too much freedom and self-governance may lead many astray into making wrong choices. Tolerance is therefore of lower value than truth.

Of course, a concern with the limits of tolerance may also be a secular one. Many think, for instance, that racism or sexism should not be tolerated because these attitudes contravene the basic right to be treated fairly and equally. At the very least, we might argue, we should not tolerate intolerance. Well, should we?

We may argue that to reject intolerance is itself to go against the principles of tolerance (another example of the so-called *paradox of tolerance*). We may again draw a parallel using pacifism: if violence is itself the thing to be rejected, then aren't we committed to *always* avoid it? And yet, it is arguably legitimate to use violence to resist attack (in self-defence) or to protect the innocent. In other words, certain values are not absolute, but exist in a hierarchy. The protection of life may therefore rate higher than the concern not to harm. As for pacifism, so for tolerance. If a racist group were to promote their views in such a way that it endangered lives, then we might be justified in censoring or prosecuting them. But we might view this not so much as an act of intolerance, but as the *protection* of tolerance. There is obviously a complex debate to be had here, for there is a judgement call to be made regarding at what point it is legitimate to protect others from intolerance. However, the point is that there need be no paradox involved as long as we do not treat tolerance as an absolute principle.

In conclusion, we can see that, whilst toleration is an increasingly vital topic for modern society, it can be interpreted in different ways: as an essential way to ensure social peace, as an admission of human fallibility, as part of a religious or Christian duty, or as a consequence of pluralism. These different approaches therefore themselves arise from different philosophical and religious perspectives, so resolving the issue once again takes us into deeper waters.

The justification of the state and its authority

We have so far talked about different political ideologies and some of the key values which we expect to find in any political system. What we haven't yet considered is a more fundamental question: what justifies the state's existence, power and authority at all?

We are so accustomed to the existence of the state that it can be an odd experience to stand back and look at just what states do. They control vast areas of our lives, regulating them, taxing them, ordering them. States control our movements between countries, they run our education and health systems, they take around half of everything we earn in tax, they fight wars on our behalf. Yet many of us go from cradle to grave without seriously questioning their right to do these things.

There are questions about how much power a state should have, but to answer these it is best to start with the more fundamental question of what gives the state any authority at all. If we can decide on what basis the state should be granted authority, the extent of this authority should follow.

Thomas Hobbes (1588–1679) offered a simple reason for why the state should exist – without it, life would be 'solitary, poor, nasty, brutish, and short'. Hobbes took a dim view of human nature, seeing mankind as greedy, violent, competitive and vainglorious. We need a state to provide a stable structure to prevent a war of all against all.

On this view, the state is justified because of the benefits we gain from its existence. Bentham, though not sharing Hobbes's profound pessimism about human nature, agreed that the state is justified on the grounds of its usefulness. In his utilitarian view, we should always try and maximise happiness and diminish suffering. This goal can be achieved more efficiently if there is a state than if there is anarchy.

Hobbes and Bentham both offer an almost common-sense justification of the state: we may not like all it does, but we would much rather have it than be without it. But the answer sketched so far leaves many things unresolved. For instance, we may agree that we need a state, but how much authority and power need it have? Is the role of the state minimal – to stop us descending into violent anarchy, as Hobbes suggested – or does it have a wider role, acting in any area of life where its intervention produces a social benefit, as Bentham suggests?

A second question concerns the legitimacy of individual governments. It may be true that we need a state, but that does not provide any particular government with the legitimacy it needs to govern. For example, it is no good a harsh dictator saying that he has the right to rule because someone's got to do it. The point is that a different form of government would do the job better. Even if the dictator was doing the best job possible, we might still think that the dictatorship lacked legitimacy if it did not enjoy popular support. Despite what Bentham says, more seems required for a government to have legitimacy than the fact that the government's existence benefits us.

What we need, then, is not just an account of why states are necessary, but some kind of account of how any particular government is justified in exercising power over its citizens. One way of doing this is by means of the idea of the social contract.

Social contract theories appear in various forms in the history of political philosophy, but most famously in Rousseau's *The Social Contract* (1762). Contrary to Hobbes, Rousseau thought that life in the state of nature was something of a lost Eden, where people enjoyed complete freedom and lived together in harmony. The noble savage lived well. But humanity has become more developed and more complex, and there is now no turning back to a time of lost innocence. In order for people to flourish now, we have to trade in some of our freedom in return for the stability and security offered by the state. Where once each individual was sovereign over herself, now individuals pool sovereignty, handing it over to the 'general will'. Our deal is that we cede personal sovereignty to the state on condition that everyone else does, to eliminate the need for conflict and to guarantee that we are all on an equal footing.

The social contract is, of course, a fiction in that no-one literally signs over their sovereignty. The contract is tacit rather than explicit. But that is not to say the deal is not real. If the state abuses its power, it breaches the contract, and individuals have the right to fight against it. If an individual breaks their contract by acting outside of the law, the state has the right to withhold its privileges from her. The theory also has the advantage of allowing for varieties of political structure. Just as long as the contract is accepted by both sides, any form of government will do, from democracy to monarchy. This means the theory does not privilege a particular form of government preferred by Western nations.

One problem with social contract theories is that they are based on a metaphor that can break down. For example, what if I want to cancel my contract? I just don't seem to be able to do this. One cannot opt out of society. So if the state does have power by means of a contract, it seems to be a contract I have no choice but to sign. But a contract signed without free consent is not a contract at all.

Similar thoughts led Hume to reject contract theories. He thought that the idea that consent, implicit or explicit, lies behind the legitimacy of the state was absurd. Someone born in a country, only able to speak its language and without riches, for example, has no choice but to live there. The idea that a person consents to live under the rule of that nation by their tacitly agreeing to its terms is a myth. Like Hobbes, Hume thought the legitimacy of the state boiled down to the fact that we cannot live without it.

Laws and law-breaking

The search for a fundamental justification for the state's existence perhaps has no better answer than this. It still leaves open the question of what form of government is best, be it democracy, monarchy, dictatorship or oligarchy. It also leaves open the question of what kinds of laws the state should be allowed to enforce and what our obligations are to follow them.

The range of laws a state should be allowed to pass follows more or less directly from considerations of political ideology. Liberals usually follow Mill's principle that the state is only permitted to pass laws restricting the freedom of individuals to prevent harm to others. For socialists, the state needs to pass whatever laws necessary to ensure that the workers themselves control the means of production. For conservatives, laws should be passed which do not greatly extend nor diminish the role of the state nor radically change the nature of society (which is why Margaret Thatcher's Conservative government in Britain was not typically conservative at all). Libertarians would want there to be as few laws as are necessary for society to function in an orderly way.

Whatever one thinks about the laws of a country and whether they are the best ones, there is always the question of how far one is justified in breaking them. In the Middle Ages, Aquinas, echoing a view which has been expressed throughout history, said that we have no duty to obey unjust laws. Indeed, he went so far as to say it is not permissible to obey a law if it contradicts God's law. Whether or not one believes in such a thing as God's law, most people would agree that it is more important to be moral than to follow the law. We admire people who refused to follow orders in Nazi Germany, even if it did mean breaking the law. And none of us likes to think that we would follow a law we believed to be deeply wrong. So it seems natural to believe that breaking laws – civil disobedience – is sometimes justified.

Yet at the same time, the whole point about the law is that it applies to everyone. If people simply followed their consciences and only obeyed the laws they agreed with, the law would cease to function as law. And without the rule of law – the law applying to everyone equally and fairly – society ceases to function. So if we accept the need for a state, and with it the need for laws, we have to accept that we may sometimes have to follow laws we disagree with.

Here, we have two contrasting views, neither of which seems quite right. It seems wrong to say that we should only follow laws we agree with, yet it also seems wrong to say we should always obey the law. To accommodate the reality of both these wrongs, we need to determine when it is permissible to break the law, given that we cannot say either that it is always or never right to do so.

John Rawls suggests there are three conditions which must hold for civil disobedience to be justified. The first is that the law being objected to is a substantial and clear injustice. We cannot permit people to break the law to protest against any law they think is wrong. In order to maintain the rule of law, civil disobedience needs to be reserved for protests against serious injustices only. Second, civil disobedience should only take place when legal avenues have been exhausted or where it is evident that there are no legal means of remedying the unjust law. This stress on following legal routes whenever possible again ensures that the general rule of law is upheld. Rawls's third condition is roughly that the act of disobedience must not undermine society so as to cause more harm than obeying the unjust law would. The idea here is that civil disobedience is only justified if the result is a fairer and more just society. So one needs to be careful that the net result of any protest will achieve this.

Rawls, following Martin Luther King, argued that civil disobedience must be a public act. Secretly not paying your taxes does not count, because that does not have the goal of ending an injustice – it simply has the aim of you personally avoiding an alleged injustice. Further, by making the protest public and facing up to the legal consequences of breaking the existing law, you uphold the general principle of the rule of law. This is essential if the protest is to be seen as a genuine attempt at reform, rather than an overthrow of the whole system. Protests should also be proportionate. For example, it would be wrong to use violence as part of one's protest if one's aims could be achieved by peaceful means.

Rawls's principles would satisfy many who are more or less happy with the system they live in and wish to reform it from within. But those who see the societies they live in as being more radically corrupt may find his arguments weak. Anyone convinced, for example, that a class war is necessary to overturn the capitalist exploitation of the workers is unlikely to think that peaceful protest over individual unjust laws is a sufficient form of protest. If the whole system is corrupt, then the whole system needs overturning. Rawls's principles only seem to apply to situations where the system as a whole is basically acceptable.

Justifications for punishment

The state does not just pass laws, it also punishes those who break them. But what are the justifications for punishment? There are essentially four: retribution, deterrence, protection and rehabilitation.

Retribution is basically revenge. Punishment is justified on these grounds because injured parties have the right to 'get their own back' on those who harmed them. There are many reasons why we might want to strike back when people wrong us, including the desire to stop that person doing wrong again or to send a signal to others that such behaviour will not be tolerated. But retribution is not justified on these other grounds. It is justified purely on the grounds that we have a right to harm those who harm us.

On the one hand, retribution seems vital to common-sense notions of justice. It just strikes us as wrong that someone can cause harm and not have to face up to any kind of punishment for it. But it can equally seem cold and barbaric to insist on retribution if no good is achieved by it. What is the point of punishing someone purely for the sake of revenge if it doesn't stop other harms occurring? For this reason, many are unpersuaded that retribution is a sufficient reason for punishment.

Deterrence is often given as another justification. We need to punish wrongdoers in order to deter other people from doing similar wrongs. If people are put in prison for robbing banks, that will make anyone else considering robbing a bank think twice. But if people were not punished for robbing banks, we would surely see banks being robbed all the time.

The deterrence argument faces some difficulties. First, it is not clear how much sentences affect the deterrent. For example, many people argue that we need the death penalty (capital punishment) for murderers on grounds of deterrence. But the evidence seems to suggest that what deters criminals is the thought that they will get caught rather than the exact nature of the sentence they would face. So although we need punishment in general as a deterrent, the nature of that punishment still needs to be decided.

A more serious problem is that the deterrence argument justifies punishment on the grounds of the crimes it will stop. But, of course, the punishment is given to the person who has already committed a crime. So the criminal is being punished, not for what they have done, but in order to stop other people doing the same. This seems unsatisfactory, because surely punishment needs to be for the wrongdoing itself, not some other purpose.

One way around this could be to combine the deterrence and retribution arguments. Retribution seems to be an exercise in justice, but if it leads to no good consequences, it seems futile. The deterrence aspect provides that missing benefit. On this view, punishment is retribution rightly taken because it will produce a benefit, which is the deterrence of future crimes.

A third justification for punishment is to protect the public. If someone is a killer, they need to be kept locked up in order to protect others. This justification follows the classic liberal position that someone's liberty may be curtailed in order to prevent harm to others. Although there seems to be little to object to here, it does need to be born in mind that many instances of punishment could not be justified in this way. Most murders, for instance, are not committed by people eager to kill again, but are one-off acts by people driven to desperate hatred against a particular individual. There is also the problem that prison tends to make people more criminally minded than when they were first put away. Prisons are almost crime schools. So if we want to protect ourselves, it seems making a lot of people who have done something wrong live in close proximity to other wrongdoers, so they can become even more imbued in the criminal life, is a pretty poor way of doing so. Protection is thus a perfectly good justification for punishment, but not necessarily of the extent and manner of actual punishment today.

A final justification of punishment is for the rehabilitation of the criminal. We can't undo what the criminal has done, but we can reform the criminal and ensure that they go on to become decent members of the community. This view also faces difficulties. First, as with the protection argument, not all criminals need to be reformed. Many committed their crimes under special circumstances and are no more likely to repeat their offence than anyone else. Also, if the aim of punishment is to reform, then aren't we more justified in punishing people who haven't yet offended, but have all the characteristics of a potential offender, than we are in punishing someone who did wrong in a moment of weakness? This seems unacceptable because we think we should only punish those who have actually done wrong. But if reform is the justification of punishment, why should it be limited in this way?

As with deterrence, we could perhaps get around this by combining the justification with the retribution argument. Punishment could be justified as retribution properly taken because of the positive end result of reform of the criminal.

It is likely that any credible theory of punishment would draw on arguments for retribution, deterrence, protection and rehabilitation. It is not to be expected that one argument alone could justify all forms of punishment. It also seems likely that any proper defence of punishment will lead to conclusions that conflict with our current penal practices. It is one thing to justify punishment, quite another to justify current policy on punishment.

Conclusion

The main questions of political philosophy overlap and inform each other in many ways. In order to maintain a consistent position it seems necessary to fix upon some basic principles. This is why issues of political ideology are so important and so divisive. If one is a liberal, for example, this will affect quite directly the ways in which one sees the proper scope and power of the state, the role of punishment and the proper use of concepts like freedom, rights and equality. A socialist's view of all these issues will also be informed by their basic socialist commitments, but they will be led to often very different answers.

At the same time, faith in the power of ideology is at an all-time low. Most people now seem to think we need to be less ideological. In Western politics we hear a lot about pragmatism, about doing 'what works', unhindered by ideological constraints. Political philosophy can perhaps serve as a caution that this kind of thinking can only go so far. We cannot untie questions of basic ideology from questions of economic justice, freedom and state authority. If we seem to be able to do this, it can only be because our fundamental ideology (a form of liberalism) is so embedded in our culture that we hardly notice it is there.

It is very important we do not forget it is there. We need to constantly subject our ideological commitments to rational scrutiny to make sure we do not fall into error. What is more, we cannot begin to understand the conflicts in worldviews between fundamentalist religions of all kinds and Western liberal democracy unless we recognise the fact that the ideology we accept is not accepted by all. To do that effectively we need to see clearly what our ideology is and how it differs from those of its critics. Political philosophy can help in this because it analyses and lays bare the ideas, arguments and concepts that form these ideologies. For that alone, the subject is well worth our attention.

Summary

Political philosophy is concerned with issues such as how we justify the existence of a state, what form and powers a state should have and what principles governments should follow.

The dominant political ideology in the West is **liberalism**, which stresses the rights of individuals to choose for themselves how to live their lives. Liberalism is based in the idea that our freedom to choose is an important part of what gives human life value, that there are many values one can live by, and that no-one has the knowledge or right to choose how everyone else should live. Critics claim liberals place too high an importance on human freedom as compared to happiness, welfare and solidarity.

Socialism is a reaction against the tendency of **capitalist** societies to concentrate wealth in the hands of the owners and away from the workers who actually produce the wealth. Socialists claim a fairer society is one where the workers own the means of production and enjoy a fair share of the wealth created. Critics claim that socialism is idealistic because people will always prefer to look after themselves more than society as a whole. They also say that socialism requires taking away too much liberty from individuals.

Conservatives are against wholesale radical change and believe it is important to preserve and maintain existing structures of society in order to safeguard our inheritance and allow for society to develop in a gradual and manageable way. Critics claim **conservatism** preserves the privileges of elites, can preserve unjust practices, and fails to accommodate the fact that the world is now changing faster than ever.

Anarchists are opposed to any form of government and private property on the basis that no-one has the right to have **power** over others. Anarchists have an optimistic view of human nature and believe that without government, co-operation will ensure a stable and happy society. Critics claim **anarchism** is utopian, although **libertarians** agree with it to a certain extent, in that they believe the role of the state should be absolutely minimal.

An important concept in politics is freedom. Freedom can be positive – the freedom to do something or to fulfil one's potential – or negative – freedom from outside interference. Both forms of freedom are desirable, but they may sometimes be in conflict with each other.

Distributive justice is everyone getting their fair share of society's goods. Many believe that a fair share is an equal share, of either actual outcomes or opportunities to obtain these outcomes. Rawls has argued that inequality is just only if the existence of that inequality makes everyone better off than they would be if things were more equal.

Rights can be negative (rights of non-interference) or positive (rights of access to services or goods). Some believe rights are natural, others that they are non-natural but inviolable, and others that they are only used by us as a means to achieve other goods and have no real existence or value independently of these purposes.

Tolerance may be seen to spring from the right to freedom of speech and **legitimate** action and is linked to liberalism. Tolerance is a value which is often associated with **pluralism** – the view that there is more than one legitimate way to live. But tolerance is not a uniquely pluralist value. It is often argued that true toleration is only of things we actively disagree with, and are not powerless to change. Others argue that the fact that I disapprove of something implies intolerance, not tolerance. These critics argue that we need in some sense to embrace the values of others, not just put up with them.

The existence of the state has been justified in several ways. One is that we need the state to prevent society from descending into chaos. Another is that the state is legitimised by an implicit **contract** between the citizen and the state whereby citizens hand over their individual sovereignty to the state in return for its protection.

The right to break the law if a law is unjust is upheld by most. However, for such **civil disobedience** to be justified, it must meet several conditions. Rawls has argued that these are that the law being objected to is a clear and major injustice, that all legal avenues have been exhausted and that the overall effect of the protest is a more just society.

States punish law-breakers to deter other people from breaking the law, to punish law breakers themselves, to reform criminals or to protect the public. The extent to which any of these provide a satisfactory justification for punishment is much contested.

Glossary

Anarchy Social organization that comes from the 'bottom up', without state control or central leadership, where there is no private property.

Authority A state or government has the authority to act on behalf of its citizens when it has a legitimate justification to exercise that power.

Autonomy The capacity an individual has to make free choices for themselves.

Capital Wealth, either in money or assets.

Capitalism The system whereby capital is owned by whichever private individuals are most efficient at generating and keeping it.

Civil disobedience Breaking the law in order to protest about a law which one feels to be unjust.

Communism A form of socialism where the state has ownership of the means and output of production.

Conservatism The belief that social institutions should be respected and preserved, and that any change should be gradual.

Distributive justice Concerning the fair distribution of goods and benefits within society.

Legitimacy An action is legitimate if it is exercised in accordance with legal or moral law.

Liberalism The view that values individual freedom, autonomy and equality of opportunity above all else.

Libertarianism The view that the role of the state should be minimal to allow as much freedom to individuals as possible.

Pluralism The view that there is more than one right way to live, and these ways may be incompatible.

Power Power is an ability to force one's will on others, whether or not one has the legitimate authority to do so.

Retributive justice Legal punishment for criminal behaviour.

Social contract An implied agreement between the state and the populace, whereby the people hand over certain freedoms and agree to certain codes of conduct in exchange for protection and security.

Socialism The view that the state should organize society, and regulate its institutions so as to preserve social equality and justice.

Further reading

Some classic and accessible texts in political philosophy include Plato's *Republic*, John Locke's *Two Treatises of Government*, Rousseau's *The Social Contract*, Mill's *On Liberty* and Marx and Engel's *The Communist Manifesto*. Mill and Plato are discussed in the companion volume, *Key Texts*.

Perhaps the two most important contemporary works of political philosophy are John Rawls's *A Theory of Justice* (Oxford University Press), which is now a classic liberal text, and Robert Nozick's *Anarchy, State and Utopia* (Blackwell), which heralded an era of great popularity for libertarianism. Roger Scruton's *The Meaning of Conservatism* (Palgrave) is pretty self-explanatory, while G. A. Cohen continues to write passionately on socialism. His *If You're an Egalitarian, How Come You're So Rich?* (Harvard University Press) is good value just for the title.

Political Thought, edited by Michael Rosen and Jonathan Wolff (Oxford University Press) is a superb reader and if you were only to buy one more book on political philosophy, this should probably be it. If it's going to be two, add Wolff's *An Introduction to Political Philosophy* (Oxford University Press).

6
Aesthetics

What is aesthetics?

The philosophy of art, or *aesthetics*, started to become a defined area of its own around the end of the eighteenth century with the publication of Immanuel Kant's *Critique of Judgement*. With some notable exceptions, such as Aristotle's *Poetics*, before this philosophers were generally more concerned with the relation of art to other areas – ethics, politics or metaphysics – than with art in its own right.

Aesthetics is concerned with a number of questions. What is art? What defines it and distinguishes it from other pursuits, such as craft, education or entertainment? In considering the purpose of art, we may ask whether it has *intrinsic* or *extrinsic* value: do we value 'art for art's sake' or as a means to something else? Is it primarily a form of expression, a vehicle for informing and improving, or merely a means of enjoyment? As we'll see, the various theories that have been put forward over the years have favoured different defining qualities, and have stressed the role of the mind, emotions, imagination and senses to different extents. But before we get into these controversies, let's ask a more general question.

What counts as art?

Before we define art we need to look at the types of thing that are generally considered to be 'artistic'. In this chapter we will use the term 'art' and 'artist' to include all art forms, including fiction, drama, dance, music, painting and sculpture, and 'audience' to describe anyone who is in a position to appreciate such work.

Firstly, there are the visual arts: painting and drawing, printmaking and sculpture. A more recent addition here is photography, which for some time was not considered a genuine art form (and still isn't by some). 'It's just pressing a button, isn't it? Where's the skill in that?' Such attitudes highlight one of the traditional assumptions about art, that it should involve some sort of expertise. The artist is in some way 'special', either in terms of skill or insight – not just anyone can be an artist. Of course, the best photographers are extremely skilful, and also possess a 'good eye' for composition and photo opportunities, but it does raise an interesting point. Many activities are skilful which we might not consider artistic. Is basket-weaving a form of art, or embroidery, or making jewellery? Perhaps we might be tempted to distinguish here between *artists* and *artisans*, between art and craft. However, there is a problem in doing that. Some of the greatest artists of the Renaissance were classed by their contemporaries as craftsmen. It stretches the concept now to think of Michelangelo as an interior decorator, even if he did paint the Pope's ceiling. However, the point is not that such artists weren't highly valued, but rather that art was then seen as subservient to other things – as a symbol of power or wealth, or as religious illustration. It is only gradually that art came to be seen as a worthy pursuit in itself, as something that might provide its own sort of insight or truth.

This problem continues when we think about other forms of art. Ballet and theatre are forms of art, but what about musical theatre or TV dramas? Such distinctions are often expressed in terms of 'low' and 'high brow', or 'pop' and 'serious' culture, and we also meet it in literature – Dan Brown vs. Shakespeare – and music – Beethoven vs. The Beatles. But what distinguishes these different levels? Some might consider the music of The Beatles or Pink Floyd to be genuinely artistic in that it attains a level of creativity and seriousness that sets it apart from other commercial pop music. But if we admit this, then what about other aspects of pop culture? What about sport, for instance? Many *aficionados* argue that Lionel Messi's divine control of a football makes him an artist. How is Messi's exquisite footwork any different from, say, that of the dancer Vaslav Nijinsky, who was widely considered an artistic genius? Isn't it just snobbery? Perhaps we can point to the fact that sport is competitive, or that it involves financial rewards, but artists too enter competitions, win prizes and receive grants. Still, isn't it the case that for artists, the aesthetic effect is the primary goal, whereas for footballers, the primary goal is, well, to score a goal, and any beauty that results is a by-product? Art has an aesthetic purpose; sport, a competitive one. But even this answer could be questioned. Some sports people would rather play a beautiful game than 'win ugly' and some artists are motivated by politics or ego, not pure aesthetic effect. Things are not quite so black and white, it seems.

One response to this is to argue that art is defined by the experts and other knowledgeable members of the art-appreciating section of society. This is known as the *institutional* theory of art, first suggested by the philosopher Arthur C. Danto, in that it sees art as defined by the social institution of 'the artworld'. Art is what appears in galleries, chosen by art critics and curators. To some, this smacks of elitism. If I like something, and think it has artistic value, then isn't my opinion as good as theirs? But the main point of the institutional theory is not that the artworld's view is better than anyone else's, it's just that its view is what defines art. Consider religion. You could say that Roman Catholicism is just what Roman Catholics say it is. That doesn't mean we think Catholics have superior theological judgement. The artworld might be full of idiots, but if they say something counts as art, it's art. That doesn't even necessarily make it good.

Another response to the elitism charge is to say that perhaps experts really do possess knowledge and taste that others don't. A wine buff may discern raspberry notes, oakey tones and the scent of summer flowers, whereas for me it's red, 13 per cent proof and was on offer at the local supermarket. Isn't it the same in art? Doesn't the expert possess more sophisticated standards of taste than me?

This type of argument was first put forward by David Hume. Hume admitted that our appreciation of art was basically a subjective experience, involving emotion and sensation rather than intellect. However, he believed that not all responses were equally well grounded. Over time, humanity has evolved various 'standards of taste' that allow us to distinguish between lower and higher pleasures. A child likes sweet things, but eventually the pleasure it gets from eating straight from the sugar bowl will lessen. In a similar way, social standards of taste evolve over time through the establishment of general consensus among people. Through experience, most realise that *Twelfth Night* is better than *Twilight*, or foie gras than faggots (for instance). But why? Even if we accept that such standards exist, we may still question them. Not everyone likes Shakespeare or prefers fine dining to more everyday fare. Should it matter that my taste differs from that of the experts?

This attitude has been challenged fairly consistently ever since the art establishment came into existence. The paintings of Monet and Renoir are now widely accepted as works of artistic genius, but the Impressionist movement that they helped to pioneer was originally a reaction against

the so-called experts who claimed to know what 'good' art should be. More radically, the *Dada* movement of the early twentieth century adopted an 'anti-art' stance in order to critique contemporary social standards, which it saw the art establishment as embodying. Visitors to some of their exhibitions were given axes and encouraged to destroy the exhibits. In more modern times, it has become even more common to question the nature and purpose of art. Such artists as Damien Hirst and Tracey Emin have challenged various traditional ideas about artistic form and content. Hirst controversially displayed various animals embalmed in formaldehyde and Emin's notorious installation, 'My Bed', was exactly that: a recreation of her bedroom at a certain time in her life, complete with dirty laundry, used condoms and other everyday detritus of human life. Both artists therefore sought to undermine accepted ideas about what an artwork should be – that it should showcase the artist's skill, that it should uplift or inform the viewer, and so on. In fact, we might say that one of the main purposes of art has become to question and explore what art actually is.

From this initial discussion, we can see that the nature and purpose of art have been controversial questions for some time. Whether something is or isn't art may be as disputed a question as whether something is good or bad art. To try to shed some more light on these issues we shall turn now to some traditional answers, of which there are three main strands: art as imitation, art as expression, and art as form.

Art as imitation

In Shakespeare's *Hamlet*, the prince gives advice to a group of actors. The purpose of acting, he says, is 'to hold, as 'twere, the mirror up to nature'. The idea here is that the job of art is to imitate, reflect or represent life in as true a manner as possible. Like a mirror, it allows us to see things objectively, rather than from in the midst of things, or from a purely personal point of view. This view is a form of *realism*, in that it assumes that art seeks to reflect some objective truth about the nature of reality or human experience, and thus inform us about the way things truly are.

This idea is quite old. We find it for instance in Plato's *Republic*, where the primary process of art is seen as *mimesis* or 'copying', which it either does badly or well. Plato has other reasons to consider art good or bad – which we'll come back to later – but he does not question the assumption that good art necessarily involves skill and *verisimilitude* – that is, a true resemblance to some object, situation or idea. We admire a painting because it captures the quality of light as it comes through the trees; we laugh in recognition at a character in a novel who reminds us of someone we know; we admire the skill with which a piece of music suggests a thunderstorm. All such examples see the value of art as allowing us to recognise certain features of common experience or truth.

However, as a theory of art, this view is quite limited. Firstly, we cannot assume that art only has value through successful imitation. In the convention of painting known as *trompe l'oeil* (French for 'tricking the eye'), the artist attempts to create a lifelike illusion. A common example would be the attempt to fool observers into thinking they were looking through a window (whereas it is actually a painting of a view into a garden or landscape). And yet, as admirable as the immense skill involved is, *trompe l'oeil* is not generally considered a form of high art, and where respected artworks are *photorealistic* (as such artistic hyper-realism is commonly called), this is not generally taken to be their most important feature. The reason for this is that imitation isn't itself enough – if it were, those people who produce the sound effects for radio programmes would be among the best artists in the world, or comedians who do impressions of celebrities, the best actors. Furthermore, this would mean that forgery itself would be high art, whereas most people would consider it a highly skilful but empty activity – and an often illegal and despicable one, to boot. We might also note that painting began to move away from realism along with the development of photography: since we can get more realistic representations simply by pressing a button, the artists realised, there must be more to art than imitation.

But there is another problem. The idea that art is imitation only fits certain types of art. Music would be a clear exception. Yes, there are instances where music attempts to imitate or represent something – Beethoven's *'Pastoral' Symphony* (no. 6) is a good example, where birdsong, cowbells and weather conditions are all suggested through musical means. However, this is one of a relatively small number of exceptions, and much instrumental music is evocative of moods and emotions without actually representing or suggesting anything tangible. Abstract art also causes a problem. It is difficult to see a painting by Mark Rothko or Piet Mondrian as imitating anything at all; they do not require us to *recognise*, but rather to *respond* – emotionally or intellectually.

Imitation also presumes that there is one way to see the world, and that the best works of art represent things more truly – as they 'really' are. And yet, if we look at what is generally considered good art, often what is admirable about it is the way in which an artist can make us see things in new and different ways. To do this, artists can employ different *conventions*, or challenge accepted ones. For instance, Pablo Picasso throughout his career rejected the traditional methods of representation – distorting perspective and proportion, showing different points of view at the same time, and so on. Part of what this does is to help us see that – for example – we are not simply looking at a picture of a violin, or of a woman, but of *a certain way of seeing* those things. It highlights the fact that art employs conventions and assumptions which we don't notice. You can watch a play, and consider it true to life, but there is generally a convention that the audience does not get involved in the action. These conventions can be challenged, of course, as they are in some modern theatre productions where involving the audience becomes part of the play. And they can also differ between time periods or cultures. In Japanese Kabuki theatre, for instance, it is the done thing to shout out a character's name at key points in the performance; such beahviour would be deeply frowned upon in Stratford at a performance of *King Lear*.

But there are more subtle conventions. When we look at a painting, we may interpret small dots in the distance as people, or blobs of white paint as reflections. But we have to learn to do this through learning what the various conventions mean. Animals are a good illustration of this. Some dogs will recognise another dog or a cat on television, whereas others perhaps simply see a buzzing box of light and sound. This ability to 'see as' is important in art, and it suggests that the artist does more than just copy; he *represents*. Increasingly, art has therefore concentrated on revealing and exploring the unspoken and assumed conventions that govern art production and appreciation.

Conventions and representation

The use of conventions in art is very important. Psychologists have discovered that very young babies can recognise a simple representation of a human face (just a circle with two dots for eyes and a line for a mouth). From early on, then, human beings learn to interpret signs and symbols using the same skills that we use to interpret experience. This is sometimes referred to as 'seeing as', which can be distinguished from 'seeing that' (a distinction first introduced by the philosopher Ludwig Wittgenstein). I *see that* something is a circle with some dots and lines; however, I *see* the circle, dots and line *as* a smiley face. 'Seeing as' therefore involves a degree of interpretation, and this is very much what happens when we appreciate art. We accept certain conventions in order to understand the things which are represented. We know the people on the stage are merely actors, but we can still cry when Juliet dies. 'Seeing as' therefore allows us to become involved without taking it all for real. A more sophisticated theory of art as imitation might therefore argue that art employs conventions in order to *represent* something. That something might not be as it appears in sense experience – a violin might not look like a violin, or a storm sound like a storm – but there is something at least to be recognised in some sense.

Coming back to Plato, whilst he rejected most forms of art, we might still adopt his approach by suggesting that art might 'represent' truth. For Plato, the real world was merely a copy of the divine ideas or *Forms* that existed separately in some otherworldly realm. So, since art often copies physical objects, then an artwork is merely a copy of a copy. What's worse, it is often done without any sound moral purpose in mind, but merely to entertain and amuse perhaps, rather than improve and educate its audience (of which, more later). However, perhaps a good artist *could* portray such ideas or feelings. Someone with the skill of a Michelangelo or a Shakespeare could help the audience to recognise certain features of reality or experience. Thus, art as representation provides us with a broader view of art than imitation theory, for if the main purpose of an artwork is to represent ideas and emotions, then it needn't 'look like' the thing it is meant to represent. The artist is also free to represent things in different ways, for conventions – the language, symbols, forms, et cetera, that we use to depict things – can change or be adapted. This is therefore a more plausible account of what art does.

However, it is often not the resemblance that we appreciate, however defined, but rather the things that the artist is using representation to say. For instance, if we consider Picasso's *Guernica*, a painting depicting a particular atrocity in the Spanish Civil War, then what gives the painting value is not its accurate portrayal of events, but the emotions and ideas that Picasso conveys in the *way* he represents them. We could say that Picasso's picture 'represents' the truth of certain aspects of war, but in what way does it 'resemble' that truth? Surely it makes more sense to say that it *expresses* that truth. 'The truth about war' is not something that exists floating around in the ether, waiting to be described or represented, but rather something which the artist thinks and feels in response to war.

If we accept this, then we are moving away from the idea that the most important thing about art is that it faithfully represents something. There might be artistic value in objectivity – an artist might unflinchingly portray the terrible reality of famine or disease, for instance. But 'realistic' in this sense does not necessarily imply 'looking like' something. And, of course, the opposite is true: resemblance does not imply reality or objectivity. Christopher Isherwood's novel *Goodbye to Berlin* opens with the famous line, 'I am a camera with its shutter open, quite passive, recording, not thinking.' This, Isherwood implies, is how a true artist works, recording things 'exactly as they are', without personal bias or interpretation. But in truth, even photography implies a viewpoint – a selection of subject, a choice of composition, of lighting, shutter speed, colour or black and white. And if this is even true of photography, then it is doubly true of more 'subjective' forms of art, where the artist must interpret how things appear and decide what they mean. After all, simply describing war is not to condemn it – a patriot and a pacifist might look at the same event and see different things. It will be their choice of words that will distinguish their viewpoints, just as artists will choose different conventions and styles of depiction. To think of art as simply describing or representing therefore seems an inadequate account of what it does.

Art as expression

There are some forms of art where it seems most natural to interpret works in terms of what the artist is trying to *express*. The value of a painter like Edvard Munch, for instance, lies not in his technical skill (which wasn't perhaps great), but in his ability to communicate a certain emotional and imaginative vision. Through his paintings, we may come to share certain feelings, or come to see the world in a different way. Perhaps, then, the value of art lies in this ability to express thought and emotion.

This approach, which is known as the *expressive* theory of art, can take various forms. One was proposed by the Russian novelist Leo Tolstoy. Art, he argued, is primarily the expression of emotion. The job of the artist is therefore to express a feeling or state of mind to the audience. Tolstoy describes this process as 'infection', as if a successful artwork were a contagious disease. But what Tolstoy really means here is that great works of art *involve* the audience. We can certainly see that this does apply to numerous works of art: the inspired painter, almost throwing paint at the canvas in his urgent desire to capture his anguish; the poet striving to craft images and phrases to express the precise nature of his forlorn love for his muse. Both seek means to provoke our sympathy and perhaps empathy. It's also true that great art often moves us – Shakespeare's great tragedies or certain of Beethoven's symphonies draw us in and affect us deeply. Related to this is the notion of *catharsis*, introduced by Aristotle, which sees art as cleansing or purifying our emotions. We are taken on a rollercoaster ride, our sympathies are engaged, and we suffer or laugh or are outraged in response to what is presented to us. Great art is therefore therapeutic, and Tolstoy – like Plato – was very particular about the sort of things that it should portray. In fact, his theory of art led him to reject his own earlier novels – including the classics *War and Peace* and *Anna Karenina* – because he no longer found the emotions they expressed to be fitting. A criticism of Tolstoy's theory is therefore that it would seem to exclude much of what we think of as art. Not only does it restrict itself to a limited emotional range, but also excludes the intellectual aspects of art. So, it might very well describe the works of a Van Gogh or a Beethoven, but what about the works of more cerebral or 'clever' artists such as M. C. Escher or James Joyce? Are such things simply 'not art'?

More flexible and sophisticated expressive accounts were advanced by R. G. Collingwood and Benedetto Croce respectively. Both philosophers argued that the purpose of art was to express the artist's personal vision. Thus, to understand a work of art, the audience must reconstruct the artist's intentions in their own mind. This is different from merely understanding what the artist was thinking about – we are not concerned here with the communication of concepts or intellectual knowledge, which both Collingwood and Croce excluded from true artistic production and appreciation. Rather, we must grasp the same intuitive or imaginative truth that the artwork embodies. In truly appreciating Samuel Beckett's *Waiting for Godot*, for example, we would seek to experience the same creative vision that drove Beckett to write the play. A successful artwork must therefore produce in its audience the same state of mind that led the artist to create it in the first place. This is more than just having emotions, however, but involves reflecting on them and seeking to give them some form in the imagination. If art's role is simply to evoke emotion, then at times it seems we may as well just look at pictures of dying puppies (or whatever). But Croce and Collingwood argue that art involves the expression of emotion at a high imaginative level. Art doesn't just make us feel sad, but causes us to be conscious of the meaning of sadness, to be involved with and reflect upon it at a higher level.

There are many subtle differences between Croce and Collingwood which we've ignored in this brief outline, but both are open to similar criticisms. Whilst their theories seem more sophisticated than Tolstoy's, they too restrict what can be considered art. For instance, Collingwood rejects art which has a purpose other than mere creativity – such as religious devotion, educational instruction or social utility. A work which aimed to improve us morally, or engage us politically, should therefore be considered 'pseudo-art'. We can see Collingwood's point – 'elevator music' or 'muzak' has the sole intention of being relaxing and inoffensive, and thus perhaps has the social purpose of putting people at their ease in a confined space. As such, it should not be considered art. Yet it would seem to be difficult to completely distinguish between pure creativity and such non-artistic or 'external' purposes. It may be argued that all art serves at least some useful end, and that a purely creative ideal is unrealistic. The *Berceuse*, Chopin's famous lullaby written for the daughter of a friend, is widely considered one of his best artistic creations. Should it be considered less so simply because it is an effective lullaby, and was partly written as such? We might make similar observations about the patriotism in Shakespeare's *Henry V*, or the anti-communist sentiments in George Orwell's *Animal Farm* and 1984, but it would seem absurd to call such things 'pseudo-art' merely on the grounds that art should not serve any functional or social ends.

There are other problems. If we are to reconstruct what the artist intended, feel what he felt, and so on, then how is this to be accomplished? How can we be sure that we have been successful? Mozart is long dead now, so how do I know that I am reacting in the right way to his *Requiem*? There is also an assumption here that there is a direct link between the artwork and the artist's state of mind. Mozart was commissioned to write the *Requiem*, and we should not assume that he was sad when writing it, or even that he called on any relevant emotion – we might even argue that writing it was a purely technical exercise, merely involving his mastery of musical language and tradition. Mozart actually compared his own process of composition to 'a sow pissing'. Anyone who has ever seen pigs urinate will understand that Mozart saw his own creative process as free flowing and easy – almost like taking dictation, as it has been described.

Worries like these led W. K. Wimsatt and Monroe Beardsley to develop the idea of the 'intentional fallacy'. As they put it, 'The design or intention of the author is neither available nor desirable as a standard for judging the success of a work of literary art'. What they say about the author could equally be said of other artists. We will see later that there are other reasons to question this idea that successful art appreciation involves discerning the artist's intentions, but the above criticisms suggest that expressionism is at least problematic as a theory of art.

Art as form

The final theory of art we shall consider is generally known as *formalism*, in that it seeks to define art in terms of its structural or formal aspects. This is especially apparent in relation to the visual arts, where shape and composition are important features of any painting, drawing or sculpture. For instance, it is well known that we find certain spatial relationships more pleasing than others, such as the 'golden ratio': when composing a photograph, a person or object situated approximately one-third of the way along will seem 'right'. However, we may apply similar rules to intervals in music, the plot structure of novels, or basically any art which has structural aspects. Some philosophers have therefore seized upon such features as defining qualities of true works of art.

Clive Bell proposed that what we value in art is what he termed 'significant form'. One consequence of this view is that form becomes more important than representation. It's not so much a question of what a work of art is 'about', or what it refers to, but rather the relationship between its various components. This is most obviously true when we look at certain types of geometric abstract art, such as the work of Piet Mondrian or the intricate mosaics of the great medieval mosques, but it can apply to a wide range of art. An appreciation of space and composition will certainly deepen our understanding of any painting, and the structure of plays, poems and novels plays a vital role in communicating the artistic message and shaping the audience's experience. Music, of course, is primarily formal – the division of time into measures and beats, the relationship between notes on a scale. If we add to this – as Bell does – that significant form produces in us a certain type of 'aesthetic emotion', then we can see how such a theory can account for much of what is distinctive in art. If we look at a beautiful Greek statue of a god or goddess, we appreciate the proportions of the body, how they fit together and complement one another. It is beautiful not because it looks like something else – an ideal in our head, or someone we recognise – but simply because of its particular shape and form. Bell's theory therefore accepts the expressionist point that emotion plays a key role in the significance of art, but denies that this can arise in relation to anything except the artwork's formal properties. Famously, he stated that, 'to appreciate a work of art we need bring with us nothing from life, no knowledge of its ideas and affairs, no familiarity with its emotions' (*Art*). It is therefore just an artwork's form which produces in us a very particular kind of aesthetic emotional experience.

Bell's approach can be traced back to the aesthetic theory of Immanuel Kant. Bell and Kant agree on a number of points. For Kant also, form is the most significant aspect of a work of art, though he even goes as far as to exclude colour (which Bell does not), which he considered only added 'charm' and was otherwise insignificant. In addition, art has no purpose other than the creation of an aesthetic emotion in the audience – as Oscar Wilde put it in *The Picture of Dorian Gray*, 'All art is quite useless.' This emotion should also be 'disinterested', meaning that it should not be connected with any practical goals or biological desires. Strong emotion or sensual desire would interest us in a way that would cease to make us objective, and might devalue the art itself. The value of art is therefore objective; we might respond *subjectively*, through emotion as opposed to reason, but a genuine work of art should arouse the same response in whoever is exposed to it. Aesthetic judgements are therefore *universal*.

The first criticism of both Kant and Bell is that their account of artistic appreciation is an extremely narrow one. It suggests a vision of sophisticated connoisseurs wandering serenely around galleries having elevated aesthetic emotions. Formalism therefore seems narrowly concerned with beauty and refined sensual and emotional enjoyment. But art can be so much more than this – it can be ugly and confrontational, it can arouse strong emotions or create great controversy. To consider something 'not art' simply because it does not leave us in a state of elevated, meditative calm seems overly restrictive.

In ignoring the historical and cultural context of art, both Bell and Kant also seem to overburden the role that form plays in art. To return to Picasso's *Guernica*, we would miss much in terms of the significance of the painting if we were to ignore the events that inspired it. Surely, our appreciation of such a work is *deepened* by greater knowledge of its historical background. Obviously, this is not always so, and sometimes we can be misled by factors which are 'outside' the artwork – for instance, we should not assume that a novel should only be interpreted in terms of an author's own life and character. However, to concentrate solely on form would seem to go too far, and to severely limit us. And what of art which is expressly created with reference to outside circumstances? Jacques Louis David's painting *The Oath of the Horatii* has strong formal elements, but we would seem to miss much of its significance by ignoring its historical context – David's relationship to the French Revolution, the contemporary interest in 'neoclassicism', and so on. Once again, like other theories we've looked at, formalism seems to want to limit what we consider as art for the sake of a neat theory.

We may also question Kant's contention that aesthetic judgements are universal. What happens when you and I do not share the same aesthetic appreciation of something? Kant would say that one of us was wrong, but it seems equally plausible that we differ for other reasons. Notions of beauty may be said to differ from culture to culture, and from one age to another. Rather than considering one response 'right', we may therefore argue that aesthetic appreciation is culturally relative – which is one more reason to relate artworks to their cultural background, or to the intentions of the artist, so that we may begin to see *why* someone might value a certain work in a particular way.

Art and society

As we have seen, none of the theories we've looked at so far is free from possible criticism. Yet, they all have something to offer. There is a sense in which we value art that informs us of 'reality', or is in some way 'true'; we also value art which expresses certain feelings or causes us to see the world differently; and we can easily appreciate the role that form plays in stimulating an aesthetic response. It would be nice if one theory could bring what is insightful in these various approaches together under one roof, in a way that reflects the true diversity of what we value in art. However, the theories discussed have mostly sought to identify what is essentially significant in art, what defines it, even if this means excluding things which most people would consider to have artistic value. Perhaps, then, in evolving a successful theory of art, we should be less concerned with what art essentially is or should be, and more concerned with analysing and understanding the role it plays in society and the lives of individuals.

Having said this, analysing the role played by art is no easy task, for it must involve a more general understanding of society and human nature. Of course, these are highly controversial issues, and there is a bewildering array of approaches that we might apply. We might think of art as stemming from early humans' religious impulse, as a form of celebration, appeasement or magic. Or, art may be seen in socio-logical terms, as fulfilling an important social function. The poet Ezra Pound wrote that 'Artists are the antennae of the race', seeking out new directions and foreshadowing new possibilities. We may also view art more cynically, as the expression of certain power structures in society. For instance, in his book, *Ways of Seeing*, John Berger criticised the traditional notion of art as the expression of high-flown ideals and tried to show how it is often driven by more earthly pursuits and

sentiments – pride in property and wealth, desire for sensual gratifica-tion, and so on. For instance, Berger sets well-known paintings from the Western tradition side by side with modern-day adverts in an attempt to reveal their similar concerns (namely, the portrayal of people, things and experiences as commodities to be owned).

As can be seen from the above examples, how we think of art will depend in part on how we think of society and human nature. Are we simply greedy, sensual mammals driven by base instincts, or are we rational souls seeking to express a higher purpose? To illustrate this in slightly more detail, we're going to briefly consider three common theo-retical approaches to interpreting art: Freudian Psychoanalysis, Marxism and Feminism.

Firstly, Psychoanalysis, pioneered by Sigmund Freud (1856–1939), proposes that we are driven by unconscious desires. Where these can-not be satisfied, they are repressed (for the safety of society, and indeed the individual concerned) and find expression through fantasies and dreams, are sublimated into other activities (shopping or sport, per-haps), and occasionally manifest themselves through psychological illnesses (hysteria, neurosis) or behavioural problems (obsessive compul-sive disorder, kleptomania). Freud himself considered artistic creations as a door into the unconscious, and considered that, since the creative process often involves irrational elements, we often find psycholog-ical conflicts appearing symbolically. For instance, an author might express an unresolved conflict with his father by projecting his quali-ties on to a character in the story, and resolving them there. In Freud's view, every man develops an 'Oedipus complex', and wants to kill his father as a rival to his mother's affections. We might therefore interpret Shakespeare's *Hamlet* (as Freud's follower Ernest Jones did) as an expres-sion of Shakespeare's unresolved Oedipus complex. From this point of view, art can be seen as a sort of safety valve. As in dreams, antisocial impulses which we cannot act upon find expression in the underlying symbolism of a story or painting, where they can play out harmlessly, unknown to the artist. Or, art may even provide a form of therapy, bring-ing unconscious feelings to light and helping to disperse them. In this latter respect, psychoanalysis has been hugely influential on artists of all types, who have seized upon its symbolic and mythic elements for their creative potential.

Marxism, stemming from the theories of Karl Marx (1818–1883), argued that society is primarily organised along economic lines, struc-tured according to wealth and means. The powerful, property-owning elite therefore utilise art as an expression of their interests, embodying their values and reinforcing the status quo – unless, of course, it is 'revolutionary art', which would seek to highlight the struggle of the oppressed workers in a capitalist society. An unsympathetic Marxist critique of *Hamlet*, for instance, would point out how it reinforces the social structure: whilst there are conflicts within the royal family, the legitimacy of the monarchy is not questioned, the general crisis within the play is seen in personal not social terms, and characters of 'lower' social class, who have only minor roles, are portrayed as coarse and uncultured.

Feminism is a broad term which describes various approaches which seek to highlight and redress what is seen as sexual discrimination against women. As such, feminists argue that society is generally structured to reflect male interests, and that social practices – art, science, politics – are geared toward expressing and maintaining male dominance, embodying attitudes that feminist thinker Kate Millett (1934–) christened *patriarchal*. As such, feminists point out that art has been primarily a male pursuit which women have not been generally encouraged or free to pursue. A feminist critique of *Hamlet* would therefore point out how its depiction of women reinforces restrictive female stereotypes – wife, widow, mother – which are defined solely in relation to their use and function for males. Furthermore, the women in the play are often portrayed in negative terms, as unfaithful, irrational, weak or untrustworthy. As with Marxism, therefore, art is seen to serve social purposes, and to express the interests of the powerful – though it also of course has the potential to serve as a tool of expression for the oppressed minority.

These are just a small selection of the different ways in which political, social or psychological theories can provide lenses with which to look at art. In practice, such critiques are more subtle than I have suggested here, and there is often a degree of crossover and intermixing between theories, as there is in Marxist-feminist critiques, for instance. However, the general problem with such attempts is that there is often a desire to make everything fit the central theory. A psychoanalytic or a Marxist approach to *Hamlet* might provide a lot of valuable insight, but we cannot assume that such approaches will exhaust what it is possible to say about the play, and in following their own agenda such interpretations may even miss something which is central. This is not to say that there *is* an essential meaning to any artwork, but merely that interpretations should not ignore the obvious, or wilfully skew a work's purpose. For instance, we can consider an interpretation of *The House at Pooh Corner* which saw the various events in the Hundred Acre Wood *only* in terms of class struggle to have missed the point.

But there are larger problems which spring from the application of such broad theories, in that such approaches require us to sign up to a general way of seeing the world. We can't accept a Marxist critique of *Hamlet* without at least in part accepting the tenets of Marxism. In one sense this is good, because it forces us to accept that art is not divorced from other concerns (as, for instance, formalism argued) but is as much a part of life as other social practices. However, the downside is that adherence to such broad theories seems to slant our interpretations in advance and forbid us from interpreting the artwork on its own terms, afresh. Of course, Marxists, feminists and psychoanalytic critics may argue that there is no such thing as an 'unslanted' perspective, for we must always come at things with certain assumptions and motives. There is some truth in this, but we should still guard against making too many assumptions about what drives a work of art, and we may also question whether it is just *those* assumptions (Marxist, psychoanalytic, and so on) that are the correct ones.

This is especially the case with psychoanalysis, for it is easy to discern the existence of symbols where they may not exist. And since we are dealing here with unconscious motivations (which the artist may not be aware of), then we cannot even point to the fact that he may not have intended them. As regards social critiques such as Marxism and feminism, the problems are slightly different. If we criticise an artwork on the basis that it reinforces the status quo (be it capitalist or patriarchal), we could miss much beauty and insight. Artworks are a product of their time and place. Shakespeare, for instance, existed in a culture where sexism, religious intolerance and racism were the norm, and where freedom of expression was strictly limited and heavily policed. This is not to excuse such attitudes, but merely to point out that it may only be natural that they exist in his plays for they are a reflection of the times. It is important to recognise this, but also to see beyond these limitations to the deeper, more enduring value of the work.

These are all important issues which cannot be avoided, but it can be seen that once we link art to society at large, then things become much more complicated for art theory. A full appreciation of art therefore takes us much deeper into philosophy and social theory, subjects which we do not have room to treat more fully here.

However, there are two interesting points here that arise from this discussion. Firstly, if artists are an expression of their age, then to what extent are they responsible for the meaning of a work? Does the audience play any role, or does meaning in some sense reside in the work itself? Secondly, can we distinguish the aesthetic value of a work of art from its moral aspects? If Shakespeare were racist or sexist, would this fundamentally detract from the regard in which we hold his plays and poetry, or might we view these things separately? Or, are morality and art in some way necessarily linked?

Authorship and meaning

Amidst the wrangling as to what role art plays, and how artworks should be interpreted, it is easy to miss a number of assumptions which turn out to be philosophically interesting. For instance, expressionism considered that the meaning of a work of art lay in trying to recreate the artist's state of mind during which the work was created. However, it's not just that it might be a challenge for most of us to put ourselves in Bach's shoes when he wrote the *Brandenburg Concerto*, or even that the artist's state of mind might not correspond to the effect the artist wished to create on the audience (as perhaps with Mozart). A more fundamental problem lies in the picture that this gives us of the way in which artworks have meaning.

Many *post-modern* philosophers argue that the idea that there is a central, authoritative meaning to a text is a myth, and that how we interpret a text depends on such things as social context and the interests of the audience. It is in this sense that Roland Barthes (1915–1980) famously proclaimed the 'death of the author'. Since both in their creation and reception artworks reflect the influence of various cultural forces, then there is really no reason to attribute a work of art to a unique individual or believe in the existence of a single 'Author-God' (as Barthes termed it). Rather, Barthes argued, each of us creates meaning each time we read a text, or look at a painting. The artist Marcel Duchamp (1887–1968), a major force in modern art, also recognised this: 'The creative act is not formed by the artist alone; the spectator brings the work in contact with the external world by deciphering and interpreting its inner qualifications and thus adds his contribution to the creative act' ('The Creative Act').

Going further than this, Jacques Derrida (1930–2004) sought to undermine the notion that there is a fixed or objective meaning to any point of view. Since all perspectives are forms of interpretation, it is impossible to favour one over another without taking certain basic values or metaphysical contentions for granted, which are themselves assumptions that can always be questioned.

There are other interesting ideas here. Often we think of the meaning of a work of art as being somehow 'in' the work itself. A poem 'contains' or 'expresses' a certain emotion or idea. If, as Kant thought, a work of art should create the same response in all people, then this meaning is, in a sense, an objective property of the poem itself. However, this is to treat the artwork as almost like some sort of sacred object. An alternative view might simply be that the artwork is a sort of 'placeholder' or sign for a shifting set of meanings, which are themselves determined by external factors – social trends and values, popular schools of interpretation, and so on. Since these are things that can change, the meaning of the artwork itself will change accordingly. This view is supported if we consider the way in which different artworks or artists can suffer ups and downs in their reputation. In philosophy, for instance, Aristotle was, at different times, venerated as the 'master of knowledge' (as Dante called him) and, during the scientific revolution, rejected as a rigid dogmatiser. Since his works themselves remained more or less unchanged over this period, we must assume that the change in meaning and interpretation was down to changes in the values and outlook of their readership.

If we accept these arguments, then there would seem to be no way to fix the meaning of an artwork either via its author, audience, or somehow in the artwork itself. You may consider this conclusion to be an unnecessarily extreme one, and you would not be alone. Many still hold to the idea that where the artwork itself is not unambiguous, then at least we can consult the artist's intentions. These may not be available to us – he or she may be dead or simply tight-lipped – but they at least present a theoretical means of solving the problem, and we can therefore work towards reconstructing what he or she might have meant.

However, there do seem to be some unavoidable problems here. Firstly, even if we assume that there is a 'correct' meaning to an artwork, it is extremely difficult to pin it down. Critics still argue over what Shakespeare meant by this or that phrase, and it is not uncommon for radically different interpretations to emerge from the same text. What's more, artists from the beginning of the twentieth century have increasingly embraced ambiguity in their work. When the Irish writer James Joyce published his magnum opus *Ulysses*, he remarked, 'I've put in so many enigmas and puzzles that it will keep the professors busy for centuries arguing over what I meant, and that's the only way of insuring one's immortality' (quoted in Richard Ellman's biography of Joyce).

Ambiguity, however, is not necessarily a negative thing, and we may point to the breadth of possible interpretation that an artwork excites as a sign of its depth and richness. As noted earlier, one of the defining features of modern art is that it reflects on the nature of art itself. As philosophers and critics question whether any fixed meaning is possible, it's therefore quite natural that this question should itself be taken up and expressed by artists themselves. So, even if interpretation wasn't such a problem, it is not always clear that an artist simply had one correct interpretation in mind.

Related to this is the idea that an artist may not always be conscious of his or her intentions. If Freud was right, then the influence of unconscious forces will mean that things are expressed in the artwork that the author did not have in mind. Some artists of course attempt to work with this process, and may consider inspiration and true creativity to be largely unconscious things. But what if an artist *explicitly* intended something? Shouldn't we then respect that? Well, it may be argued that intentions and outcomes are potentially separate things. I may intend not to create offence with my joke, but that is something that is at least partly out of my control (I cannot control others' sensitivities). Also, there is a sense in which the conventions that artists use – symbols and shapes, words and metaphors, musical instruments and scales – are public property. In using them I am relinquishing a degree of private control simply in order to communicate. Perhaps, then meaning is not the private and fixed thing that some take it to be.

In summary, given these problems, it therefore remains a controversial issue as to where the meaning of an artwork resides and therefore if such a 'true' meaning exists. Given the strength of these objections, it also appears that these are problems that will remain with us, and cannot be easily swept aside.

Art and morality

Finally, we turn to the relationship between art and morality. Oscar Wilde famously claimed that morality had nothing to do with art at all. A book is 'well written, or badly written. That is all.' (*The Picture of Dorian Gray*) But as our discussion of the role of art within society showed, it is obvious that art can and does play a role in promoting or challenging moral values. It is difficult to express some view on life through a work of art that does not have at least some consequences for what we think is right or wrong. This might not always be explicit in an artwork – you may paint a picture which depicts the beauty of the natural environment, which by implication may be taken to mean that you would oppose deforestation or would like to see tighter controls on industrial pollution. It *might* not: what looks like a celebration of nature may be a parody of our romanticisation of it, but that too would give the work an ethical dimension. We may also observe that the production of art has moral consequences. If an artist employs female nude models, it may raise issues of the objectification of women, or perhaps concerning worker exploitation and the need for a minimum wage. A recent example involves the film version of Alex Garland's novel *The Beach*, which generated controversy through its landscaping of the island where it was filmed (Koh Phi Phi Leh near Thailand). So, the general point is that it is difficult to completely divorce aesthetic and ethical concerns, and most art has at least some indirect moral impact.

There is also the question of freedom of expression. Some hold the attitude that art is somehow exempt from regulation, and that any form of censorship is a restriction upon true creativity. This last bit may be true, but it still needs to be shown why art should be exempt from regulation. Art is a social activity, and as such may cause offence or encourage anti-social attitudes. Some therefore argue that an artist whose work was racist or sexist should perhaps be prosecuted in the same way as any general member of the public would be had they promoted these views, whilst others point out that once we begin to interfere with artistic expression, for this or that reason, it is difficult to stop, for there is always *someone* who will be offended. Better, then, to simply leave art relatively unregulated.

Related to censorship is the idea that genuine art should promote the correct moral values. This goes all the way back to Plato, who allowed into his ideal society only those art forms which could be regulated so as to encourage the development of proper moral sentiments – such as courage, honesty, temperance, and so on. As such, poetry was completely banned. Since poets traditionally choose images, metaphors and phrases that heighten the reader's experience and involvement, then Plato considered them to possess a powerful means of influencing the passions and emotions and undermining the rational mind. He therefore considered poets to be somewhat irresponsible, presenting (for example) gods and heroes in unfavourable attitudes, depicting them drunk or mad, or as responsible for immoral and selfish actions. If we are to have such stories, then they should be written by the proper people, those trained in the moral virtues and possessed of the wisdom to employ such techniques responsibly (i.e., *philosophers*). Thus, art is replaced by propaganda.

Plato's vision has been quite influential, and his recognition of the power of art in shaping and influencing society was shared by the totalitarian regimes that emerged over the course of the twentieth century. Through Communism in Russia and China, and Nazism in Germany, all forms of free expression were repressed and art was put into the service of aiding 'social progress' and 'cohesion'. Communist art is generally termed Socialist Realism, in that it sought to depict and glorify the lives of everyday workers in fulfilling their heroic duties to the motherland. Similarly, Nazi art promoted an ideal of health and physical vigour, presenting an ideal racial specimen of worker-cum-soldier (this is sometimes known as *Heroic Realism*).

Regarding Socialist and Heroic Realism, it must be noted that 'realism' here did not mean 'realistic'. Nazi and communist art did not portray things 'as they really are' but 'as they should be'. Charitably put, it was the promotion of an ideal; more cynically, a barefaced lie. In Soviet Russia at its height, there might have been no food in the shops, and poverty and disease might be widespread, but propaganda posters and newspapers depicted happy, healthy and well-fed workers toiling in well-organised factories and farms. It is easy to see, then, how, even with honourable intentions, the use of art for State-controlled moral purposes quickly turns into a propaganda and 'spin' machine for manipulating the populace. Art here loses what is arguably one of its essential features, that of creative free expression. Denied the ability to tell the truth, or even to express how they feel, artists simply become liars, or lackeys of political control. So, even if the vision of art as a vehicle for moral improvement is a personal vision – as it was for Tolstoy – then the influence of such a vision would seem to have the same effect: the restriction and narrowing of creative expression, and a restrictive definition of what is 'true' art.

This leads us nicely back to the first point, regarding whether it is ever legitimate to restrict artistic expression on moral grounds. An interesting take on this is supplied by John Stuart Mill, who argues that free expression should only be curtailed when absolutely necessary – if someone were to seek to deliberately incite violence or social unrest, for instance. His argument is that if an opinion or viewpoint is wrong, then it will do us no harm for it to be expressed, where it can be publicly debated and refuted; if correct, then we owe it a debt of gratitude. Suppressing it can only cause resentment and allow errors and prejudices to fester on unaddressed. Applied to art, this approach has some merit. The attempt to ban a work has often given it more publicity, and sometimes more attention than it deserves, and a work or artist that would otherwise be neglected and allowed to fade into obscurity becomes a *cause célèbre*. Religious believers may object here that certain things are sacred and must be protected, but aside from the technical question of whether a non-believer *can* blaspheme, it would be difficult to formulate laws protecting religious belief that did not also make it immune to criticism – which would in turn lessen freedom of speech within society in general.

We must therefore be tolerant of the odd insensitive idiot in order to retain the greater benefit of free expression.

A counter-argument to the above might point out that art is in especial need of regulation because of the great influence it has (which was Plato's point). This leads us to the question of whether – for instance – the portrayal of violence or other anti-social and immoral acts necessarily influences those who are exposed to it. The short answer is that it's difficult to say. Studies to date seem to leave matters inconclusive, and for every murderer that has been influenced by films which glorify sadistic violence, there are thousands who are unaffected, or even who have their distaste for violence reinforced. In fact, we might just as easily argue that the link between violent films and violent people goes the other way: potentially violent and sadistic people *seek out* violent films *because they enjoy them*, and such people would have been that way whether they watched such films or not. However, whilst the debate remains an open and ongoing one, a general point against Mill might be that he places too much emphasis on people's rationality. It's all very well to say that free expression is healthy and encourages debate, but it assumes that everyone is willing and able to partake in such a debate. But perhaps this is simply too optimistic. If so, then unregulated free expression might in fact do more harm than good, for harmful opinions or values, left unchallenged, may exert an influence that legitimate censorship would otherwise deny them.

Conclusion

Aesthetics is a rich and complex subject, study of which leads us into many broader and deeper topics within philosophy. The question of what art is and how we should understand it is therefore not a marginal interest that need only concern artists or intellectuals, but, in many regards, a vital concern that should engage everyone. Defined in its broadest sense, we all make daily use of art, and our attitudes to it reflect our larger assumptions to do with education, entertainment and politics, morality and religion. As such, whilst it is a complex and controversial field, the philosophy of art involves consideration of issues vital to us all.

Summary

'What is art?' Can it be distinguished from craft or other skilful activities (such as sport)? The **institutional** theory of art proposed that art is defined by the experts in the 'artworld' (Hume's 'competent judges').

The **imitation** theory assumes that art copies or represents reality (it is therefore a **realist** theory), but there would seem to be more to art than faithful copying. A development of this view allows us to explain how different **conventions** can be employed to 'represent' a more general truth. However, aside from the fact that not all art is **representational** (music, dance), this suggests that what is important is *how* subjects are represented.

Expressionism, versions of which were advanced by Tolstoy, Collingwood and Croce, is the view that art seeks to express the artist's emotional or imaginative vision. This accounts for some art forms, but seems to rule out others as 'pseudo-art', giving it limited applicability. It also makes the questionable assumption that art has meaning through a communication of the artist's intentions.

Formalism, associated with Immanuel Kant and Clive Bell, rejects the historical and representational aspect of art and concentrates on shape, composition, the interrelation of elements and other formal features. This reduces art appreciation to a particular '**aesthetic emotion**'. Kant's assertion that aesthetic responses were universal is put into question by the fact that concepts of beauty have been shown to differ between cultures and ages.

Different religious, educational, sociological, political and psychological perspectives can also affect how we see art. Psychoanalysis sees it as largely an expression of unconscious desires, Marxism as a product of the economic structure of society, and feminism as a reflection of the alleged **patriarchal** nature of culture.

Some argue that it is possible for an artwork to have a fixed interpretation, determined either by the author or somehow communicated to the audience by the artwork itself. Both these assumptions have been questioned, on the basis that an artist's intentions are often impossible to know and also that the meaning of an artwork is determined by the culture in which it is received, and so is beyond the control of the artist.

Although some reject the idea that art should be judged in moral terms, it is often impossible to completely divorce artistic concerns from moral or social ones, and artistic activity can have indirect ethical implications. On the question of freedom of expression and censorship, the use of art by governments for 'social improvement', or any attempt to restrict free expression, should certainly be questioned.

Glossary

Aesthetic emotion   The emotional response produced in the audience by the appreciation of a work of art.

Convention Any of a number of established ways of presenting or appreciating art, concerning matters of style or representation, but also artistic 'rules'.

Dadaism An anti-art movement originating in the early twentieth century in Switzerland and Germany.

Expressionism/expressivism The theory of art, associated with such thinkers as Tolstoy, Collingwood and Croce, that sees art as primarily expressive of the artist's emotion or imaginative vision.

Extrinsic (As applied to the value of art) pertaining to things 'outside' of true artistic concerns (such as social function or education); the idea that art serves some purpose external to itself.

Forms Plato's theory that our grasp of truth is dependent on the existence of objective and independently existing ideas (Forms). Not to be confused with *formalism.*

Formalism The theory of art, associated with Kant and Clive Bell, that the value of art lies in its formal features (shape, composition, relation of parts, and so on).

Golden ratio A mathematical relationship (1:1.6) that is considered to contribute to the beauty or aesthetic quality of objects.

Imitation The theory, associated with Plato, that the value of art lies in its ability to faithfully represent reality.

Impressionism An art movement originating in France toward the end of the nineteenth century that sought to move away from slavishly representative art and concern itself more with light, colour and form.

Institutional theory The idea that art is defined by the experts that make up the 'artworld'.

Intrinsic (As applied to the value of art) pertaining to things 'internal' to true artistic concerns; the idea that art has value for its own sake.

Mimesis The act of copying or mimicking; associated with the imitation theory of art.

Neoclassicism A cultural movement, spanning the late eighteenth and most of the nineteenth century, that drew inspiration from the art and culture of ancient (classical) Greece and Rome.

Oedipus complex In Freud's theory of psychoanalysis, a boy's repressed and unconscious feelings of sexual attraction towards his mother, with a corresponding desire to kill his father.

Patriarchy A social structure where male interests and authority determine status, rank and power.

Photorealism A term often used to describe the extreme realism of a work of art (i.e., like a photo).

Realism (Within aesthetics) the idea that art should represent the 'real' world, and that 'good' art in some way represents things as they really are.

Representation Generally, a means of using one thing to stand for or represent another (artistic symbols, shapes, and so on). A representational approach to art is a form of realism.

Romanticism A cultural movement originating in the second half of the eighteenth century that constituted a reaction against the Industrial Revolution and the extreme rationalism of the so-called 'Age of Enlightenment' and advocated emotional expression and a love of nature.

Seeing as/that   Terms used by Ludwig Wittgenstein to suggest the difference between seeing as a form of interpretation (seeing as) and seeing in a less ambiguous way (seeing that).

Significant form   Clive Bell's term for the precise formal features of an artwork that give it artistic value.

Socialist Realism   The cultural movement dominant in communist countries such as Soviet Russia and China which attempted to reinforce the communist ideal through depiction of social subjects (such as happy and healthy workers). The Nazi equivalent is sometimes termed *Heroic Realism*.

trompe l'oeil   (French) Literally, 'deceiving the eye'. Used to denote artworks that attempt to fool the viewer into thinking that what they are seeing is real (such as a view through a window).

verisimilitude   A term used to describe an artwork's faithfulness to life (associated with imitation theory).

Further reading

A good general introduction to the subject is *Aesthetics: An Introduction to the Philosophy of Art*, by Anne Sheppard (Opus).

Arthur C. Danto's institutional theory is first outlined in his essay, 'The Artworld'. David Hume's views on aesthetics are primarily found in his two essays, 'On the Standards of Taste' and 'Of Tragedy', but his general views on ethics and human nature are also relevant. Many of the older readings (Plato, Tolstoy, Hume, Mill, Freud) will also be available free as e-texts, which can be easily tracked down by an internet search.

Plato presents his theory of art as imitation in *Republic*, Books II, III and X, and also in *Ion*, where he argues once more that poets are unfit to relay truth because they are inspired by divine madness (and are therefore not very faithful copiers). Ludwig Wittgenstein's comments on 'seeing as' can be found in the *Philosophical Investigations* (Blackwell), and are also discussed in Chapter 2 of Sheppard's book.

Leo Tolstoy's expressionist theory appears in his essay, 'What is Art?' Other forms of expressionism can be found in R. G. Collingwood's *The Principles of Art* (Galaxy Books), and Benedetto Croce's *The Aesthetic as the Science of Expression and of the Linguistic in General* (Cambridge University Press). 'The Intentional Fallacy' is an essay by literary theorist W. K. Wimsatt and philosopher Monroe Beardsley.

The two key texts on formalism mentioned are Immanuel Kant, *Critique of Judgement* (Oxford World's Classics) and Clive Bell, *Art* (Book Jungle).

Art and society: Terry Eagleton's *Literary Theory: An Introduction* (Blackwell) is an excellent introduction to the various theories discussed (obviously, from a literary approach), plus a great deal more. For a broader perspective, you could look at E. H. Gombrich's *The Story of Art* (Phaidon), which is pretty much the classic history of the subject from prehistoric to modern times. For Ernest Jones's Freudian view on *Hamlet*, see *Hamlet and Oedipus* (Norton). John Berger presents his critique of the traditional view of art in *Ways of Seeing* (Pelican), a very readable and highly recommended combination of text and photo-essay.

On authorship and meaning: we don't recommend tackling Derrida in the original, but Roland Barthes is slightly less intimidating, and his essay, 'The Death of the Author', can be found in the collection *Image-Music-Text* (Fontana Press). However, Eagleton's book is very useful on both these authors.

On art and morality: Plato's views on censorship and propaganda are once again presented in *Republic*. J. S. Mill's views on freedom of speech and censorship can be found in *On Liberty* (Oxford World's Classics).

Finally, *Aesthetics: A Comprehensive Anthology*, edited by Stephen M. Cahn and Aaron Meskin (Blackwell), is an excellent resource, containing excerpts from pretty much all the major contributions to aesthetics from ancient to modern times, including almost all those discussed here (Plato, Hume, Kant, Tolstoy, Croce, Bell, Collingwood, Danto, and Wimsatt and Beardsley).

Glossary

A glossary for each theme is found at the end of each chapter. Here are a few more general philosophical terms that are found throughout the text.

Abduction   Argument to the best explanation.

A posteriori   Reasoned from experience.

A priori   Reasoned from first principles, the truth of which are not established by the evidence of experience.

Contingent   Not necessarily the case or true, but dependent on certain factors.

Deduction   A form of reasoning where, if the premises are true, the conclusion must also be true.

Empiricism   The style or school of philosophy which takes as the starting point of knowledge the data of experience.

Epistemology   The branch of philosophy concerned with questions of knowledge and its foundations.

Existentialism   The style or school of philosophy which takes as its starting point the idea of the necessity for humans to choose their own values.

Induction   A form of reasoning that uses the experiences of the past or future as evidence for truths about the past, present or future that cannot be established by more direct means.

Logical positivism   An early twentieth-century approach to philosophy which claimed that any proposition which could not be verified by logic or by experience was meaningless.

Premises   The starting points of arguments, from which conclusions are derived.

Rationalism   The style or school of philosophy which believes the most important and fundamental truths can be established by the correct operation of reason, without reference to experience.

Realism   The view that things have an existence independent of human thought and consciousness. One can be a realist about a number of things, including the external world, morality and beauty.

Sound   An argument which is both valid and the premises of which are true.

Valid   A successful deductive argument where the truth of the conclusion follows necessarily from the truth of the premises.

Further Reading

Suggestions for further reading for each theme are provided at the end of each chapter. Here are a few more general recommendations.

The companion volume to this book is *Philosophy: Key Texts* (Palgrave Macmillan). It adopts a similar approach to this book but looks at works by Nietzshce, Mill, Plato, Descartes, Hume and Sartre.

The *Philosophers' Magazine* is a quarterly aimed at general readers as well as professionals. Julian Baggini is its co-founder and editor-in-chief, and its website is www.philosophersnet.com

The best single-volume reference book on the subject is the *Oxford Companion to Philosophy*, edited by Ted Honderich (Oxford University Press).

If you want to start reading original philosophical texts, the best place to start is probably with Nigel Warburton's excellent anthology, *Philosophy: Basic Readings* (Routledge).

The Philosopher's Toolkit, by Julian Baggini and Peter S. Fosl (Blackwell) is a comprehensive guide to the techniques of philosophical thinking and argument.

Index